THE CHALLENGE OF D. H. LAWRENCE

The Challenge of
D. H. Lawrence

Edited by

MICHAEL SQUIRES

and

KEITH CUSHMAN

The University of Wisconsin Press

The University of Wisconsin Press
114 North Murray Street
Madison, Wisconsin 53715

3 Henrietta Street
London WC2E 8LU, England

5   4   3   2   1

Printed in the United States of America

Library of Congress Cataloging-in-Publication Data
The Challenge of D.H. Lawrence/edited by Michael Squires and
    Keith Cushman.
    228 pp.   cm.
        1. Lawrence, D.H. (David Herbert), 1885–1930—Criticism and
interpretation.   I. Squires, Michael.   II. Cushman, Keith.
PR6023.A93Z62128 _____ 1990
823'.912—dc20   89-40537   72360
ISBN 0-299-12420-7   CIP
ISBN 0-299-12424-X (pbk.)

Contents

Acknowledgments

We are indebted to James C. Cowan and Charles Rossman, who wrote splendidly helpful reports for the University of Wisconsin Press. Their scrupulous critical engagement with these essays merits our special thanks.

We have benefited from Dennis Jackson's advice and longstanding friendship. Tamera Shepherd and Helen Hatcher cheerfully typed the manuscript. The College of Arts and Sciences of Virginia Polytechnic Institute and State University and the Research Council of the University of North Carolina at Greensboro provided financial support. On behalf of the Estate of Frieda Lawrence Ravagli, Gerald Pollinger has kindly granted permission to use quotations from D. H. Lawrence's works.

We are grateful to Lynn and Deb for sharing with us "the deepest of all communions."

Wayne C. Booth's essay, though composed for this volume, appeared in shortened form in his *The Company We Keep: An Ethics of Fiction* (1988) and is reprinted by permission of the University of California Press.

Abbreviations

References to the works of D. H. Lawrence are cited parenthetically in the text by abbreviated title and page numbers. Where available, the Cambridge editions are quoted.

CD	*The Captain's Doll. Four Short Novels.* New York: Viking, 1965. 181–266.
CP	*The Complete Poems of D. H. Lawrence.* Ed. Vivian de Sola Pinto and F. Warren Roberts. New York: Viking, 1971.
CSS	*The Complete Short Stories of D. H. Lawrence.* 3 vols. New York: Viking, 1961.
EC	*The Escaped Cock.* Ed. Gerald M. Lacy. Los Angeles: Black Sparrow, 1973. Originally published as *The Man Who Died.*
JTLJ	*John Thomas and Lady Jane.* London: Heinemann, 1972.
LCL	*Lady Chatterley's Lover.* New York: Grove, 1959.
R	*The Rainbow.* Ed. Mark Kinkead-Weekes. Cambridge: Cambridge UP, 1989.
SCAL	*Studies in Classic American Literature.* Harmondsworth, Eng.: Penguin, 1983.
SL	*Sons and Lovers.* Ed. Keith Sagar. New York: Penguin, 1981.
SM	*The Symbolic Meaning: The Uncollected Versions of "Studies in Classic American Literature."* Ed. Armin Arnold. Arundel, Eng.: Centaur, 1962.
STH	*Study of Thomas Hardy and Other Essays.* Ed. Bruce Steele. Cambridge: Cambridge UP, 1985.
WL	*Women in Love.* Ed. David Farmer, Lindeth Vasey, and John Worthen. Cambridge: Cambridge UP, 1987.

THE CHALLENGE OF D. H. LAWRENCE

Introduction

From the outset D. H. Lawrence's writings challenged conventional taste and expectations. One reviewer of his first novel, *The White Peacock,* distressed by Lawrence's "brutality," complained that "something of miasma belongs to the book." Another reviewer anticipated recent controversies about Lawrence's sexual politics by noting his "sympathetic understanding" of both male and female psychology. Many readers have not been comfortable with a novelist who, as Henry Savage said in another early review, "intends only to tell the truth as he sees it" (Draper 41, 36, 43). Lawrence's prickly insistence on telling the truth was a lifelong habit.

Lawrence remained controversial throughout his career; he is still so today. As gifted a reader as Edward Garnett, his early mentor, was unable to appreciate the challenges posed by *The Rainbow,* with its linguistic innovations, its affront to Christian orthodoxy, and its exploration of erotic mysteries. After *The Rainbow* was banned, *Women in Love,* the masterpiece that followed, went the rounds of London publishing houses before reaching print, then in the United States had to survive a court action for obscenity. Even an ardent admirer like Amy Lowell advised Lawrence in 1918 to be "a little more reticent" and apply "an India rubber in certain places" (Healey and Cushman 67). At the end of Lawrence's career, problems with censorship were common. D. W. Harding, reviewing the Penguin edition of *Lady Chatterley's Lover* in 1960, found Lawrence making a "determined effort . . . to challenge the proprieties of his time" (736).

But if Lawrence's continuing notoriety results from his attempt to introduce "the normality and significance of physical passion" (Mudrick 34) into the English novel, this is but one element of the ongoing challenge he offers readers. In a large, diverse body of work Lawrence explores most of the important questions that have perplexed our century. His writings ask us to consider what it is to be part of the darkly mysterious universe that is ours. He raises questions about modern society and community, about freedom and

3

constraint, about gender and human identity, about love and power, about language and truth. Lawrence's prose and poetry explore ceaselessly what it means to be alive and fully human. The search itself is more important than the provisional answers he offered during his lifelong "thought-adventure."

F. R. Leavis's *D. H. Lawrence: Novelist* (1955) is the essential landmark that established Lawrence's critical reputation, although it is rarely recognized that as early as 1930, the year Lawrence died, Leavis had written a pamphlet proclaiming Lawrence's distinguished literary achievement. "To read Lawrence's best work is to undergo a renewal of sensuous and emotional life, and to learn a new awareness," Leavis concluded (32). Harry T. Moore's pioneering biographical and critical studies also helped rescue Lawrence from the relative oblivion of the 1930s and 1940s, as did Moore's edition of Lawrence's collected letters (1962).

Lawrence's rise to critical preeminence is interestingly reflected in the two editions of David Daiches's *The Novel and the Modern World*. The 1939 version included chapters on Galsworthy, Mansfield, and Huxley. In the 1960 revised edition, Daiches eliminated these writers, added two chapters on Lawrence, and declared "that the giants of the modern English novel are Conrad, Joyce, and Lawrence" (*Novel* vii–viii). In the last twenty years, Lawrence, Joyce, and Woolf have emerged as the central figures of modern English fiction. Robert Kiely's *Beyond Egotism* (1980), a comparative study of these three novelists, assumes that they matter most. Such multi-author studies as Elizabeth Tenenbaum's *Approaches to Identity in Stendhal, D. H. Lawrence, and Malraux* (1977), Daniel Albright's *Personality and Impersonality: Lawrence, Woolf, and Mann* (1978), and Margot Norris's *Beasts of the Modern Imagination: Darwin, Nietzsche, Kafka, Ernst, and Lawrence* (1985) demonstrate that Lawrence keeps impressive critical company.

It can be argued that Lawrence is currently less fashionable than Joyce and Woolf. His emphatic individualism has found less favor in the reactionary 1980s, and his fiction, morally urgent rather than self-consciously formalist, is less receptive to contemporary theorizing. The agenda of feminist politics, which has cleared new space for Woolf but little for Lawrence, has also affected his reputation.

Still, Lawrence's status as a modern master is secure. Following Leavis and Mark Spilka (*The Love Ethic of D. H. Lawrence*, 1955), Julian Moynahan in *The Deed of Life* (1963) praised Lawrence for never abandoning "the conviction that life creates value and is somehow self-sanctioning" (xx). Lawrence wrote in defense of the life principle and individual integrity, in opposition to repressed or sterile feeling and compromised selfhood. Spilka and Moynahan, two of the most enduringly influential spokesmen for this "life-affirming" Lawrence, are represented in this volume by their most recent, reconsidered thoughts about Lawrence the moralist. But the great healer who exhorts us to "destroy our false, inorganic connections" and to "dance with rapture that we should be . . . part of the living, incarnate cosmos" (*Apocalypse* 149) is also the great nay-sayer, challenging complacency about our society, our personal relationships, ourselves. Lawrence repudiates our conventional, unexamined beliefs.

Some have found Lawrence's challenge unsettling. The scarcely concealed animosity of critics like Eliseo Vivas (*D. H. Lawrence: The Failure and Triumph of Art*, 1962) and Emile Delavenay (*D. H. Lawrence: The Man and His Work*, 1968), or even Kate Millett (*Sexual Politics*, 1970), suggests that these critics felt fundamentally and uncomfortably challenged by Lawrence. A man of strong, often impolite opinions, Lawrence has always provoked strong opinions. But his greatness is ultimately not explainable by his unconventionality or the pummelling he inflicted on orthodox morality.

Lawrence's work is direct, assertive, forceful. The response to life articulated in his novels, stories, poems, and other writings emerges unswervingly from the deepest levels of his being and insists on engaging the reader with an answering depth and intensity. As David Daiches wrote for a popular audience, Lawrence's "challenge seems to go beyond that which is normally asserted by a work of art. It is difficult to escape the challenge; to make any attempt to respond fully to what he is saying is to be drawn into his world, forced to share his vision" ("Introduction" 2110). And as we share his vision, we are stirred to ponder the most abiding human concerns.

The centenary of Lawrence's birth in 1985 served as an opportunity to rethink his art and thought. The ambitious Cambridge University Press editions of Lawrence's works and letters have conferred new status on the writer while providing reliable tools for the scholar and critic. Such key works as *The Rainbow* and *Women in Love* are now available. Meanwhile Cambridge has issued most of Lawrence's letters. When complete, this edition of letters will offer a modern literary self-portrait of unparalleled detail, complexity, and fascination. The time is therefore propitious for a serious reconsideration of Lawrence's achievement.

The essays that make up *The Challenge of D. H. Lawrence* ask what it means to be a serious reader of Lawrence. Implicitly they examine the grounds on which mature readers can return to Lawrence and find in his work reasons for ongoing engagement. Enriching our sense of his creative accomplishment, these essays are not largely concerned with rereading or exegesis, but with the challenge of Lawrence's achievement. The Lawrence who emerges from these pages is large, substantial, inexhaustible. The critics assembled here bring a variety of perspectives— historical, cultural, theoretical, feminist, contextual, critical—to their scrutiny of Lawrence. Their essays illuminate individual works as well as vital issues that transcend individual works. Collectively they demonstrate that Lawrence is able to sustain the highest level of critical attention.

If in the past Lawrence has attracted commentators equipped with traditional methodologies, *The Challenge of D. H. Lawrence* demonstrates the value of bringing more contemporary systems of inquiry to bear on his literary achievement. The poststructuralist psychoanalyst Jacques Lacan, who, like Lawrence, found new ways to probe the human psyche, figures in these pages, as do the philosopher of knowledge Michael Polanyi and the literary theorist E. D. Hirsch. Lawrence's art survives well its encounter with these thinkers, and they provide valuable new paths into familiar works. The Lawrence who emerges from these pages is very much our contemporary.

At the same time, as Julian Moynahan states in his essay, Lawrence is "a great conservator as well as a major innovator" (page 29). The essays by Moynahan, Michael Squires, and Janice H. Harris show how firmly Lawrence was rooted in tradition and literary convention even as he advanced into terra incognita. If Lawrence culminates Leavis's great tradition, he also persists as a living presence, as demonstrated both by Mark Spilka's reading of Lawrence amid current attitudes about sexuality and by Alan Golding's discussion of Lawrence and contemporary American poetry. Lawrence is at once conservative and radical.

In assembling this collection, our main goal was to gather strongly original essays that would also cohere as a group. We include essays by both major critics of twentieth-century fiction and younger, newer critics. It was not our aim to offer one essay on each major work by Lawrence—the usual case with collections—yet the essays do cluster around Lawrence's greatest fictional achievements, *The Rainbow* and *Women in Love,* and treat such major works as *Sons and Lovers, The Fox,* and *Lady Chatterley's Lover.* Insightful analyses are also offered of such lesser-known works as *Touch and Go,* "Strike-Pay" and "Fanny and Annie," "The North Country" and "Red-Herring," "The Wild Common" and "Thought," *Study of Thomas Hardy* and *Studies in Classic American Literature.* The thirteen critics represented here range knowledgeably across Lawrence's fiction, prose, and poetry, thereby strengthening the significance of their conclusions.

The volume has two parts. The first concerns Lawrence and other writers; the second, organized chronologically across Lawrence's career, addresses individual works. In this way readers may gain a sense of historical depth before moving along the span of Lawrence's career, so that a useful perspective informs these readings.

The essay that opens the collection is Wayne C. Booth's keynote address for the 1985 Lawrence Centenary Conference at Tufts University. Although Booth wittily discusses his long-term difficulties in appreciating Lawrence, he defines the novelist's particular achievements with the zeal of a convert. In so doing, he establishes a perfect frame for the essays that follow.

Both Julian Moynahan and Michael Squires place Lawrence within the historical context of the English novel. Moynahan defines Lawrence's career in terms of his revitalization of the idea of conscience. Squires juxtaposes Dickens's *Dombey and Son* with *The Rainbow* and *Women in Love,* illuminating the novels as they play off one another, then freshly defines the extent to which Lawrence works within the central tradition of English fiction.

Janice H. Harris also stresses historical concerns. She examines *The Rainbow* in the context of emergent ideas about women at the turn of the century. In this perspective Lawrence's novel becomes at once a product of its times and a transcendent achievement.

Paul Delany and Robert Kiely probe the issue of Lawrence and industrialism in essays that effectively complement each other. Delany shows how Lawrence's critique of the industrial system draws on a version of the pastoral myth. Kiely analyzes the language Lawrence chooses to express his complex attitude toward the working class.

M. Elizabeth Wallace explores the conceptual congruences in the writings of Lawrence and the philosopher of knowledge Michael Polanyi, showing how insights drawn from Polanyi clarify Lawrence's epistemology and enhance our reading of his fiction. John N. Swift, focusing on *Women in Love,* offers a succinct Freudian analysis of Lawrence's stylistic repetition, offering a provocative argument about the author's language and his awareness of death.

Jane A. Nelson approaches Lawrence's intriguing novella *The Fox* from the perspective of Lacan's psychoanalytic theories, producing a reading with striking new implications. Frederick P. W. McDowell reassesses *The Captain's Doll,* another major novella of the early ''leadership'' years, and contributes the fullest reading yet of that text.

Lydia Blanchard demonstrates that Lawrence as a critic shares some of the assumptions of E. D. Hirsch and that Lawrence's most ambitious work of criticism, *Studies in Classic American Literature,* possesses a stronger methodological base than has been recognized. She also demonstrates the continuing relevance of Lawrence's reading of American literature to an understanding of our literary past.

Mark Spilka's discussion of vaginal and clitoral sexuality in *Lady Chatterley's Lover* provides an eloquent defense of Lawrence's vision of human contact and understanding. Spilka argues the enduring pertinence of Connie Chatterley's praise of her lover for his courage and tenderness. To conclude the volume, Alan Golding trenchantly examines Lawrence's influence on contemporary American poetry, showing that Lawrence's impact as a poet has been more widespread and various than is customarily assumed.

These essays, then, give us a provocative, original, vital Lawrence. They freshly measure both the nature of his understanding and the quality of his art. They demonstrate the depth of his thought and the brilliance of his artistic skill. They allow D. H. Lawrence to "roar out challenge on the world" (*CP* 327).

WORKS CITED

Daiches, David. "Introduction to D. H. Lawrence." *The Norton Anthology of English Literature*. Ed. M. H. Abrams et al. Vol. 2. 5th ed. New York: Norton, 1986. 2107–10.

Daiches, David. *The Novel and the Modern World*. Rev. ed. Chicago: U of Chicago P, 1960.

Draper, R. P., ed. *D. H. Lawrence: The Critical Heritage*. New York: Barnes & Noble, 1970.

Harding, D. W. "Lawrence's Evils." *Spectator* 11 (1960): 736.

Healey, E. Claire, and Keith Cushman, eds. *The Letters of D. H. Lawrence and Amy Lowell: 1914–25*. Santa Barbara: Black Sparrow, 1985.

Lawrence, D. H. *Apocalypse and the Writings on Revelation*. Ed. Mara Kalnins. Cambridge: Cambridge UP, 1980.

Lawrence, D. H. *The Complete Poems of D. H. Lawrence*. Ed. Vivian de Sola Pinto and Warren Roberts. New York: Viking, 1971.

Leavis, F. R. *D. H. Lawrence*. Cambridge, Eng.: Minority Press, 1930.

Moynahan, Julian. *The Deed of Life: The Novels and Tales of D. H. Lawrence*. Princeton: Princeton UP, 1963.

Mudrick, Marvin. "The Originality of *The Rainbow*." *D. H. Lawrence: A Collection of Critical Essays*. Ed. Mark Spilka. Englewood Cliffs, N.J.: Prentice-Hall, 1963. 29–49.

CHAPTER 1

Confessions of a Lukewarm Lawrentian

WAYNE C. BOOTH

I

We enact here, as I look out at you Lawrentians,[1] an ancient ritual or myth: the story of the prodigal son. Because in a wild moment of long-distance telephone tomfoolery I thought the alliteration of "lukewarm Lawrentian" appealing, I find myself now returned from my un-Lawrentian prodigalities to confess my sins and to ask forgiveness. I did object in that telephone conversation that I was not a Lawrentian in either sense of the word, neither an expert nor an enthusiast. But I was told that nothing could be more appropriate for a Lawrence conference than absolute sincerity, even ignorant sincerity: my very reluctance was the clearest sign that I should let myself go. So here I am, feeling released from my scholarly inhibitions by that word "confessions" in my title.

As the good sons and daughters who have been minding the store all these years, you may feel resentment when the prodigal son returns to announce discoveries that you made long ago. But this homecoming may finally be pleasant enough, so long as you remember that it is better to rejoice over the return of one lost sheep than over the faithful attendance of the ninety-and-nine.

In 1975 I was living in Sussex, trying to write a novel of my own. While avoiding my task, I ordered some books from Blackwell's, including an edition of Lawrence's letters. About a week after they arrived I was reading through the letters, often with admiration but often with a rending of garments and gnashing of teeth, when suddenly, at page 77, I found a tiny scrap of paper with the following message scribbled in red ink: "Dear Professor Booth: The novels of D. H. Lawrence are better than you think."

Now isn't it a pity that the anonymous, disinterested young packing clerk is not here to see what he (or was it she?) hath wrought.

---

1. I have preserved throughout this essay the evidence of the occasion that prompted me to address Lawrence again, after a quarter century of neglect, at a Lawrence centenary conference at Tufts University.

If my later *mea culpa*'s are to be intelligible, I must first make clear that my critic had greatly overgeneralized my criticism. After all, my point in *The Rhetoric of Fiction* had been not to attack Lawrence but to defend certain narrative techniques sometimes dismissed as "telling rather than showing." My inability to engage fully with *Lady Chatterley's Lover*, I argued, would not be cured by removing the authorial commentary, since the real trouble arose from my quarrels with the character of the implied author:

> If we finish the book with a sense of embarrassment at its special pleading, if we read Mellors' final pseudobiblical talk of "the peace that comes of fucking" and of his "Pentecost, the forked flame between me and you," with regrets rather than conviction, it is ultimately because no literary techniques can conceal from us the confused and pretentious little author who is implied in too many parts of the book. (Booth 81)

After a passage like that, I can hardly blame Blackwell's employee for overlooking the evidence that I had found a quite different implied author in *Sons and Lovers* and some other earlier works. My tone was, after all, condescending and dismissive, concluding like this: "Even our memory of the very different author implied by the better novels—*Women in Love,* say—is not enough to redeem the bad portions of this one" (81).

Are the novels of D. H. Lawrence indeed better than I had implied? After agreeing to think about Lawrence again, I was determined to play fair: I would go back and reread the major novels with no ax to grind. And where better to start than with *The Rainbow* and *Women in Love,* generally said to be the best? I had a dim memory of reading them both decades ago, with some pleasure (lukewarm, of course), but I soon discovered that they were in effect entirely new—so new that I can't believe that I ever did more than a speed-reading for some assignment, as student or teacher. I found a few old pencil marks here and there: an "n" for "narrator's intrusion," an "i.a." for "implied author." But nothing echoed as something previously *experienced.*

I wish I could report that my first efforts led to instant enthusiasm. But my actual experience was much more troubled. Though I found marvelous passages in both novels, I also experienced, reading with an audience of Lawrentians in mind, many moments of anger, disgust, even contempt—and of course of mounting anxiety. Reading dutifully, reading in the worst possible way (with pencil in hand), I became more and more depressed. This author *is,* I found myself saying, too often a pretentious little preacher who thinks he knows more than he does.

On first try I didn't even get beyond the middle of *The Rainbow,* so annoyed was I by Lawrence's nagging. And *Women in Love* led me, on first try, to an exasperated few hours when I found myself taking extensive notes on the worst stuff, preparing to do a hatchet job.

A few weeks later, I am reading *Women in Love* aloud to my wife as we drive into the countryside. This is my third reading since I agreed to try to open my mind, and I have come to the scene where Birkin goes to Ursula's home to propose and finds himself instead in an angry encounter with her father. I pause to say, "Isn't that wonderful? What other novelist could have managed a scene like that? I completely overlooked the wonder of it last week."

So we have now my full confession of incompetence as a first reader of *Women in Love*. What could account for such a slow awakening?

Increasingly anxious about how to answer that question, I began to ask colleagues and friends in Chicago and New York how they felt about Lawrence. I could not find a single Lawrentian. Wherever I turned, I met people who once read him with enthusiasm but had not gone back to him. Their responses did not please me. By now Lawrence was important to me, so I settled down to some serious thinking about him.

II

It's never easy to assign blame when readers and authors fail to meet. As we enter a novel, we all carry the burden of our special situations, our personal incapacities, and our cultural moment. Part of what it means to "learn to read well" is to get beyond our local deficiencies in order to achieve a full meeting with something that is "other," beyond, larger than what we bring. As the reader-response critics have rightly insisted, we never manage to travel very far from our home base. Lawrence, both in his weaknesses and in his powers, asks me—as a professor of English and a literary critic—to travel a long way from home. Without pretending to be entirely clear about where the blame lies, let me describe some of my problems.

First, I am a slow reader and Lawrence is a fast writer—an extremely uneven stylist. His way of revising en bloc left a lot of copy editing unattended to. What major novelist, other than maybe Dreiser, provides more invitations to stop reading and start complaining about style?

Sometimes the trouble results from pure carelessness. What kind of writer can write of "the activities of her heart"; of "a clang of mistrust and almost anger in his voice"; of "a perfect fire that burned in all his joints"? And what of sentences like these:

"She lifted her face to him implicitly." How do you *do* that?

" 'He's very dirty,' said the young Russian swiftly and silently." Surely that's the neatest trick of the week.

"It was rather wet everywhere, there was a stream running down at the bottom of the valley, which was gloomy, or seemed gloomy." In this scene

Birkin is alone. Lawrence wanted to say only that it seemed gloomy to Birkin. He wrote it wrong first, then corrected it, but retained both versions.

If you offer a pedant like me enough clumsy stuff like that, he is sure to take as careless much that is actually deliberate and fresh. It was essential to Lawrence's purposes, as he himself said in his foreword to *Women in Love*, to repeat key words that had for him unusually powerful meaning: words like *blood, uncreated, dissolution, self, dead, mindless, naked, sinister, organic*. Such repetitions, when combined with relentless hyperbole and dash, can leave the reluctant Lawrentian laughing or groaning rather than soaring— mistakenly adding these deliberate touches to the collection of boo-boos. "Her subtle, feminine, demoniacal soul knew it well"; "He could move into the pure translucency of the grey uncreated water."

But troubles with style are only the beginning. Even more difficult to sort out are the ideological differences between us that spring from our different generations. I am near retirement, living at the frazzled end of a terrifying century. Lawrence was in his twenties when be began to work on "The Sisters," just before the outbreak of World War I; he published *The Rainbow* at thirty and *Women in Love* at thirty-five. They are books of a young man, about young people, characters initially conceived in a climate of hopes and despairs very different from ours.

At first the characters seem immaturely obsessed with problems of coupling and decoupling, as those problems appeared to bright young people early in this century. And while my interest in sex has not radically declined, my interest in talk about it has been more than satiated by the sexual revolution that Lawrence helped to inspire. It is sometimes said that an intellectual is someone who has found something in life more interesting than sex. I am actually—perhaps shamefully—more interested these days in how people face aging and death, and the likely death of us all, than I am in how they couple. I could not finish Updike's *Couples* when it came out some years ago, and I have not been able even to start Mailer's *Ancient Evenings*. We have by now had generations of novelists and psychologists claiming to save the world through some sort of phallic redemption, and Lawrence's prophetic talk about such matters has lost the freshness that it once had. If I had read these books at twenty, I would no doubt have felt myself in the presence of a sure and infinitely knowing guide. Reading of Birkin and Ursula's intercourse after the exciting Schuhplatteln dance, I might not have guessed what kind of "bestial" copulation Lawrence had in mind, but I would probably have felt exhilarated in sharing Ursula's own sense of liberation into the enjoyment of "bestiality":

She was fascinated. . . . What would he do to her?

He was so attractive, and so repulsive at once. . . . And she gave way, he might do as he would. His licentiousness was repulsively attractive. But he was self-respon-sible, she would see what it was.

They might do as they liked—this she realised as she went to sleep. How could anything that gave one satisfaction be excluded? What was degrading?—Who cared? Degrading things were real, with a different reality. And . . . she balked at her own thoughts and memories: then she added—so bestial? So bestial, they two!—so degraded! She winced.—But after all, why not? She exulted as well. (*WL* 412–13)

But after decades of such talk, after the multiplying sex manuals and *Playboy* philosophizings, such freedom-talk can seem old hat. Again and again on first reading I found myself simply bored.

Even the direct and skillful portrayals of sexual experience are, I think, harder to enjoy in our time than would have been true in the twenties. The excitement of reading Lawrence in earlier decades was in part an excitement at discovering an author daring enough to attempt to make readers feel what the characters felt in the act of love. Decades of increasing explicitness have removed much of the delicious shock, even from the most explicit passages of *Lady Chatterley's Lover,* another work that I have recently reread and found to be much better than I had thought. They have certainly reduced the pleasure of titillated curiosity in the novels before *Lady Chatterley:* "What exactly *is* a loin?" "Does that stuff about the base of the spine actually mean an erection?" "Where exactly *is* her hand at this moment?" "Front or rear?"

My resistances extend beyond the sexual nostrums to the whole range of panaceas offered in the "Salvator Mundi" vein. It is very difficult to take as seriously as Lawrence would like the quest of a young prophet for some spiritual revolution that will save the world. For reasons that make it impossible for me to reread Hesse's *Siddhartha,* I find many aspects of Birkin's and Ursula's quests informative at best, boring at worst. I am now suspicious of all epochal claims and all passionate struggles for perfection. To me it doesn't much matter what Lawrence thinks about the faults of the whole human race or about the certain doom for us all that lies ahead. Improvised sweeping indictments and cures irritate me whether they go this way or that. The result is that I cannot read most of the critical work that has been devoted to detecting Lawrence's precise position on prophetic issues. And though his own words are usually preferable to critics' guesses about what they mean, I find too often that his overblown diagnoses and prognoses have dated badly.

This problem is of course not just stylistic, and it's not confined to differences easily datable and then dismissed. Even the staunchest Lawrentians have had their troubles. F. R. Leavis, who says in his still impressive appreciation of 1955 that Lawrence "is incomparably the greatest creative writer in English of our time . . . one of the greatest English writers of any time" (5), confesses that it took him many years and many rereadings to discover the greatness. And he adds that Lawrence too often betrays, with his insistent jargon, an uncertainty not just about himself but about "whether a valid communication has really been defined and conveyed."

Many of the passages that I initially objected to are finally redeemed when we recognize the deliberate but subtle ironies that Lawrence has embodied (I shall have more to say about that later). But what do we make of a passage like this, found *after* Birkin has achieved his full love with Ursula? "Don't I [want other people's love]?" Birkin asks of Ursula.

"It's the problem I can't solve. I *know* I want a perfect and complete relationship with you: and we've nearly got it—we really have.—But beyond that. *Do* I want a real, ultimate relationship with Gerald. Do I want a final, almost extra-human relationship with him—a relationship in the ultimates of me and him—or don't I?" (*WL* 363)

I can forgive Lawrence for having fixed this use of the word "relationship" into the vocabulary of our young folks, who can no longer talk of *loving* each other, or use any of the eulogistic or pejorative terms for marriages and trial marriages, but must talk only of "relationships." But surely I must deplore his pointing the way to those lost contemporary souls who devote themselves to worrying about how to get in touch with their feelings and achieve an "almost extra-human" something or other.

To someone like me, even returning as a prodigal son, the hyperbole is especially troublesome when it throbs in Lawrence's destructive vein. I understand and share Lawrence's horror over the effects of modernism and industrialism on the lives of both the exploiters and the exploited. His portraits of the various forms of "uncreated" life have never been surpassed. But there is a great difference between feeling hatred for destructive institutions and expressing unadulterated and unmediated contempt for those who have their being within those institutions. His novels, essays, and letters are full of hatred for this or that kind of human being—to say nothing of his deplorable eagerness for revenge.

Whole classes of people are often simply wiped out by contemptuous reference: Jews, old people, especially if they are in the least conventional, and certain kinds of women—Hermione, Mrs. Bolton. And I belong to too many of those classes. Perhaps most obviously I'm the wrong kind of intellectual, a professor as critic. I have spent a lifetime trying to learn how to think about literature—to think consciously, even linearly. I believe not only in the value of mind, but in the value of a kind of mental work that Lawrence seems to abhor: the work of worrying consciously about contradictions and inconsistencies. Though good thinking about human affairs always requires us to respect our emotions, I am much more skeptical than he is about what my gut tells me, especially if it tells me something that my mind abhors. And though I now agree with Leavis that Lawrence is both highly intelligent and even in one sense an intellectual, he doesn't make things easy for a reader brought up, as it were, on Aristotle and Austen.

I can now easily recognize that I earlier misread Lawrence on this matter.

When Birkin, for example, lashes out at the stupid and vicious Hermione's effort to obtain knowledge about life, I felt, on first reading, that he was blatantly cheating: what she was blamed for doing was surely what Lawrence himself was doing—trying to encompass the world with her mind. Why so much vitriol against a passion for learning that Lawrence himself obviously in other contexts must share? So that when I arrived at the climax of the wonderful wrestling match between Birkin and Gerald Crich and found the phrase "mindless at last" (*WL* 270), I thought that maybe I'd found the title for my strictures against this troublesome man. Mindless at last, indeed!

It is not just groups of people—it's often the whole human race. "Humanity itself is dry-rotten," says Birkin. "Mankind is a dead tree, covered with fine brilliant galls of people." Ursula protests, "But even if everybody is wrong—where are *you* right? . . . Where are you any better?" And Birkin replies, "My only rightness lies in the fact that I know it. I detest what I am, outwardly [note that he does not say "what I am, inwardly"!]. I loathe myself as a human being. . . ."

> "So you'd like everybody in the world destroyed?" said Ursula.
> "I should indeed."
> "And the world empty of people."
> "Yes truly." (126, 127)

Soon Ursula herself is thinking how pleasant it would be to view a world emptied of people.

In short, it's not surprising that passionate Lawrentians have often confessed, with Leavis, that many rereadings were required before they could see how the novel as a whole transforms such moments into something less appalling.

III

By now you must be wondering: how did this reluctant reader manage to find virtues strong enough to overwhelm the obstacles?

As you know, I am not the first to defend Lawrence after describing his faults. Usually the redemptive claim is that Lawrence teaches some deeper truths, either in spite of his excesses, or even because of them. Diana Trilling, in her lukewarm introduction to *The Portable D. H. Lawrence*, finally forgives Lawrence because he presents a "metaphor against doom," "a possible procedure for a fierce surgery upon our ailing world and selves" (32). The trouble is that Trilling does not buy that "possible procedure," that "fierce surgery," just as Leavis does not think that Lawrence is finally as intelligent as he, Leavis, is. I don't think that the path of truth is the one on which we will find Lawrence at his best.

Instead I would finally praise him for two quite different achievements: his special brilliance and subtlety in the handling of point of view—though that term is misleading—and the special ethical relation that this allows him to build between the reader and the implied author.

Avrom Fleishman has recently argued that Lawrence's style suffered a sea change in the twenties under the influence of Giovanni Verga, three of whose books Lawrence translated between 1920 and 1927. Lawrence's narrative voice, Fleishman argues, became more "dialogical," in Bakhtin's terms, as he learned from Verga how to achieve a many-voiced narrative tone. From *Sea and Sardinia* on, Fleishman claims, we find Lawrence "orchestrating a multitude of voices, each one of which is capable of itself becoming such an orchestrator" (167):

It is my larger contention that Lawrence is a grand master of the oral, dialectical, parodic, and polyglot manner that Bakhtin has established for Dostoyevsky and that Lawrence creates in normal English diction an equivalent of the narrational hetero-glossia distingushing encyclopedic authors from Rabelais to Pynchon. Indeed, in at least one text, *St. Mawr,* Lawrence manages an extended construction in what Bakhtin calls "dialogized heteroglossia," the interchange and opposition of competing lan-guages or linguistic registers. (169)

I don't question Fleishman's thesis that Lawrence became more dialogical or "heteroglossic" after his second Italian experience. But I do want to claim that much of my initial distress in reading *The Rainbow* and *Women in Love* came from my failure to recognize just how often Lawrence attempts double-voiced narration in these earlier fictions as well. I fell into the very trap that I've spent a lifetime warning my students against—assuming that a charac-ter's words and judgments belong to the implied author.

Lawrence was experimenting radically with what it means for a novelist to lose his own distinct voice in the voices of his characters, especially in their inner voices. In his practice, all rules about point of view are abrogated: the borderlines between author's voice and character's voice are deliberately blurred, and only the criticism of the whole tale will offer any sort of clarity to the reader seeking to sort out opinions.

The effect is most acute when we dwell for extended passages in the minds of central characters like Ursula toward the end of *The Rainbow,* Birkin in *Women in Love,* and Mellors in *Lady Chatterley.* Since their opinions often sound like opinions that Lawrence himself sometimes expressed directly, it has from the beginning been easy for readers to do what I did a few months ago: that is, to assume that because the narrative voice enters enthusiastically into the feelings and beliefs, appropriate to a given moment, and does not often say anything about how those feelings or beliefs are limited, D. H. Lawrence must identify with them. For such readers it does no good for

Lawrence to insist that we "trust the tale, not the teller." We thought we found the trouble *in* the tale.

This is not simply the traditional problem produced by subtle but stable irony. It is true that we find in his works many traditional stable ironies— moments when characters give themselves away by speaking or thinking in ways that Lawrence expects the reader to see through and deplore. Almost everything said or done, for example, by the sophisticate Halliday and his crowd is portrayed in a manner that leaves us in no doubt about where we should stand. When Halliday reads aloud Birkin's passionate letter to the hooting hateful bohemians and Gudrun snatches the letter and flees, we know where we stand. But frequently we are offered ironies that must be called unstable—if we are to call them ironies at all. Again and again Lawrence simply surrenders the telling of the story to another mind, a mind neither clearly approved nor clearly repudiated yet presented in a tone that demands judgment. I don't know of any novelist, not even Dostoyevsky, who takes free indirect style further in the direction of a sustained surrender to a passionate mimicry that gives us two or more voices at once: the author's and the independent character's. The result inevitably blurs our picture of just where the implied author stands. As Bakhtin says about Dostoyevsky's surrendering to his characters, it is as if the author became simply one of many characters, one voice among many, having given up his right to total control (xxii–xxiii).

Notice how the surrender occurs in the following passage from *Women in Love:*

> As the day wore on, the life-blood seemed to ebb away from Ursula, and within the emptiness a heavy despair gathered. Her passion seemed to bleed to death, and there was nothing. She sat suspended in a state of complete nullity, harder to bear than death.
>
> "Unless something happens," she said to herself, in the perfect lucidity of final suffering, "I shall die. I am at the end of my line of life." (191)

So far we are clearly observing, with Lawrence, as Ursula thinks and feels in her despair: she said to herself—quote, unquote. But the clues are quickly abandoned, so that we cannot tell, when the judgments come, whether or not Lawrence speaks for himself as well as for Ursula.

"Darkly, without thinking at all, she knew that she was near to death." Well, *is* she near to death, or is this a portrait of how a young woman exaggerates when in despair about love? "She had travelled all her life along the line of fulfillment, and it was nearly concluded. She knew all she had to know, she had experienced all she had to experience, she was fulfilled into a kind of bitter ripeness, there remained only to fall from the tree into death. And one must fulfill one's development to the end, must carry the adventure to its conclusion. And the next step was over the border into death—" (191).

Who is this "one," by now? It sounds like Lawrence. Yet almost certainly this is now Ursula's thought only, in her premature despair. Surely this is still pure Ursula. Lawrence cannot want us to believe, still less than halfway through the book, that "she had experienced all she had to experience" or that she is really "fulfilled into a kind of bitter ripeness." Is she not going too far? Where are we? And where is Lawrence in the following?

> After all, when one was fulfilled, one was happiest in falling into death, as a bitter fruit plunges in its ripeness downwards. Death is a great consummation, a consummating experience. It is a development from life. That we know, while we are yet living. What then need we think for further? One can never see beyond the consummation. It is enough that death is a great and conclusive experience. Why should we ask what comes after the experience, when the experience is still unknown to us? Let us die, since the great experience is the one that follows now upon all the rest, death, which is the next great crisis in front of which we have arrived. . . . If a man can see the next step to be taken, why should he fear the next but one? Why ask about the next but one? Of the next step we are certain. It is the step into death. (191–92)

Who is the "one" who speaks here, who the "we," who the "man"? The impersonation is so complete that a first reader, already unclear about what the implied author might believe about life and death and love, is almost sure to assume that Lawrence has taken over and is inviting us to share *his* final truth that Ursula has discovered.

After my first reading of passages like this, I would have said, "Lawrence has lost control; he is intruding his own thoughts about life and death onto Ursula's experience—and they are thoughts that I reject." Now I would put it differently: Lawrence has so fully surrendered to imagining how such a moment of despair would feel to an Ursula, he has so fully granted Ursula her freedom, that her trance becomes his own, for the moment, and for the moment ours. This is how the struggle between life and death works, for her.

Even now I cannot say that Lawrence is blameless when readers take such passages as undoctored Lawrence. I would not even claim that he knew, in any ordinary sense, whether or not he agreed with Ursula's views here. No doubt in some moods he thought and talked this way. But the *novel,* considered as a whole, places the meditation as only one of many rival intensities— one that must be granted its reality, its otherness. It must not be accommodated to a simple, consistent, propositional portrait of what Lawrence believed.

The temptation to a misleading identification is strongest, of course, when we encounter the thoughts of a Birkin. Because Birkin bears so many resemblances to what we know or guess about Lawrence himself, the reader is tempted to assume that whenever he launches into a tirade or thinks deep idiosyncratic thoughts, we are hearing Lawrence. On first reading, for example, I took Birkin's ecstatic roll in the dewy flowers at Breadalby as Lawrence's own silly romanticism. You'll remember Birkin's discovery, in the primroses and trees, that people did not "matter altogether," that it was "quite right of Hermione to want to kill him," that he need no longer "pretend to have anything to do with human beings," that "he wanted nobody and nothing but the lovely, subtle, responsive vegetation, and himself, his own living self"—all this seemed pure excessive Lawrence, and I could well understand the revulsion of the early critic who quoted, in alarm, Birkin's claim that "he preferred his own madness, to the regular sanity. . . . He rejoiced in the new-found world of his madness. It was so fresh and delicate and so satisfying" (107–8).

But then comes a curious passage, underplayed on my first reading:

As for the certain grief he felt at the same time, in his soul, that was only the remains of an old ethic, that bade a human-being adhere to humanity. But he was weary of the old ethic, of the human being, and of humanity. He loved now the soft, delicate vegetation, that was so cool and perfect. He would overlook the old grief, he would put away the old ethic, he would be free in his new state. (108)

How could I have missed, on first reading, that all of this expresses Birkin as he thinks and feels *before* Ursula, Birkin at his most isolated, most misanthropic? The ecstasy is genuine, but the thoughts are for Lawrence himself half-baked. Lawrence does not trouble to say so. He does not say, "This is the way an ecstatic fusion with nature feels to a man who has almost been killed by his jaded mistress—a man who has long been surrounded by phonies, an intelligent, sensitive man choosing (rightly) to repudiate the empty world of Breadalby—a man desperate for human love." He leaves it to us both to feel the temptations of Birkin's vegetable love and to discover its limitations as the novel progresses.

Lawrence may have been deliberately playing a tricky narrative game with us here, one that yields a dangerous kind of irony. Birkin and Ursula are both expressing, in the passages I have just quoted, the full threat of the modern world as it appears to anyone who meets it as an isolate. In the search for an authentic self, any sensitive modern spirit living without love must end either in despair like Ursula's or in a half-mad ecstasy like Birkin's. By dramatizing their conclusions as if they were conclusive, Lawrence tries, consciously or unconsciously, to build in us a longing for the only condition that he thinks can save us—a longing for what he elsewhere calls the "Holy Ghost" of self-purged selfhood.

He knows that human beings cannot be saved except in loving others, yet he has discovered that the wrong kind of love for others is the greatest threat to genuine selfhood. We readers must long for the fruition of love between Birkin and Ursula if the novel is to work at all, much as in reading earlier

fiction we longed for that fruition for an Elizabeth Bennet or for the young
Catherine Linton. But we must never make the mistake of thinking that
romantic love is enough to save us. What will save us, for Lawrence, is only
a self-transcendence that is quite inexpressible in propositions and quite unlike
any of the traditional efforts to transcend the body and its death in a domain
of spirit. And if that is so, we must experience the various temptations of our
central characters as authentic temptations, not as errors already judged to be
wanting and thereby distanced.

It is a mistake, then, to talk of Lawrence's deliberately blurred handling of
point of view as "simply" a technical innovation. Whether we see the innovation as occurring before or after the point fixed upon by Fleishman, it
carries strong implications for Lawrence's general importance. Every technical maneuver in a novel obviously produces changes in effect; we can never
separate technical choices, even of the most minute kind, from general effects: one clumsy move can turn tragedy to farce, heroism to mockery.

The chief effect of any technical choice is likely to be a change in our
relations with the implied author, "Lawrence." As flesh-and-blood readers,
we either meet the implied author where we think he lives—and the main
clues about his dwelling are his technical choices—or we refuse the meeting,
as I almost did in my recent efforts to renew acquaintance. No matter how far
we fall short of meeting the author as he intended, every reader encounters
some version of an implied author and in one way or another makes a choice
about whether to continue the relation—whether to build a lasting friendship
or keep the author only as a casual acquaintance. Even if the Lawrence I think
I construct from the text contradicts in every crucial respect what D. H.
Lawrence himself intended, I still cannot avoid a decision about whether or
not to go along with the demands of this would-be friend.

In meeting those demands, I invariably build an ethical relation with that
person—ethical in the sense that *my* character, my ethos, meets this new
character. The ethos of *my* D. H. Lawrence, the person who made all of the
choices necessary for producing any given story, encounters my ethos, and I
must make choices in return—*ethical* choices not only because they reveal my
character but also because as I respond to the author's invitations or demands,
I experience effects in my character—changes in or reinforcements of my
habits of choice.

The argument for thinking of such relations in ethical terms is made more
easily when dealing with Lawrence than with, say, Samuel Beckett or even
James Joyce. Lawrence is quite open in his claims, made both within his
fictions and in his criticism, that he wishes to place his art in the service of life
and that the writing and reading of fiction find their justification in the kind
of people we become as we write or read. Thus no reader who refuses to
engage with Lawrence in ethical debate could ever claim to be reading him in

his own terms. We can assume that Lawrence would accept without question my assertion that his way of handling technical choices, his way of extending free indirect style to produce a deliberate confusion of moral viewpoints, has ethical consequences.

IV

But what is the ethical relation that he builds? In reading him, I find myself conversing with a peculiarly insistent, intent, passionate, and wide-ranging friend, one who will respond in some challenging way to every important question I can pose. There is surely something special about a friend to whom one can go with any kind of question in the expectation of a good conversation.

Considered under this metaphor of friendly conversation, Lawrence's overlapping narrative voices give us a steady stream of invitations to converse. Because of the intensity with which he explores the opposing experiences and speculations in each situation, we are again and again left with the *kinds* of irresolution that life itself presents, but with a broader *range* of irresolutions, and a deeper engagement with manifold possibilities, than life itself is ever likely to present to any one of us unassisted.

Almost thirty years ago Leavis made a similar point in showing how Lawrence consistently presents dramatic conflicts in which the reader must feel the legitimacy of more than one side. Using as example the quarrel about religion between Will and Anna in *The Rainbow,* Leavis concludes, "It is impossible not to register, in the upshot of the argument, that criticism has been established against both parties to the conflict—against both sides of the enacted argument" (149). But I would stress even more the generosity of Lawrence's engagements. I discovered, on a second and third reading, and especially on reading *Women in Love* aloud, an astonishingly just and lively distribution of human sympathy for widely disparate views.

What I want to praise Lawrence for, then, is not any body of truth that he offers; I suspect that I still disagree with more of his opinions than I accept. I am also quite sure that I would not have had much success in trying to converse about most of them with the real Lawrence: our opinions are too different, our styles of argument too much in conflict. But what I cannot disagree with is the importance of the topics he raises in our times together, or the sheer miracle of his sympathetic skill in cutting through to the central complexities under each topic. I think that Leavis refers to something like this skill when he grants to Lawrence the virtue of "supreme intelligence"—"the power to pursue an organizing process of thought through a wide and difficult tract, with a sustained consistency that is at the same time a delicate fidelity to the complexities of the full concrete experience" (391).

I can only sample the topics that illustrate Lawrence's range. The kind of conversational friendship Lawrence provides, when I attend seriously to what he says, is perhaps unique among novelists in English, both in its range and in the depth achieved in each presented topic. Here I can illustrate only the range and not the depth.

Item: Suppose I want to talk with someone about the powers and corruptions of formal education, of how it feels to try to teach but fail, of how it feels to have one's first slight success as a teacher, of how it feels to see naive educational ideals corrupted before one's eyes by actual teachers and students. Now I happen to disagree with much that Lawrence seems finally to say about such matters. I'm personally disturbed by his downgrading of "elementary ed" as he shows Ursula and Birkin blithely violating their responsibilities to those elementary school kids in order to work out their private salvation. But where can I find anyone to surpass the depth and poignancy of experience that Lawrence gives to the young Ursula as she beats her rude charges into belated submission—and with the beating loses her idealism about herself? Most novelists who take the trouble to look at education with any vigor or seriousness (and few of them do) reduce its problems and joys to the level of most textbooks on the history and theory of education—crude caricatures of incredibly joyful rewards, or even cruder caricatures of comic failure. But Lawrence remembers, and captures, the full range and intensity of motives and emotions that go into pedagogical triumphs that are simultaneously defeats:

> So the battle went on till her heart was sick. She had several more boys to subjugate before she could establish herself. . . . And at length they were afraid of her, she had them in order.
>
> But she had paid a great price out of her own soul to do this. It seemed as if a great flame had gone through her and burnt her sensitive tissue. She, who shrank from the thought of physical suffering in any form, had been forced to fight and beat with a cane and rouse all her instincts to hurt. And afterwards she had been forced to endure the sound of their blubbering and desolation, when she had broken them to order. (*R* 376)

Item: Suppose I want to have a serious conversation about the fate of religion in the modern world and its likely role in any future, a conversation that will not cheat by resting from the beginning on ready-made assumptions for or against belief. Lawrence saw that the essential religious questions had not been solved by modernist moves against traditional doctrines and establishments. He saw that the essential quest for each of us is still to find a self responsible to a cosmos that we did not make. And he knew in his bones how it feels to try out and then painfully reject the traditional answers. He explored these issues in such works as *Sons and Lovers*, *The Rainbow*, "The Woman Who Rode Away," and *The Man Who Died*. His quest for a larger self that would truly reject "the other"—the *others* who inadequately represent Him or It—is to me the most impressive effort at religious fiction of this century, at least in English.

Most forms of individualism, in his time and ours, tout a self smaller than everyone's actual experience—a self that is only a tiny core of private reality that is left when all otherness has been peeled off. Lawrence urges me to build a self bigger than "myself," a self somehow not reducible to known psychology or typology, or to any "conjunction of forces, physical and chemical." Nowhere in literature is there a more wonderful evocation of our quest for such a self than Ursula's in the chapter "The Bitterness of Ecstasy" in *The Rainbow*. Looking at some "plant-animal" under the microscope, she muses:

It intended to be itself. But what self? Suddenly in her mind the world gleamed strangely, with an intense light, like the nucleus of the creature under the microscope. Suddenly she had passed away into an intensely-gleaming light of knowledge. She could not understand what it all was. She only knew that it was not limited mechanical energy, nor mere purpose of self-preservation and self-assertion. It was a consummation, a being infinite. Self was a oneness with the infinite. To be oneself was a supreme, gleaming triumph of infinity. (408–9)

Now as an answer to cosmological questions this is pretty minimal. Ursula's answer is at best temporary; she is headed for more darkness and confusion and misery than she can now dream of. But if I want to remind myself of how it *feels* to grapple seriously with religious issues divorced from established answers, I'll reread that portion of *The Rainbow* rather than, say, Paul Tillich. Or perhaps I should say "along with," not "rather than": I don't expect to find in Lawrence, or any other novelist, a full encounter with careful theological reasoning, and I want some of that, too, along with Lawrence's kind of spiritual drama.

Item: Suppose I have become interested in recent talk about death and dying, and I'd like to hold a conversation about how I might think of my own aging and death and of modern ways of dealing with them. I can certainly find many modern novelists who will tell me that death is a tragedy or a farce or a dirty trick played by God. And I can find a few religious novelists who will tell me that I should not worry about death because it is transcended by an afterlife. But where will I find anyone who will show me convincingly how it feels to die unanointed and unaneled, as Thomas Crich dies, mute, uncomprehending, "uncreated," in effect cheated of a death of his own? Or as his son Gerald dies, never having found, or created, himself in love of another?

"He should have loved me," [Birkin] said. "I offered him."
[Ursula], afraid, white, with mute lips answered:
"What difference would it have made!"
"It would!" he said. "It would."
. . . Birkin remembered how once Gerald had clutched his hand, with a warm,

momentaneous grip of final love. For one second—then let go again, let go for ever. If he had kept true to that clasp, death would not have mattered. Those who die, and dying still can love, still believe, do not die. . . .

And Gerald! The denier! (*WL* 480)

Item: Suppose I am interested in how movements in modern art relate to the rest of our interests. Not only does Lawrence raise the right issues in vivid form, as we look at Gudrun's art, at the African sculpture that graces Halliday's apartment, and at the art created by Loerke. Lawrence also engages me in precisely the conflicts of form and ideology that are still, today, at the forefront of critical debate.

Item: Suppose—to come to what may be the most troublesome issue for us today—suppose I am interested in feminist criticism. I am in fact not only interested; I am convinced that most male novelists have debased women. One could easily make a case against Lawrence as a sexist—indeed most of the women I have talked with about him say that he offends them, too often, with his way of talking about how each woman can or must play the hen to some man's cock. I personally find him shifting about on this issue. He fails, for example, to repudiate clearly the way Gerald and Birkin talk about women in general, and especially semi-whores like Pussum: "There's a certain smell about the skin of those women, that in the end is sickening beyond words—even if you like it at first," says Gerald, and Birkin replies, "I know" (*WL* 95).

Yet with this said, where could I turn for an encounter as serious as Lawrence's with the struggle for an equal relation between men and women as one finds in novel after novel, story after story? Where could any woman turn, looking through novels by men, for a more serious, exhaustive search for forms of life tolerable to an intelligent, sensitive woman? And where would I look for a more serious search by a male author for a male role that is not sexist?[2]

I am impressed by Lawrence's capacity to dramatize rival positions in all these matters, oppositions that become emotionally and psychologically plausible and engaging, because of the author's vigorous penetration of the souls of those he tells about. And I could add many more topics: Lawrence's profound engagement with the psychology of unconscious motivation—he's the first English novelist to recognize the full challenge to traditional narration

2. One mark of any novelist who, like Lawrence, is a remarkable "conversationalist" is the range of subjects critics have chosen to see as the center of *their* responses. It is hard to think of any important general topic about which there is not a book or article with a title roughly in the form "Lawrence and [That Topic]." About religion, for example, see Murfin; about the formation of a self, see Howe; about the question of feminism, see Simpson. I have not yet sought out works on his "marriage counseling" or on the industrial revolution or on his views of death and dying, but I know they would be easy to find.

offered by the Freudian revolution; or his serious grappling with the ethics of art; or his prophetic and deep engagement with the changing nature of labor, for both men and women, as technology spreads and people increasingly measure their lives in terms of material comfort; or his penetrating and surprisingly "inward" portraits of the new industrialists (like Gerald Crich) whom he professed to hate as a class; or his sensitive realization of the challenge and appeal of scientific inquiry, particularly of biology; or his splendid studies of what we now call "marriage and the family"—all of these are topics explored in the essays that follow mine.

I even enjoy talking with him about parenting—what other childless novelist has ever done as much justice to the joys and pains of being a parent? The prolonged scene between Tom Brangwen and his stepchild Anna, early in *The Rainbow,* as he first tries to silence her uncontrollable sobs with angry reproach, then carries her tenderly with him to the barn and the nightly chores, and finally lulls her to sleep, having at last calmed her fears about losing her mother—where could that marvelous scene have come from, in Lawrence's experience?

He put the child into bed wrapped as she was in the shawl, for the sheets would be cold. Then he was afraid that she might not be able to move her arms, so he loosened her. The black eyes opened, rested on him vacantly, sank shut again. He covered her up. The last little quiver from the sobbing shook her breathing. (77)

We could easily go on. Can we think of any topic that Lawrence does not enliven and illuminate? And who can rival this breadth? Remember, it is not a matter of discovering whether he or his rivals actually talk about a given topic. I suspect that Aldous Huxley or Norman Mailer could rival him in sheer coverage of up-to-date topics, as could John Dos Passos or even John Updike. But how deep do they go—on more than two or three topics?

Range and depth are only two of many standards we might apply to proffered friendships, in literature as in life. We might, if space allowed, discuss the remarkable difference between Lawrence and most other modern ideological novelists in the difficult matter of "vitality." Because Lawrence shows so many characters on so many occasions inveighing against life, readers have from the beginning often misread him. In the much abused terms used in debates between philistines and the avant garde, he has seemed to be "life-denying" rather than "life-affirming" or enhancing.

But everyone who dwells with him long finds him to be finally energizing. He yields a renewed confidence in the ability of the individual artist (and reader) to resist even the most adverse social and political circumstances and to do something with them. I think that this effect may spring in part from his special theory of how art relates to life. Unlike a large number of modern novelists and poets, Lawrence sees art as serving life rather than merely compensating for it. The artist cannot escape responsibility for the effects of his art, and his art is to be judged by its connections with life as lived—as expressed, for example, in Ursula's response to Loerke's sick art. The final effect of reading his novels is to feel that here is one artist whose work serves life rather than bleeding it in the name of art.

V

We have been considering, then, the ways in which this proffered friendship is ethically rewarding. It is not that Lawrence is edifying or morally bracing according to one specific code. I'd be surprised—indeed I'd be alarmed—if any reader found all of Lawrence's nostrums palatable. But the particular pronouncements that I once found troublesome do not now seem to matter, except as stimulus to conversation with him. In his range of sympathies, his depth of courageous engagement with others and "the other," and his ultimate commitment to making each life count, Lawrence has won me.

Of course, some of us may still be tempted to dismiss him as a friend because he would not make a good fellow guest at a cocktail party. Sullen, opinionated, sneering, he sulks in a corner, condescending to talk with me— provided I'll give him his head—but fulminating against most of the other guests: they are dead, "inorganic," "uncreated." But if I can bring myself to follow him when he slams out of the door in disgust, if I can learn to tease him, as Ursula teases Birkin and Birkin teases himself, for "Hamletizing" and for the Salvator Mundi tone, I know that I can count on a good conversation—about how the people at the party betrayed themselves in their talking, about how their secret notions belied not only their open talk but their conscious *arrières-pensées;* about how their ways of thinking and feeling represent their class, their profession, their family origins, and their sexual history—to say nothing of the political history of their time and the history of the human race.

It is still true that if my new friend were to attack me for an act of stupidity or immorality, the attack would not make me lose as much sleep as would a similar criticism from, say, Jane Austen or Henry James or Flannery O'Connor. Lawrence's particular expressions of anger and contempt might amuse me, as his particular expressions of passion often merely amuse me or at best goad me to thought. The great man is still a creature of his time and particular history, and I must not ask him to be as large and permanently prophetic a creature as he himself aspires to be. But how he stretches my notions of the possibilities of life in my century! How he dwarfs most of his imitators and rivals in the game of prophetic fiction!

So I must conclude my confessions as something a good deal warmer than a lukewarm Lawrentian. The novels of D. H. Lawrence are indeed, as the anonymous young critic at Blackwell's insisted, better than I had thought. I may still be divided and often confused in my responses to this giant, but he has blasted me once and for all out of the camp of the Laodiceans.

WORKS CITED

Bakhtin, Mikhail. *Problems of Dostoevsky's Poetics*. Minneapolis: U of Minnesota P, 1984. Introduction by Wayne C. Booth.

Booth, Wayne C. *The Rhetoric of Fiction*. Chicago: U of Chicago P, 1961.

Fleishman, Avrom. "He Do the Polis in Different Voices: Lawrence's Later Style." *D. H. Lawrence: A Centenary Consideration*. Ed. Peter Balbert and Phillip L. Marcus. Ithaca: Cornell UP, 1985. 162–79.

Howe, Marguerite Beede. *The Art of the Self in D. H. Lawrence*. Athens: Ohio UP, 1977.

Lawrence, D.H. *The Rainbow*. Ed. Mark Kinkead-Weekes. Cambridge: Cambridge UP, 1989.

Lawrence, D. H. *Women in Love*. Ed. David Farmer, Lindeth Vasey, and John Worthen. Cambridge: Cambridge UP, 1987.

Leavis, F. R. *D. H. Lawrence: Novelist*. New York: Knopf, 1956.

Murfin, Ross C. *Swinburne, Hardy, Lawrence and the Burden of Belief*. Chicago: U of Chicago P, 1978.

Simpson, Hilary. *D. H. Lawrence and Feminism*. DeKalb: Northern Illinois UP, 1982.

Trilling, Diana, ed. *The Portable D. H. Lawrence*. New York: Viking, 1947.

CHAPTER 2

Lawrence and the Modern Crisis of Character and Conscience

JULIAN MOYNAHAN

> When the depths find voice we stand aghast, knowing neither ourselves nor those whom we have lived with always.
>
> George Moore, *Evelyn Innes*

Alone among the great modern English writers, D. H. Lawrence assumed the burden of the defense of character and conscience against the onslaughts of modernism. Writing to Edward Garnett in June 1914, he agreed that he could do without "the old stable ego of the character" but must take his stand with character deeper down, with a self that was of the core, energized, dark yet vivid, "physiologic," "inhuman" (*Letters* II: 183). He felt that he had come to the bottom of the human person but refused to call what he had discovered there either psyche or the soul, according to accepted meanings of those terms.

This dwelling on the essential and radical aligns Lawrence with all the generations of writers in a Christian culture whose sense and presentation of character, in terms of constancy, resistance, and conscience, ultimately depends on a belief in the soul and its immortal destiny. At the same time, Lawrence sharply diverges from this tradition in evincing a loathing as powerful as Blake's directed against the dualisms of mind and body, soul and body, form and substance, idea and its embodiment that have shaped Western thought from its foundations. After this distaste for dualism has been made clear, Lawrence is prepared to give the name of soul to the deeper character he has discovered. In the foreword to *Women in Love,* he speaks of the "creative, spontaneous soul" and the "deep, passional soul" sending forth "promptings" that are the characters' "true fate" (*WL* 485). These promptings, sometimes felt in the blood, and sometimes struggling into verbal expression in the conscious and scrupulous arrangements of literary art, sound suspiciously, even eerily, like the prompting voice of a conscience.

By developing more profound conceptions of character and conscience, Lawrence rescued or, better, refounded the central moral traditions of English fiction when these had come to be disrupted and at a loss early in the present century. He is then a great conservator as well as a major innovator. That is my argument.

Let me begin by entering a qualified dissent from the currently fashionable view which holds that all thought, and presumably all feeling as well, is a total obscurity apart from verbal expression. We find this in Chapter 4 of Saussure's vastly influential *Course in General Linguistics* (1916): "Our thought—apart from its expression in words—is only a shapeless and indistinct mass. . . . Without the help of signs we would be unable to make a clear-cut, consistent distinction between two ideas. Without language, thought is a vague, uncharted nebula. There are no pre-existing ideas, and nothing is distinct before the appearance of language" (111–12).

As Mark Twain said of Wagner's music, this isn't as bad as it sounds; not nearly as bad as some of Saussure's more rigid followers have made it sound, for whom all meaning resides in the verbal sign—which of course he does not say. What I dislike is Saussure's offering as fact what is really only a rule. That is, in order to operate the language system as he conceives it—and he conceives it as a game very like chess—there must be an arbitrary ruling out of meanings that fall between squares, or that take themselves off the game board altogether yet remain undying elsewhere, in space which the Saussurian language game does not encompass or comprehend. After all, it can be said with equal plausibility that confusion *enters* human thought and feeling with the appearance of language. Even the comparison of language to chess probably creates as much confusion as it clears up. For one thing, a chess game is diachronic if it is anything. But Saussure made his analogy between language and chess in order to illuminate language in its synchronic aspect.

We need this measure of relief from the Saussureans if we are going to get on with Lawrence and the various problems that his meanings pose. However, I cannot forgo this opportunity to show that the English poet-novelist and the Franco-Swiss linguistic scientist were really blood brothers. In his essay of 1919, "The Two Principles," Lawrence writes:

When we postulate a beginning, we only do so to fix a starting-point for our thought. There never was a beginning, and there never will be an end of the universe. The creative mystery, which is life itself, always was and always will be: It unfolds itself in pure living creatures. (*SM* 176)

But this is almost exactly what Saussure claims for language. Substituting *langue* for Lawrence's "life" and "universe" we get this:

When we postulate a beginning of language, we only do so to fix a starting-point for our thought. There never was a beginning and there never will be an end of language. The creative mystery, which is language itself, always was and always will be. Language unfolds itself in the utterance (*parole*) of successive though interpenetrating generations of speakers.

Who will claim that this falsifies Saussure's thought in any essential way?

There is still another connection to be drawn between the linguistic scientist and the life worshiper. Saussure's notion of the phoneme depends upon his notion of difference. The first difference is between sounding and not sounding. That is, the primary phonemic utterance is contoured by, differentiated into, significant existence, not by other sound but by the silence preceding, following, surrounding it. We find this same duality between utterance and silence in Lawrence's most fundamental reflection. But there is a difference. For Saussure the silence is empty and a nothingness. It is merely an enabling condition to permit language (*langue*) to begin actualizing itself in speaking (*parole*). For Lawrence, the silence is full, rich, a universe by itself. That is one reason why he ends his letter on "blood-knowledge," written to Ernest Collings in 1913, by saying, "I'm like Carlyle, who, they say, wrote 50 vols. on the value of silence" (*Letters* I: 504).

Conscience we commonly understand as a faculty of the moral, rational, and volitional subject. Not surprisingly, Lawrence defines this faculty as residing in the deepest self, in the blood in fact, where "we have our strongest self-knowledge, our most powerful dark conscience." Again I'm quoting from "The Two Principles" in Armin Arnold's edition of the early versions of Lawrence's essays on classic American literature, entitled *The Symbolic Meaning*. On page 187 of this edition the word *conscience* is misprinted as "consicense," a trisyllable. The word appears to be mutating on the page into the word *consciousness*. If one had to present Lawrence's main sense of our modern dilemma in ten words or less, one could do worse than aver that it is the appropriation of conscience by consciousness. Where blood-knowledge was, ego shall be!

Even our printers, not to mention the hucksters of pop psych infesting the airways, magazines, agony columns, and best-seller lists, share this conspiracy of conscience appropriation. In mining metaphor the process may be described as turning up the miners and closing down the mine for good after the black colliers emerge blinking into the light. In agricultural metaphor it's bulldozing the wild common and seeding the plowland with condominium developments and retirement villages.

Ordinary dictionaries agree with Lawrence in stressing the largely intuitional character of conscience. *Webster's New World* instructs me that conscience is "a knowledge or feeling of right and wrong with a compulsion to avoid wrong and do right," and explains that the word replaces the medieval and Anglo-Saxon *inwit,* meaning conscience as knowing within and deep down. The *OED* adds that this knowing and feeling about right and wrong is with and in oneself alone, and that conscience has long been called "the God in the bosom."

Emphasis on the individuality, privacy, and singleness of conscience reminds us that it is the Protestant faculty par excellence. It is sometimes said of Catholics, usually by Protestants, that they put their consciences in the keeping of their confessors, or of the entire church with its thick manuals of moral rules and dogmatic pronouncements. Following the Reformation, and especially in the seventeeth century, "cases of conscience," the writing up of difficult and delicate questions of conduct and motive, became popular. These exercises were perhaps the characteristic form of Protestant casuistry, especially in so thoroughly reformed and protestantized a national culture as Britain's. Among others the *OED* gives allusions to such cases from the writings of Jeremy Taylor and Oliver Cromwell.

From written-up cases of conscience, real or imaginary, to prose fiction where the conscience of individual characters plays a determining role is not a big step. Given the rising English novel's fascination with epistemology, its powers of penetration into mind, feeling, and the more intimate recesses of the self—along with its rapidly developing powers of analysis directed at tangles of motivation and at nuances and idiosyncrasies of acting and being in both public and private spheres—it was bound to happen that a major artist of conscience in fiction would emerge. I take that artist to have been Jane Austen. Though Lawrence's "dark conscience . . . in the blood" may seem indescribably remote from Austen's "cases" in *Pride and Prejudice, Emma,* and *Mansfield Park,* his is still a development—some might say a devolution—from her starting point. Though Lawrence could disparage Jane Austen, comparing her unfavorably to Fielding and accusing her of a certain lack of robustness, it must also be acknowledged that he paid her a considerable if indirect compliment in his finest novel, *Women in Love.* That comes in the scene where Birkin and Ursula, hunting furniture—or so they think—find a perfect chair amid the Victorian bric-a-brac at the outdoor market in Beldover and confess the pureness and beauty of its design, while acknowledging that it was produced in Jane Austen's England.

The most important figure of conscience in *Pride and Prejudice* is of course Elizabeth Bennet. From the time she receives Darcy's long letter of explanation and partial apology for his behavior—while she is visiting Charlotte at the Collinses' vicarage near Rosings—we see her carrying out the work of conscience, rethinking and refeeling her attitude toward Darcy, Wickham, and others in the light of what she discovers more and more compellingly to be the case. It takes time, it's painful, it's humiliating, with more humiliation to come after Lydia's elopement with Wickham. But of course, since Austen is writing comedy, things work out to a happy issue.

Lawrence liked to call this scrupulous process of moral and affective recognition, with its attendant deep changes and refocusing of feeling, a "realizing." In Austen conscience is at least as important as the influence of family, social circle, education, friendships, and assorted mentors, such as Emma's Mr. Knightley, in schooling the feelings of her young heroines to a point of fineness where no iota of strength or liveliness has been sacrificed. Indeed, Elizabeth takes after her father, in intelligence and even in witty and playful temperament. Mr. Bennet, however, is an inveterate evader of conscience. He hides out in his book-insulated study, holding the world and his own dependents at arm's length with his satiric barbs and sarcasms when he should be opening himself to realization. There is a price to be paid for this moral shirking. By the end he is a shrunken and meager figure when set beside his splendid daughter, who put herself to school at her own conscience and emerged a great lady, equal if not superior to the great gentleman she marries.

Among Jane Austen's novels *Mansfield Park* gives conscience its greatest scope and most impressive determining power. Through conscience Fanny Price, the "creep-mousey" poor relation and adoptive daughter of the troubled Bertram family, accomplishes nothing less than the family's moral regeneration. Since the Bertrams in their estate setting represent the traditional landed aristocracy as a whole, it becomes possible to say, in the words of David Monaghan, that "the survival of the old order depends entirely on her" (95), that is, on the order of a hierarchical agrarian society devoted to land cultivation and living in a state of amity with the circumambient wild nature out of which farms and orchards, gardens and "hahas" have been shaped. Though Fanny is raised amid urban squalor at Portsmouth, and spends her years at Mansfield Park as a quiet, untraveled, unregarded member of the household, she appears to grasp the central values of the country tradition by instinct—or should we say blood-knowledge? On her first excursion away from Mansfield Park, to Sotherton, she observes and appraises from the carriage window the changing zones of cultivation, with their varieties of soils and growth, exhibiting the directed curiosity and expertise of an experienced cultivator. At the great house, she immediately appreciates and acutely analyzes it as the architectural embodiment of an organic, Burkean social tradition, and her walks about the grounds reveal that she understands landscape design and estate planning as if to the manor born.

Such mastery cannot all come from reading books and engaging in solitary reflection in the East Room at Mansfield Park. Most of it comes from her total identification of self with the organic tradition that has produced both Mansfield Park and Sotherton. She draws moral strength from that identification.

That is how she is able to defend and finally to rescue the "old order" from urbane worldlings like the Crawfords.

When Connie Chatterley in *Lady Chatterley's Lover* makes her motor tour through the industrial wasteland of the Midlands, from manor to manor and return, she is not unlike Fanny Price traveling from Mansfield Park to Sotherton and returning. Connie too has been aroused to the defense of organic values, not those associated with great houses of course, for the manors, like the woods and fields, are going down "under the rolling and running of iron" (167). Actually her version of an organic tradition, based upon warm and loving bodies—hers and the gamekeeper's—coming together in the celebration and creation of life, is the oldest one of all.

It can be argued that Jane Austen established a line of conscience for English fiction that stands up well throughout the nineteenth century, at least through the novels of Thomas Hardy. In this line the faculty appears as a primary aspect of the character, lying deep, functioning more or less like an organic instinct, sometimes expressing itself inchoately, as dogged resistance or persistence. It also seems self-begotten and self-monitoring. Non-English people, reading this body of fiction for the first time, must occasionally be dumbfounded by the staggering moral ordeals assigned to very ordinary characters, some of them poor and scantily educated, many of them children, or orphans, or unprotected young women—the "mere young things" of James's preface to *Portrait of a Lady*. But such readers may be equally surprised by the essential self-possession these same characters display as they set about making their own destinies.

The final fate of Hardy's Michael Henchard illustrates this line of conscience. For all his misdeeds and blunderings he ought to die effectively silenced. But no, he *will* write his testament, an absurd and touching document that gives lordly directions, all negative, to his survivors: "That Elizabeth-Jane Farfrae be not told of my death . . . that no sexton be asked to toll the bell . . . that no man remember me. . . . To this I put my name" (*The Mayor of Casterbridge* 336). What a marveolus moral resistance to fate disguising itself as utter submission! His last will is a monument of conscience, even in its sheer perversity, which guarantees him a place in everliving legend.

Writing of Dickens and the nineteenth-century English novel, Hippolyte Taine, the great French historian of British literature, pointed out that although children are "wanting in French literature," they not only frequently appear as major characters in English fiction but also embody central values of English tradition, in particular the spontaneous and intuitive moral sense (ix, 159–65). One recalls little Jane Eyre surviving the horrors of those early months at Lowood School and the bitter loss of her only friend, Helen Burns, without turning savage, self-defeating, or even self-doubting. Where does

David Copperfield discover the strength of resistant character to decide to walk alone the many miles from London to Aunt Betsey Trotwood's, never mind the physical strength to survive the journey? It doesn't come from outside influences—neither from his association with the Micawbers, nor from his having witnessed his widowed mother fall prey to Mr. Murdstone and Murdstone's terrifying sister.

In the case of Jude Fawley, we first encounter him at age eleven, dreaming of mastering Latin, working as a living scarecrow, frightening off the birds in a farmer's fields. Consumed with pity for the birds' hard lives, he feeds them grain and earns a severe beating as his reward. This leads to his thinking, "As you grew older, and felt yourself to be at the center of your time, and not a point in its circumference, as you had felt when you were little, you were seized with a sort of shuddering . . . All around you there seemed to be something glaring, garish, rattling, and the noises and glares hit upon the little cell called your life, and shook it and warped it. If he could only prevent himself growing up! He did not want to be a man" (*Jude the Obscure* 17).

We may want to refer the last part of this to Hardy's reading in the philosopher Hartmann about "the coming universal wish not to live," but what is most impressive is this child's self-acknowledged moral autonomy and his very concretely felt moral sensitivity. He is affected by stresses from his harsh environment. Yet his strong and tender conscience is no gift from the environment. Is it innate? Who can say? Taine would have claimed that Jude's conscience emanates from the passionate, moral Germanic character which, he imagined, underlay the facade or mark of thrift, industry, and pragmatism in every English person (Taine 159ff.). Despite Jung and his school, most of us reject this vaguely "racial" way of thinking common in the late nineteenth and early twentieth centuries. The main thing is that Jude has an undeniable conscience *somehow* and that the faculty lies deep in his boyish nature.

I may be claiming no more than that English novelists are apt to leave their heroes and heroines sufficiently free to shape their own fates, to find destiny on their own. So the fascination of watching an almost wholly admirable character like Dorothea in *Middlemarch* conscientiously muddle into her marital disaster with Casaubon is that no one makes her do it. She illustrates to perfection Lawrence's axiom—"We can go wrong in our minds. But what our blood feels and believes and says, is always true" (*Letters* I: 503). The fascination of the rest of her story is watching Dorothea wake up to what her blood had been telling her all along; only, before she got to see the Reverend Casaubon bare she was too high-minded to listen.

This letting the character off the author's or narrator's leash—letting the character run—seems rarer in the European novel. A marvelous figure like Stendhal's Julien Sorel is never free of his creator's devastating irony and his nostalgic cult of Napoleon. Even Julien's sudden breaking out and breaking down at the end of his career of rising and deceiving appear to telescope the last moves in Napoleon's career as a dynast and world conqueror. Tolstoy is more like the English in allowing his characters to make their own terrible or sad mistakes and find their own accommodations to life. A form of the deep, indwelling organic conscience is operative in the careers of Anna Karenina and Prince Andrey, shaping their ultimate fates. But that is not true for Dostoyevsky. Many of his characters are maimed spirits who have been programmed with virtually insane criminal compulsions to act out, so that they may then confess to their sins on short notice and at great length. Dostoyevsky's ideal reader should be one part priest, one part criminal, and one part policeman. Probably only Dostoyevsky himself fills the bill.

After Hardy, conscience in the English novel is in crisis. Can we blame the crisis on the near disappearance of the organic society, the bewildering complexity of modern urban growth, multiplication of roles and role-playing in society, Britain's morally compromised position as an aggressive imperialist power? Conscience as deep instinct lapses, reappearing at the top of the diagram of mind as Freud's "superego" and "ego ideal." We enter the era of Henry James, "historian of fine consciences," an era of novels depicting characters who draw on conscience to create a shambles. My illustrations are from James himself, from Conrad, and from Ford Madox Ford.

In *The Turn of the Screw* the governess strives conscientiously to save the adorable children from the malign influence of the ghosts of Quint and Miss Jessel, who in life had subjected them to what nowadays we would call sexual abuse. But the governess's management of the little boy in the story's closing pages suspiciously resembles sexual abuse as well, and when she finds that in order to save him it will be necessary to allow him to be destroyed in the flesh, she may well remind us of American military logic in the management of Vietcong-dominated villages in South Vietnam during the 1960s. What else could she have done? She could have taken the kids and run. Never mind her instructions from the mysteriously absent master. The appropriate gloss on this celebrated and overinterpreted novella comes in *Women in Love*. Gudrun and Ursula are talking about the childhood accident in which little Gerald Crich shot his brother with an old gun that was supposed to be unloaded. Gudrun says,

> "It seems to me the purest form of accident."
> "No," said Ursula. "I couldn't pull the trigger of the emptiest gun in the world, not if someone were looking down the barrel. One instinctively doesn't do it—one can't."
> (49)

It is this kind of instinct which the governess lacks and which seems to be in critically short supply in the era of fine consciences.

Consider Conrad's *Lord Jim*. Jim's professional conscience, his mental

image of how he should act in a crisis, is so idealized and technicolored that
when crisis comes he cannot act at all. This happens twice, once at the training
school and again on board the *Patna*. After Jim's public disgrace and his long
period of conscientious self-torment, he gets his chance at restitution when he
is sent by Stein to oversee that mysterious capitalist's commercial interests in
remote Patusan. But again Jim goes wrong, idealizing himself as the benign
white lord, or *Tuan,* of these simple native folk when he should be remembering the utterly compromised terms on which white economic enterprise and
colonial domination exist in these underdeveloped territories. Dressed all in
white, according to his refurbished ideal self-conception, he is a ready target
for the visiting buccaneers and survives just long enough to be the main cause
of a good deal of suffering and loss of life among the natives.

Jim's deficiencies are scarcely emphasized in the book's later sections.
Indeed, certain paragraphs about the destiny of nations suggest that Captain
Marlow, the narrator, thinks that white rule is right rule by virtue of white
European superiority in material civilization. Where Conrad himself stands on
this isn't altogether clear. What is clear is that no one in the book has the sense
to say with Ursula, "One instinctively doesn't do it," whether "it" is abandoning a breached ship filled with sleeping passengers or acting out one's
romantic self-conception at the expense of innocent bystanders.

Finally, there is Ford's *The Good Soldier.* The book is a farce of conscience. Every conceivable tradition of conscience—Protestant, Catholic,
gentlemanly, military, Yankee—is wheeled out and flourished, while the four
principal characters behave worse and worse, more and more crazily, more
and more destructively and self-destructively. By the end, only the mad girl
who keeps saying "shuttlecocks" seems morally sane. So ends, in a debacle,
the era of fine consciences in English fiction.

After this debacle Lawrence faced a hard task. That was to rediscover the
organic conscience, giving it radical redefinition, and reestablishing its decisive position at the roots or core of the self. He seems to have grasped quite
early, certainly by 1914, that this project would work a revolution in his
fiction, in the dynamics of character, plot, language, and structure. He knew
this when he wrote his important letter to Edward Garnett on the carbonic self
or ego and its implications for fiction. About this time his great Irish contemporary, Joyce, was beginning to unsettle received notions of fictional
character with Leopold Bloom, but in an entirely different way. Bloom is the
first literary character conceived as inflatable sculpture or constructed like an
Identi-Kit. In himself he is nothing ("Noman") or everything ("Every-
man"). It comes to the same thing. He is entirely the creature of the written
style and thematics of each of the fifteen episodes in which he appears. Does
he have a conscience? Only where conscience has been scripted for him. Yes,
in "Cyclops," where he stands up bravely to the anti-Semitic Citizen and

defends love and humaneness. No, in the previous episode, "Sirens," where he is resolved to a quasi-musical phrase—"Bloo-bloom"—in a quasi-fugal structure.

But JoyceinBloom is not our problem. Let me try to say how Lawrence handled his. In "The Wild Common," his first truly visionary poem, the speaker discovers and raptly annunciates the self as sheer substance and immediacy. Soul or psyche is so entangled with, so mixed into the body's life, that henceforth the two can never be pulled apart. The poem's context in experience is Lawrence's recent recovery from life-threatening illness. Now Lawrence can say with Blake, "the notion that man has a body distinct from his soul, is to be expunged" (*The Marriage of Heaven and Hell,* plate 14), but mean by it the exact opposite of what Blake means. The Collings and Garnett letters make programmatic what the poem celebrated. In the "pollyanalytic" language of "The Two Principles," "the plasm of the human body is identical with the primary human psyche" (*SM* 176). The importance and difficulty of rendering this intuition in the language of conscious art are taken up— briefly—in the foreword to *Women in Love.* Whatever its scientific status, Lawrence remained ever faithful to the intuition itself.

The wild common is a place, but it also provides an emblematic image of the fundamental self, which I take to be virtually identical with what I have been calling the organic conscience at its strongest and most vital. This same common, complete with stream and sheep-dipping pool, reappears in the important story "England, My England." The common lies just behind the formal garden shaped by Egbert, where he shirks his life responsibilities, where he leaves lying out the sharp scythe which will wound and eventually lame his daughter. This accident will in turn lead to the destruction of his marriage and to his terrible yet greedily sought-after death in battle. Accidents in Lawrence have the most drastic consequences, even where it is being urged that there is no such thing as accident. (Birkin, for instance, "did not believe that there was any such thing as accident. It all hung together, in the deepest sense" [*WL* 26]).

Egbert is one of a long line of Lawrence characters, a majority of them male, who are flawed at the core, exhibiting an illness, a disruption, or an utter nullification of the organic conscience. Mostly they bring the trouble on themselves by refusing to become deep realizers or by botching personal relationships. Some, however, have the misfortune to have been born into distressed family situations or defective traditions, like the Morels and the Criches. Luckily, except for the nullified ones, recovery is often possible, sometimes on one's own, sometimes by entering into Lawrence's own version of exogamy, which might be called "mating with the stranger." There are many examples from his work—Tom Brangwen and Lydia Lensky, Kate Leslie and Don Cipriano, Lady Chatterley and the gamekeeper—and a crucial illustration from life—Lawrence's union with the German baroness Frieda von Richthofen—to confirm my point.

Most readers of Lawrence will agree that Gerald Crich in *Women in Love* is his most impressive, most complex representation of the "organically flawed" character. Gerald has a sort of tragic grandeur, and in many respects the book plots itself out like a five-act Shakespearian tragedy. The formal climax and anagnoresis—the knowledge that nothing can be done to controvert doom—comes in "Water Party," the supreme point in all of Lawrence's imaginative writing and itself plotted like a five-act tragedy in miniature. We see there and in the long agonizing aftermath how much power Lawrence has restored to fiction by repositioning the force of fate within character. Gerald acts against himself but also for himself. He does not dance on anyone's string, certainly not on Lawrence's.

Lawrence's most important artistic innovations as a twentieth-century novelist develop from his wrestling with the problem of representing in words the deep character and its promptings, as well as its transactions with the world. As the depths found voice—I am drawing from the epigraph by George Moore at the head of this essay—the contemporary reader, aghast or not, was forced to learn a new, difficult, and often disturbing language of revelation. In this effort the critics tried to be helpful but often didn't succeed. Certainly those with simplistic ethical, psychological, or sectarian axes to grind and, more recently, those eager to hail Lawrence as the prophet of a good-sex, feel-good revolution have had their empty say. There is a better critical tradition, of course, perhaps stemming from Leavis's redefinition of the Lawrence novel as a "dramatic poem," which emphasizes the poetics of his fiction. Here the focus is on tone, style, and rhetoric: on Lawrence's extraordinarily free and sometimes baffling treatment of point of view, as explored in the preceding essay, his webbing together of dominant images, metaphors, and symbols, his shadowing forth of mythic traces in the mental life and situations of some of his characters, his sometimes choreographic representation of characters in action and relationship, his painterly effects in depicting landscapes and soulscapes. The approach through poetics sounds rather untidy—and often is. But a lifetime of reading Lawrence convinces me there is no better way. Freud has said that dream analysis is the royal road to the unconscious. The way to the heart of Lawrence's imagination is through confrontation with the dense, fraught idiom of his verbal art.

Even so, there is no end. Every revisiting—Leavis's term was "frequentation"—of a Lawrence text brings fresh revelation. While rereading *The Rainbow* recently, I began noticing a systematic deployment of images, carrying through the book, in which an energized, even molten core, center, or hub was set in contrast and tension with a hardened surface, rind, or rim. Once remarked, these images and their quite systematic transformations seem an essential part of the burden of revelation the book carries. So I wonder how I overlooked them, or minimized their importance, many years ago when I worked hard on *The Rainbow* while writing my book *The Deed of Life*. I have noticed only lately that when one looks at the Brangwen saga as a totality, there appears a progressive etherealizing or abstracting of images of the man-woman connection, from the early brick and stone arches, to the rainbow arch with its earthly footings, to the remote celestial bodies cautiously orbiting each other in space, as Birkin's theory of "star-equilibrium" requires. This pulling back from direct contact seems important now that it has been identified. It may connect with Lawrence's anguish over the Great War, his growing despair for the future of English society and culture, for the future of Europe altogether.

Not that touching is enough in Lawrence's drama of character and conscience, his lifelong championing of the "deep" soul and its "promptings." We grasp that from the powerful postwar story "The Blind Man." There Bertie, a man who is all integument (or civilized consciousness), is broken down by being forced to touch the blinded war victim Maurice, a man who has become mostly core (or preconscious inchoateness), while Maurice's wife, Isabel, a woman containing, linking, and balancing the two extremes, is like a personified conscience as she scrutinizes and worries through the desperate ironies of the situation.

Did Lawrence give the etiolated and life-deficient character the name by which he had been known in his own family circle out of some reflex of despair, or was it part of his continuing feud with Bertie Russell? Actually such choices are frequently overdetermined. Yet Maurice as well is something between the monstrous and the manly, with his ugly scarred eye sockets, his harboring in solitude and darkness at the remote country house, his merely phallic physical presence: "For a moment he was a tower of darkness to her, as if he rose out of the earth. . . . When he stood up his face and neck were surcharged with blood, the veins stood out on his temples" (*CSS* 354). There is also his confession, "Sometimes I feel I am horrible" (363).

On the whole, Maurice is easy to connect with the poor bewitched beast of "Beauty and the Beast" and—since that old story is a secularized version of the Persephone myth—with Persephone's Underworld captor. When these connections are made, the precisely calculated imprecisions of Lawrence's opening description of the married couple's life together come alive. "Immediate contact in darkness," "a whole world, rich and real and invisible," and "unspeakable intimacy" (*CSS* 347) together evoke the closeness underground that haunted the imagination of the coal miner's son until close to his dying day, at least until he was done with writing the poems "Bavarian Gentians" and "Glory of Darkness." Still, someone might claim that "unspeakable intimacy," a phrase twice repeated in the next two pages, is just a careless way of saying that the couple prefer not to talk about, or don't know how to talk about, their intimacy. That is only part of what is meant. "Unspeakable" is essential for its connotations of the awful, the tabooed—and the indecent, just supposing silence were breached. Certainly these connotations are operative at the end, when the wretched Bertie recoils from Maurice's proffered and quite ceremonious mysteries of the tactile, becoming "like a mollusc whose shell was broken" (365).

In the famous letter to Garnett already cited, Lawrence disclaims that it is his "cleverness" which will bring the deeper self and its promptings into the scope of artistic treatment, but he is very clever just the same. Consider merely the stagecraft of "The Blind Man." Maurice Pervin's house, the Grange, is a typical civilized upper-class residence, filled with books, a piano, and beautiful furniture where it fronts the highroad. But at the back it is a farmstead occupied by the Wernhams, tenant farmers who double as house servants. Behind, but still partly lighted by light from the kitchen windows, lies the main enclosure or yard where the animals are tended to, and behind this space—far behind, like Egbert's common—is the great dark barn where Maurice comes fully into his own. Here he tends the milk cows and other cattle by touch, knowing them and their positions in the stalls entirely by sensory means. As the story develops, those issues which can be contested and settled in the light of civilized consciousness are argued out at the dinner table or at the fireside in the living room, but the deeper issues are divulged and acted upon "blindly" in the barn where Maurice, for all his pathos, is master. In one of these night-for-day scenes, Isabel goes to find Maurice at his chores and is shaken to discover how, back there, she is the blind and blundering one. The experience does her no harm. The result of Bertie's visit with Maurice back there is of course quite different. It finishes him.

It is often claimed now that literature is intransitive, that books are at bottom "about" the verbal arrangements comprising the text. Granted that language is a great and powerful mystery, I do believe that Lawrence got deeper down than language and had the strength and endurance, at least for a time, to report back to us what he uncovered. That these reports are couched in words does not make them merely about words. In this essay I have claimed that they constitute a radical exploration into the fundamentals of character and conscience. Others will want to use other terms. Just so long as we agree that language, before which there has been so much deep bowing of late, is not all there is.

WORKS CITED

Blake, William. *The Marriage of Heaven and Hell.* Ed. Geoffrey Keynes. London: Oxford UP, 1975.

Hardy, Thomas. *Jude the Obscure.* Boston: Houghton Mifflin, 1965.

Hardy, Thomas. *The Mayor of Casterbridge.* New York: Rinehart, 1948.

Lawrence, D. H. *The Complete Short Stories of D. H. Lawrence.* Vol. 2. New York: Viking, 1961.

Lawrence, D. H. *Lady Chatterley's Lover.* New York: Grove, 1962.

Lawrence, D. H. *The Letters of D. H. Lawrence.* Vol. 1: *September 1901–May 1913.* Ed. James T. Boulton. Cambridge: Cambridge UP, 1979.

Lawrence, D. H. *The Letters of D. H. Lawrence.* Vol. 2: *June 1913–October 1916.* Ed. George J. Zytaruk and James T. Boulton. Cambridge: Cambridge UP, 1981.

Lawrence, D. H. *The Symbolic Meaning: The Uncollected Versions of "Studies in Classic American Literature."* Ed. Armin Arnold. Arundel, Eng.: Centaur, 1962.

Lawrence, D. H. *Women in Love.* Ed. David Farmer, Lindeth Vasey, and John Worthen. Cambridge: Cambridge UP, 1987.

Monaghan, David. *Jane Austen: Structure and Social Vision.* London: Macmillan, 1980.

Saussure, Ferdinand de. *Course in General Linguistics.* Trans. Wade Baskin. New York: McGraw-Hill, 1966.

Taine, Hippolyte. *History of English Literature.* Vol. 4. Trans. H. Van Laun. New York: Colonial, 1889.

CHAPTER 3

Lawrence, Dickens, and the English Novel

MICHAEL SQUIRES

D. H. Lawrence and Charles Dickens died sixty years apart, Dickens in 1870, at the center of Victoria's reign, Lawrence in 1930, while modernism flourished. As the gospels of literary history have it, the novelists epitomize their different historical periods. Whereas Dickens is distinctly Victorian, Lawrence is thoroughly modern, "the great writer of our own phase of civilization" (Leavis v). Yet their differences have blurred the important assumptions that modern and Victorian novels share, and have obscured the extent to which a modernist like Lawrence, though radically and brilliantly new, sustains the work of his predecessors.

Lawrence is widely regarded as breaking with tradition—in probing consciousness, in attempting to represent impersonality, in experimenting with rhetorical forms, in exploring male bonding, and in opening up fictional endings. But he absorbs much of the tradition from which he broke. A preeminent novelist like Dickens provides a superb test of Lawrence's art because Dickens exemplifies what tradition has come to mean—in plot construction, character analysis, and role differentiation. Although many contrasts emerge, so do remarkable continuities, and Lawrence's break with tradition is, I conclude, less decisive than is often assumed. Since measuring the depth of that break is part of Lawrence's critical challenge, I focus on three areas: the problems of freedom and language, the characterization of males and females, and the issue of male bonding in *Women in Love*.

I propose to examine the "middle" work of Lawrence and Dickens. I focus on the first major novel of broad scope that each author wrote. For Dickens the choice of *Dombey and Son* (1848) is arguable. Several large novels preceded it, notably *Oliver Twist* (1837), *Nicholas Nickleby* (1839), and *Martin Chuzzlewit* (1843). But *Dombey* marks the first fully serious work of Dickens's maturity—rhetorically impressive, artistically coherent, deeply felt. For Lawrence the choice of "The Sisters" is less arguable, since among

Lawrence's important works only *Sons and Lovers* (1913) had appeared. Lawrence began "The Sisters" in 1913, rewrote it several times, then split the unwieldy draft into *The Rainbow* (1915) and *Women in Love* (1920). I also propose to link these works to a single useful concept: the tension between constriction and release. Historically it is a central tension—between the decay of social and personal power that constricts freedom, and the joyful release of feeling that nurtures personal growth.[1] This dialectic informs *Mansfield Park, Wuthering Heights, Middlemarch, Far from the Madding Crowd, The Mayor of Casterbridge,* and *A Portrait of the Artist as a Young Man.* But nowhere is it better embodied than in Dickens and Lawrence.

The two writers share biographical similarities.[2] Both had struggled out of the working class in spite of the resistance of one parent; as youths, both had briefly held jobs in factories—Dickens pasting labels on shoeblack bottles, Lawrence handling correspondence for a dealer in artificial limbs. Both were humbled by their fathers' inept handling of money. And their common experience of poverty and rejection had created a strongly developed social conscience, from which sprang their mutual reverence for the vitality of life; at mid-career both shared a tarnished optimism. Like George Eliot and Hardy, both had given up a profession—legal reporting for Dickens, schoolteaching for Lawrence—in order to write. Each author had married in his twenties; and later, both wrestled with the threat of adultery. Both traveled restlessly, seeking stasis and fulfillment.

It is no surprise that their biographies provide paradigms of differences in their respective novels. Having married early and grown unhappy, Dickens eventually met a younger woman, Ellen Ternan, and in anguish separated from his wife Kate. Lawrence, however, openly refused to marry Jessie Chambers, the Kate-like figure to whom he became unofficially engaged; instead, he met an older woman, Frieda Weekley, and eventually married her, rejecting his native England. The stripping of social obligation occurs first in Lawrence's life and then in his art. His characters—Anna, Ursula, Birkin, Connie—are open, challenging, breaking constraints, as imaged in *The Rainbow* by bursting acorns. Indifferent to social values, they are free to follow the impulses of their own natures, especially passions only half acknowledged; the Brangwens are separate from the world, isolated, "a law to themselves" (*R* 97).

By contrast, Dickens's characters are psychologically closed, like Dombey and Carker, or are, like Florence and Edith, capable of slight change. In

---

1. Weinstein puts this tension differently: mid-Victorians "imagine the protagonist becoming himself—achieving freedom—by subordinating the givens of his natural body," whereas modernists "envisage the protagonist's freedom and self-enactment in his capacity to affirm desire and to resist . . . his culture's injunctions" (4). For Weinstein freedom is possible in both positions.

2. A number of noted critics—F. R. Leavis, George Ford, Mark Spilka, H. M. Daleski—have written books on both Dickens and Lawrence.

Dombey, the narrative provides little "space" and feels constricted: objects and images stifle characters like Mr. Toots or Mrs. MacStinger or Mrs. Skewton so that their gestures become emotional prisons—Skewton's pose, Toots's chuckle, Edith's hauteur, Major Bagstock's choking laugh, Captain Cuttle's glazed hat, even Florence's sweet smile; and the ticking clock, heard often, or the waves rocking to and fro, are "closed" images of cycles and circularity—like Hardy's in *The Mayor of Casterbridge* or *Tess of the d'Urbervilles*. Moreover, coincidence, as insistent in Dickens as in Fielding, is the form of plot closure that reduces the "space" between the characters and limits their freedom by binding them into a network of social relations.

II

The rhetorical problem that each novelist faced reflects the differences in the freedom of theme and narration that each exercised. As others have noticed, what distinguishes Dickens and those novelists who emulated Fielding is not only a reliance on plot as organizing principle, but on the mediating rhetorical voice, which converts private experience into public prose. In spite of Dickens's ability to move an audience, his narrator's voice is "aloof" and "closed," distanced from the characters, treating them as objects of strong feeling—pity or scorn.

What distinguishes *The Rainbow* is Lawrence's immense freedom to move from narrative exposition to indirect discourse to free indirect discourse.[3] Lawrence's social range is narrower than Dickens's because he more deeply penetrates his characters' psyches. His aim is well expressed in a passage found in the holograph manuscript of *Lady Chatterley's Lover* (1928). As Connie reaches sexual fulfillment with Mellors, the narrator reports that her sharp cries "were like the language of the first wild gods crying out before argument began, like the shouts of the first angels, strange yelping noise of incipient music" (Squires 208). Consciousness is imagined as preverbal ("before argument") so that Connie's responses are chaotic sensations unshaped by rhetorical strategy. There lies the individual's *pure* character—"deeper down than language" (Moynahan, page 40). It is then shaped—even sullied—by the narrator's intervening language, which mediates between pure consciousness and audience adaptation. Although Lawrence's narrator recognizes the need to mediate, he often takes the reader back toward this "language" of incipient beauty—as when Paul Morel confronts an enormous orange moon, when Louisa Lindley touches Alfred Durant's back, when March gazes at Henry Grenfel: or when any of the admired characters make love. At such times

---

3. Indirect discourse clearly marks the narrator's presence ("He said that he loved her"); free indirect discourse greatly reduces it ("He loved her").

Lawrence modulates the narrator's rhetorical voice to a more personal and sensuous form in which the privacy of sensual experience can be maintained. The characters are, as it were, shielded from public scrutiny.

Dickens also takes the reader back, but into a consciousness where characters like Paul and Florence Dombey are attuned to a preternatural mystery. That mystery is comparatively schematic, a way for worthy characters to hear messages of Christian comfort. Dickens's attempt to connect characters to a sort of racial memory offers less a means to truth than another rhetorical device, in which the waves become a metaphor for a choric voice: another way for the narrator to comment indirectly.

Both novelists encountered opposite sides of the same problem. For Dickens the problem was how to communicate a character's inner emotional integrity while using strategies such as a complicated plot. For Lawrence the problem was how to get far enough outside a character's private emotional experience to make it intelligible within a larger artistic design. Whereas Dickens conceived of his novels in response to what his characters *did* to each other, in a web of social threads, Lawrence viewed his novels as responses to what his characters *felt*, at the eye of the web, cutting the burden of social threads to pursue self-fulfillment—as Ursula does when she rejects Mr. Harby's authority in order to establish her "personal self" (*R* 351).

Whereas differences in narrative freedom separate the two novelists, so do differences in the freedom with which they explore language. In *Dombey* Dickens is intrigued by nonverbal language: Captain Cuttle communicates with gesture; Paul deciphers messages in the patterned wallpaper; the waves speak to admired characters like Paul and Florence. Paul often tries to understand the waves' repetitions or the river's rolling to sea, and at the close the waves murmur to Florence of "love, eternal and illimitable" (976; ch. 61). Dickens reaches for the same external key to unlock the meaning of human experience that Casaubon and Lydgate seek in *Middlemarch,* that Lyell and Darwin sought in science, that Frazer sought in myth, that Lacan and Foucault have sought in language.

In Lawrence's *Rainbow* nature also speaks a language intelligible to the admired characters. In the cows' chuffing, Tom and Anna hear sounds of harmony and integration. In the biology lab Ursula finds a message in a single, autonomous cell: "a consummation, a being infinite" (409). Later she enters a trancelike communion with the moon and the stars, "filled with the full moon, offering herself," wanting "consummation" (296); still later the stars seem to enter "the unfathomable darkness of her womb" (431). Artistically and philosophically, however, these passages of waves and moon are remarkably different. What has intervened is Thomas Hardy's fiction, where the rhythms of agricultural life linked to such characters as Oak, Winterborne, and Tess have aroused a fresh bond of sympathy in spite of nature's cold indifference. What has also intervened is a new assumption about symbolic language in which the distance between subject and object has radically changed. For Dickens the waves, even when richly evocative, remain expository, a "speaking" symbol, inert. The waves convey a message, a statement of universal truth, applicable to characters and reader alike.[4] Dickens thereby preserves the kind of distance that typifies his fiction: characters are kept physically and emotionally separated, doors and windows and walls block their emotional gratification, males and females are sharply differentiated, single identifying gestures distance reader from character.

For Lawrence the distance between subject and object shrinks, as when Ursula embraces the moon. In such passages critics have located Lawrence's attempt to reach the bedrock of character or to overcome nature's indifference.[5] What also needs saying is that human subject and natural object fuse, symbolically reaching back into the kind of eternity represented by Dickens's waves—not to hear a message but to achieve a new identity, impregnated with a new selfhood, cleansed of corruption.[6] For Lawrence this impregnation suffuses the new self. Yearning for something unknown, Ursula passed "far away, into the pristine darkness of paradise, into the original immortality" (R 418). After sex with Skrebensky, she lies "motionless, eternal" (445). In a review of Frederick Carter's Dragon of the Apocalypse, Lawrence makes the connection explicit: "To enter the astronomical sky of space is a great sensational experience. . . . It is the entry into another world. . . . And we find some prisoned self in us coming forth to live in this world" (Phoenix 293). For Lawrence this freshly discovered fusion of human subject and natural object opens up an array of narrative freedoms—the use of habitual action instead of simple incident, the subordination of plot, and a narrative structure based on stages of physical attraction which Dickens would have disliked. Unlike Lawrence, Dickens looks out, not down, into a social web distanced from the narrator. Their essential difference is imaged in the waves' contrasted meanings: for Dickens the waves bear tidings of shared comfort, for Lawrence's Connie Chatterley they bring internal assurance, the "dark waves rising and heaving," putting "her whole darkness . . . in motion" (LCL 229).

4. Miller observes that the sea, its fluidity breaking up the solid and the enclosed, symbolizes "that realm beyond this earth where the seemingly inescapable separation between people will be transcended and the reciprocity of love will be possible" (149).

5. Daleski is representative: "The passage [of moon consummation] is a brilliant example of the 'carbon' of character in action" (112). Miko, however, finds the scenes of moon consummation "the most puzzling in the book" (173). For him the new light imagery implies a different but uncertain direction for Ursula.

6. As Perloff writes about Birds, Beasts and Flowers: "For Lawrence, there is no longer a distinction between subject and object, consciousness and the external world. Rather, the new space is one in which the mind and its objects are present in a single realm of proximity" (127).

III

The tension between freedom and constraint helps determine the treatment of both male and female characters. I start with female. In Victorian literature narrative constraints have a social equivalent called duty, which appears in Trollope, Charlotte Brontë, George Eliot, and Hardy, and which affects both men without power, like John Carker, and most of Dickens's female characters. In his fiction Dickens inculcates strong allegiance to parental figures, covertly reinforcing the social hierarchy. Early, the dying Paul protects his father's feelings by crying, "Indeed I am quite happy!" (295; ch. 16). Florence is obsessed with duty. Less extreme are Mrs. Pipchin, James Carker, Walter Gay, Susan Nipper, Mr. Toots, and Rob Toodle. Rob, for instance, gravitates from one parental figure to the other, and Paul, Florence, Toots, and Walter all seek closure in parental figures. Because social integration precedes self-integration in Dickens's novel, these characters hunger for protection. Since self poses a burden, society offers an escape, as when Florence rescues her father from the terror of being alone. On the other hand, Ursula's early experiences with her father—swinging at the fair, swimming dangerously, planting potatoes—free her to pursue self-realization as a personal responsibility. "Slowly, slowly, the fire of mistrust and defiance . . . burned away her connection with him" (*R* 249). After a quarrel, "she was free—she had broken away from him" (338). Ursula's parental experiences leave her "hard and impersonal" (367). As Janice Harris says in the essay that follows, "Lawrence deserves his reputation as the voice of the time proclaiming a woman's liberation" (page 70).

Lawrence wrote in 1913, "the cruelest thing a man can do to a woman is to portray her as perfection" (*Letters* I: 549). Like Thackeray and Trollope, Dickens continued to work in the tradition of Richardson and Fielding, idealizing women and limiting their power to act. Despite the narrator's claim that Florence lacks "art or knowledge of the world" (477; ch. 27), her inability to challenge the forces in her environment, or to interpret her own experience, limits her capacity to grow and her human appeal. She yearns to love her father but cannot recognize his atrophied feelings, which resemble Clifford Chatterley's. Dickens's narrator, instead of demonstrating the sources of Dombey's human failure, harangues: "Let him remember [his rejection of Florence] in that room, years to come. . . . Let him remember it in that room" (327; ch. 18).

Compared to Florence, Edith Skewton Dombey is better realized—more intelligent, more courageously opportunistic, more willing to challenge the marketing of women: "There is no slave in a market: there is no horse in a fair: so shown and offered and examined and paraded . . . as I have been, for ten shameful years" (473; ch. 27). But even Edith must be made a fallen woman.

For six chapters (chs. 48–53) Dickens leads the reader to assume that she is Carker's mistress: after shedding her jewels, like Becky Sharp, she flees to Dijon, then visits London after Carker's death, socially ruined, her pride dissolving into penitence. Edith resembles Tess Durbeyfield—running from her pursuer, justified in spurning the man who tries to seduce her, yet still reduced to death.

Lawrence approaches female character differently. As the stable Victorian world gives way to colliding perspectives on truth and reality, Lawrence comes to Anna and both Ursulas from an altered perspective, seeing each woman as a character successively redefining herself, stage by stage, as the "adventure in life" unfolds.[7] Anna progresses from love to religious zeal to maternal fulfillment, Ursula from religious probing to the wonders of knowledge to the ecstasy of "impersonal" sexual revelation; and many of Lawrence's other heroines move similarly from withered hope and stunned sensibilities to richly integrated selves.

Here, abridged, is a piece of Ursula's sensual response to Skrebensky:

> He seemed like the living darkness upon her. . . . She quivered, and quivered, like a tense thing that is struck. But he held her all the time, soft, unending, like darkness closed upon her, omnipresent as the night. He kissed her, and she quivered as if she were being destroyed, shattered. The lighted vessel vibrated, and broke in her soul, the light fell, struggled, and went dark. She was all dark, will-less, having only the receptive will.
>
> He kissed her, with his soft, enveloping kisses, and she responded to them completely, her mind, her soul gone out. Darkness cleaving to darkness, she hung close to him, pressed herself into [the] soft flow of his kiss, pressed herself down, down to the source and core of his kiss, herself covered and enveloped in the warm, fecund flow of his kiss, that travelled over her, flowed over her . . . so they were one stream. . . . (R 413–14)

This beautiful passage, almost a chant of primal feeling, turns volatile: Ursula feels "as if she were turned to steel"; then gradually, like Kate Leslie and Connie Chatterley in the later novels, she dissolves into a stream of feeling. Human touch, like heat, transforms the self from one phase of realization to another. But here Ursula's aroused self also penetrates to the "core" of Skrebensky, taps the "source of him"; he cannot keep himself separate and individual, so she must shed him.

Whereas Lawrence, as he creates, listens mainly to the bodies of his female characters, Dickens listens mainly to his audience. Choosing not to gauge the body's muttering and incoherent spontaneity, Dickens offers superior rhetorical control: he *thinks* what his characters feel, whereas Lawrence, often

---

7. As Jarrett-Kerr has said, "Even hostile critics are agreed that Lawrence's supreme achievement was to find expression for states of being hitherto almost unexplored" (146–47).

rejecting tradition, reckons with the new knowledge about evolution, instinct, and will, and freshly gauges new stresses on the individual that accompany the new modes of surveillance which Michel Foucault has analyzed. And because Lawrence sees things in a new way he can say them in a new way. Hence in the last half of *The Rainbow* Lawrence splendidly renders Ursula's sensations, urges, and perceptions—as when she canes Williams, devours Skrebensky with her will, or hallucinates about the rhythmic assault of wild horses. Lawrence's extraordinary emotional sensitivity means, however, that some narrative segments are not conventionally coherent. Whereas Dickens in a long novel like *Little Dorrit* uses images of the prison to ensure unity, Lawrence composes differently. The novel's major scenes of "Stacking Sheaves," "Lincoln Cathedral, "The Moon as Consummation," and "Wild Horses" do not share a cumulative set of images; instead, the material world provides the hard surface on which the novelist can set strong emotion, like cups on a table, for stability. Rather than alternating plots, Lawrence projects passionate feeling, then pauses with interludes of summarized action. The logic is internal rather than external.

In Dickens intense feeling can also typify the exchanges between male and female, but the intensity is less felt than it is seen and overheard. Take Edith encountering Carker in their hotel room at Dijon:

He was coming gaily towards her, when, in an instant, she caught the knife up from the table. . . .

"Stand still!" she said, "or I shall murder you!"

The sudden change in her, the towering fury and intense abhorrence sparkling in her eyes and lighting up her brow, made him stop as if a fire had stopped him. . . .

They both stood looking at each other. Rage and astonishment were in his face, but he controlled them, and said lightly,

"Come, come! . . . Do you think to frighten me with these tricks of virtue?" . . .

"I have something lying here that is no love trinket; and sooner than endure your touch once more, I would use it on you . . . with less reluctance than I would on any other creeping thing that lives."

He affected to laugh jestingly. . . .

"How many times," said Edith, bending her darkest glance upon him, "has your bold knavery assailed me with outrage and insult? How many times . . . have I been twitted with my courtship and my marriage? How many times have you laid bare my wound of love for the sweet, injured girl [Florence], and lacerated it? How often have you fanned the fire on which, for two years, I have writhed; and tempted me to take a desperate revenge[?]" (854–56; ch. 54)

Characteristically, Dickens prefers dialogue, a stiff spoken rhetoric, and dramatic gestures like the ready knife. The repetitions are Ciceronian, public. Dickens's narrator watches Edith from the outside, mesmerized by her pride, not as he understands it but as she reveals it. He observes her at a distance, giving her portrait a coldness like that given to Dombey himself.

There is another difference. Whereas Lawrence often concentrates an emotional response *within* the characters in *The Rainbow* and *Women in Love*, Dickens usually divides an angry response to power or oppression *between* the characters and the narrator. When Florence seeks her father's affection as he lies wounded and asleep, the narrator punctuates the scene with these words: "Awake, unkind father! Awake, now, sullen man! . . . the hour is coming with an angry tread" (698; ch. 43). And when no character can articulate Dickens's diatribe on poor sanitation, the narrator offers it himself, lambasting "the thick and sullen air where Vice and Fever propagate together, raining the tremendous social retributions which are ever pouring down" (738; ch. 47). Thus when Dickens's narrator can, himself, struggle against oppressive conditions, Dickens's characters need not: so that the thin texture of the characters' lives is exaggerated by Dickens's choice of narrative method.

Of course, Lawrence can also use this method, as he does when Ursula is disillusioned with the university's professors and curriculum. Yet he can perfectly concentrate struggle within a character like Ursula—can intensify her reactions and penetrate deeply into her consciousness, as in the extraordinary passage where she hears horses "looming in the rain, not near yet. But they were going to be near. . . . She knew the heaviness of her heart. It was the weight of the horses. . . . Like circles of lightning came the flash of hoofs. . . . Her feet faltered. . . . It was the crisis" (*R* 451–53). The rhythmic motion of the horses is a sustained metaphor of anxiety, anxiety over male power[8]—the equivalent of Carker's insinuating power over Edith. Yet Lawrence captures Ursula's anxiety with fewer rhetorical concessions to his reader. He turns the narrative camera inward, reducing the narrator to one who organizes (using in/out structures), who patterns (using a series of enclosures), but who does not engage in the three forms of explicit commentary that Chatman (237–47) has identified: interpretation, judgment, and generalization. Lawrence can therefore portray female frustration as an attractive vulnerability, as encompassing great personal risk, leading, it seems, only incidentally to Ursula's loss of her baby as a plot solution. Gordon says perceptively that in *The Rainbow* and *Women in Love* "Lawrence invents new ways of presenting character and organizing plot that reduce the pressure of

8. Martin Green sees Ursula's anxiety differently: "Ursula's dream of a circle of threatening horses . . . surely must mean, in the context of the novel, the world of men. By a Freudian interpretation, of course, it *must* mean male sexuality, but this is a good example of the limitations of such interpretations of Lawrence. Ursula is not afraid of male sexuality. . . . What she is afraid of . . . is the world of institutions and public events, the world of the school, the army, the war, the police, the factory. These are what surround and threaten Ursula symbolically, and these are what she is destined triumphantly to elude" (358).

cause-and-effect logic and give greater sanction to the immediacy of feeling, before it is exposed to reflective judgment'' (245).

IV

Although Dickens and Lawrence differ in their use of narrative ''space'' and conceive of admired females differently, the two novelists share important similarities. These similarities hold special critical interest because they demonstrate the extent to which Lawrence indirectly endorsed traditional literary values: in his attitude toward assertive females, in his treatment of male power, and in his use of artistic closure.

Both writers express an aversion to willful, dominating women who affect youth and sexual allurement. Creating caricatures, both continue a tradition that includes Lady Bellaston in *Tom Jones,* Mrs. Dobbs Broughton in *The Last Chronicle of Barset,* and Mrs. Charmond in *The Woodlanders.* Both share a preference for repetition as the chief verbal signal of dislike—a technique that Lawrence may have learned from Dickens.[9] For Dickens repetition identifies and tracks characters so that the reader instantly links ''chuckle'' with Mr. Toots, ''make an effort'' with Mrs. Chick, or ''the black-eyed'' with Susan Nipper; for Lawrence repetition often expresses the emotional pulsation that characterizes his mature style and signals his profound faith in intuitive feeling. In *Dombey* Dickens's satire most effectively targets Mrs. Skewton, a prototype of both Lady Dedlock in *Bleak House* and Lady Tippins in *Our Mutual Friend;* Lawrence's satire targets Hermione in *Women in Love,* but it extends to Mrs. Hepburn in *The Captain's Doll,* Mrs. Witt in *St. Mawr,* Pauline Attenborough in ''The Lovely Lady,'' and Lina M'Leod in ''The Blue Moccasins.'' At once, Mrs. Skewton, posturing and febrile, is reduced to the metonymy ''Cleopatra,'' much as Lawrence labels Mrs. Fawcett ''the little Jewess'' in *The Virgin and the Gipsy.* With Mrs. Skewton, and with her alone, are associated a series of striking verbs—simpered, minced, lisped, drawled—that become a kind of template for Lawrence's own ''sang Hermione,'' which, like a drum, punctuates Hermione's speech in *Women in Love.*

Female power offends both writers. Mrs. Skewton, like Mrs. Brown, barters her daughter for wealth and position: both Alice and Edith have had to disguise their natural feelings of rage, having been taught to covet not male power, but the power that males can confer. For classic characters like Moll Flanders, Pamela Andrews, Lydia Bennet, and Becky Sharp—as well as for Alice and Edith—the preferred means to power is sex: disguised as coquetry

---

9. In ''The Future of the Novel'' (1923) Lawrence recalls ''the loony Cleopatra [Mrs. Skewton] in *Dombey and Son,* murmuring 'Rose-coloured curtains—' with her dying breath, old hag'' (*STH* 153).

in Mrs. Skewton (" 'You aggravating monster,' said Cleopatra, giving one hand to the Major, and tapping his knuckles with her fan" [447; ch. 26]), disguised as cold hauteur in Edith. To peel off the disguise is the stuff of comedy in Fielding, but in Dickens a layer of poignant humiliation lies exposed—for Edith as well as for Miss Tox, both cruelly exposed as husband-hunters. Indeed, Edith is undone not by her polished recital of attractions but by her unguarded anguish, in which Carker, hiding, sees that within her "some passion or struggle was raging" (458; ch. 27), his knowledge of her painful secret growing malignant in her breast.

Lawrence's Hermione Roddice is a husband-hunter too; and like Cleopatra she is a broker in mockery and an advocate—if ironically—of spontaneity. Hermione "want[s] to clutch things and have them in [her] power" (*WL* 42). Like Mrs. Skewton parading her daughter, Hermione parades her houseguests through the park: " 'This way, this way,' sang her leisurely voice at intervals" (87). Both writers reveal a knot of antagonism toward powerful females who coerce—including Mrs. Markleham in *David Copperfield,* Miss Havisham in *Great Expectations,* Mrs. Clennam in *Little Dorrit,* and the castrating wives that both Aaron Sisson and Oliver Mellors escape. Such women threaten male integrity and identity.

Both novelists are also alike in their mistrust of male power, whether industrial or personal. Mr. Dombey's accumulated power is subverted by his deceitful ally Carker; urban renewal topples Staggs's Gardens; and at the novel's close the rushing train, a concentrated image of industrial force—and "the symbol of real power in the novel" (Humphreys 413)—bears down on Carker with relentless speed, killing him. Similarly, in *Women in Love* the raucous, smoking train bears down on Gerald Crich's sensitive mare, imprisoning her between the train's iron wall and Gerald's iron will. In *The Rainbow* the religious power of the church oppresses, and Lawrence evokes Wiggiston's industrial energy as a cancer of the spirit which lures Uncle Tom and Winifred Inger, with their "marshy, bitter-sweet corruption" of homosexual sterility (326). For all of Dickens's reforming art, Lawrence resists industrial energy more forcefully, has an angrier sense of its destructive power, sees with more loathing its paralyzing havoc.

As powerful, symbolic males, both Carker the Manager in *Dombey and Son* and Gerald Crich in *Women in Love* are treated ambivalently—attractive on the surface, destructive beneath. Relishing their power, both have a strong sense of vocation, Carker efficiently managing Dombey's firm, Gerald his father's mines. Both arrange liaisons with unmarried women—Carker with Alice Marwood, Gerald with Pussum—after which both men achieve an intimacy that each is unable to consummate: Carker physically, with Edith; Gerald spiritually, with Gudrun. And both are clothed in striking imagery, Carker cool and feline and smiling, "sharp of tooth, soft of foot, watchful of eye" (372–73; ch. 22), Gerald all electric, "with a subtle friction of electricity," "as if struck by electricity" (73, 440). Like Heathcliff or Casaubon, both males, deficient in sympathy, exploit others. As Casaubon uses Dorothea in *Middlemarch,* so Carker uses Alice, casts her off, then uses Edith to revenge Dombey; similarly, Gerald, spurring his bleeding mare, sees her, like his mine workers, as an object "for my use" (139).

Both males are caught in the same plot direction, thereby confirming their human failure. Carker, like Bradley Headstone in *Our Mutual Friend,* moves from a public life of respectability to a private life of intimacy, guilt, and disintegration; Gerald, like George Saxton in Lawrence's first novel, moves also from a public life of respectability to a private life with Gudrun that leads to violence and disintegration. Both writers capture the men's deaths impressively from the inside, Dickens (atypically) burrowing into Carker's consciousness as Carker escapes Dombey and collides with the express train, Lawrence piercing Gerald's consciousness as Gerald escapes Gudrun and falls asleep in the snow, as weary and disoriented as Carker.[10]

These similarities lead to a deeper understanding of tradition as it defines Lawrence's achievement. It is, for example, instructive to compare these two inside renderings of male deterioration. Near the close both Carker and Gerald go abroad with the women they love—Carker to France, Gerald to Germany; afterward, both women respond violently, betray their lovers, and leave them distraught. To capture Carker's fractured mental state, Dickens writes a rhetorically brilliant chapter (ch. 55) in which Carker's paranoia, caught in sentence fragments, rolls outward in evocative waves. Lawrence's portrait of Gerald's deterioration, though less assured, is also evocative. Both male characters are portrayed escaping others; both are numb with fatigue; both, in terror of falling, fear they will be murdered ("Somebody was going to murder him," thinks Gerald [473]); as if trapped, both move desperately, Carker back and forth, Gerald up and down; and both experience a revelation before death, Carker spying Dombey on the train platform, Gerald seeing a little Christ "at the top of a pole" (473). As a reader might now expect, Carker is gradually constrained by the external sensory world, Gerald gradually released from it, wanting only sleep.

To move from Carker and Gerald to a consideration of Rupert Birkin will show how strongly tradition molds Lawrence's conception of character, for Birkin may be located in the same context of mistrusted males. Since he is greatly admired in *Women in Love,* this claim may seem surprising, but it will

---

10. In Lawrence's later work the conflicted character, doomed by internal flaws and thus desiring death, reappears in Egbert ("England, My England"), Cathcart ("The Man Who Loved Islands"), and the Woman Who Rode Away. All receive enlarged narrative sympathy as their deaths approach.

show the effects of tradition in just the area—male bonding—where Lawrence is credited with major innovation. In *David Copperfield* (1850) Dickens had examined the issue of male bonding with special sensitivity—developing the relationship between David and James Steerforth, tolerating David's strong infatuation with his handsome friend, admitting that Steerforth "carried a spell with him to which it was a natural weakness to yield" (157; ch. 7), and allowing David, when he hears Steerforth's footstep in Chapter 28, to feel "my heart beat high, and the blood rush to my face" (485): Dickens only then revealing the worm in their bond, for Steerforth, like Carker, is a traitor who seduces David's childhood friend, Little Em'ly, already betrothed to another. In a sense Dickens punishes David's attraction to Steerforth. But Lawrence makes an advance over Dickens by characterizing Birkin not as a classic seducer like Steerforth but as a complex, ambivalently attractive figure whose impulses are partly blocked, partly expressed, so that the undertow of authorial hesitation is built into Birkin's characterization—not explicitly, as in Dickens, but implicitly.

Like Steerforth, both Carker and Birkin are, in a sense, also emotional thieves who reject male-to-male bonding. Whereas Carker betrays Dombey's trust and friendship in order to steal Edith's affection, so does Birkin curry Gerald's friendship and then, with little encouragement, seek (if ambiguously) a *Blutbrüderschaft* that has the potential to become sexual: "he had been loving Gerald all along, and all along denying it" (206)—just as Lawrence himself, in 1916, was plagued by his erotic feelings for Middleton Murry. Lawrence, says Paul Delany, "could neither keep them entirely hidden, nor express them in plain words—still less in any direct physical way" (223).[11] Critics usually argue that Gerald is incapable of returning Birkin's offer. Charles Ross is typical: the "failure [of Birkin and Gerald] to consummate is an inevitability of Gerald's character" ("Homoerotic Feeling" 181). While their friendship develops, then cools, the narrator slowly sabotages Gerald's selfhood by exposing his deficiencies: "He held himself back" and becomes "as if fated, doomed, limited," succumbing to "a sort of fatal halfness"; he "could never fly away from himself" (207). In this way Victorian constraint gets reinscribed into Gerald's character. Later his inert, dead body elicits "disgust" (477). I submit that in Birkin's earlier, coarser, more cynical avatars in the English novel—in Squire B or Lovelace or Wickham—he would have dallied not with a Gerald but with a woman like Lydia Bennet or Hetty Sorrel or Winifred Hurtle, whom the narrator could gradually reveal as unsuitable or inadequate— as Austen and Eliot and Trollope do. Hence the novel tradition helps identify Birkin as a potential seducer who tries to appropriate what isn't his.

11. To Murry, however, Frieda Lawrence wrote on 6 August 1953: "I think the homosexuality in him was a short phase out of misery . . . and that he wanted a deeper thing from you" (360).

How might this claim affect our reading of *Women in Love?* In two ways. To see Birkin as a potential seducer is to make fresh sense of the emotional "muddle" that he faces midway through the novel, when he says to Ursula, his face full of perplexity, "It's the problem I can't solve" (363). Birkin is muddled not only because he is working out a difficult polarization of his feelings, such that even when he passionately desires Ursula, he feels the "unyielding anguish of another thing" (187). He is also muddled because part of him—perhaps an unacknowledged part—wants to seduce Gerald, finding him "physically" beautiful (273), but without knowing how to justify that desire within a social frame.[12] What is unavailable is punishable. It is not enough to say that Birkin flies to Gerald because their friendship offers a haven from entanglements with destructive women, for Gerald soon becomes a victim like Edith. As Edith rejects Carker's advances, so Gerald rejects Birkin's, lacking the strength to swear his love. Early in the novel, in what I regard as a critical pronouncement, Birkin says (though not to Gerald), "You've got to lapse out before you can know what sensual reality is . . . and *give up your volition*" (44, emphasis added). "Do you *want* to be normal or ordinary?" Birkin later demands of Gerald (205). But Gerald cannot give up his volition: to do so would be an act of foolish vulnerability, a violation.

Yet the pressure remains, and when, in "Man to Man," their eyes meet again, "Gerald's . . . were suffused now with warm light and with unadmitted love, Birkin looked back as out of the darkness . . . with a kind of warmth, that seemed to flow over Gerald's brain like a fertile sleep" (210). This "fertile sleep" is hypnotic, potentially seductive, designed to induce a deeper intimacy. Still later, when Birkin pleads that they "admit the unadmitted love of man for man," Gerald hesitates and then adds, in a clarifying passage inserted as late as September 1919 (Ross, *Composition* 129): "Surely there can never by anything as strong between man and man as sex love is between man and woman. Nature doesn't provide the basis" (352). That is the classical Christian

---

12. On the problem of homosexuality in the novel, Sagar writes: "I believe Lawrence dropped 'Prologue' . . . and the whole theme of deadly homosexuality, primarily because he came to see that the position to which he had committed himself was not quite honest. He had lacked the courage to accept the implications of the most honest passage in 'Prologue' . . . and . . . had allowed his horror of sodomy . . . to blind him to the possibility that other, more creative, forms of contact, even physical contact, might be possible, even desirable, between men. And he had invested so much in his marriage that he was loath to admit to himself that it was not enough" (174). I disagree with Donaldson, who argues that in Lawrence's novel "what besets Birkin in the Prologue—the homosexual impulses he cannot deny and will not accept—do[es] not seem to be Birkin's trouble in *Women in Love*" (49). Cowan intelligently concedes the "homoerotic motive in scenes involving sensual touch between men" but urges that "something other and more profound than simple homosexual desire" also emanates from them (130). Cowan would distinguish between a sexual motive, whether conscious or unconscious, and an intention to act out that motive in overt sexual behavior.

objection to homosexuality, enunciated by Clement of Alexandria and Saint Augustine (Boswell 140–50). Birkin replies, "Well, of course, I think she does"—that nature does provide the basis for something as strong between man and man as sexual love between man and woman. We will never be happy, Birkin continues, "till we establish ourselves on this basis"—meaning, I take it, on the basis of love, even sexual love, between man and man.[13] To this intellectual argument Gerald replies, "Only I can't *feel* it, you see" (352–53). That response is fair and precise; it is also lame. But it shows that Gerald has, like most males, long before internalized the Western prohibition against homosexuality into an emotional response compounded with fear.[14] Whereas Birkin is caught between ambivalence and expression, Gerald is caught between ambivalence and suppression. Yet Lawrence immediately follows this exchange with an apparent gloss: Gerald "was ready to be doomed"— doomed, one presumes, because he *feels* he must choose marriage ("the seal of his condemnation") and hence the "established order" (353). The real problem, I submit, is that the narrator cannot respect Gerald's position, partly because it conveys an emotional rejection too close to Lawrence's recent personal experience with Middleton Murry, and partly because he cannot effectively rebut the underlying charge that "nature doesn't provide the basis." As Donaldson says, "Lawrence never gives Gerald's doubts and mistrust their due" (55).

"Doomed" and "condemned," Gerald now faces banishment to the snowy Alps as Edith is banished to Italy or Alice to death. Gerald's psychological doom is only a modern version of the social doom that hounds the fallen figures of earlier English novels, in which a constriction of self is the fruit of the narrative's judgment. Gerald, we are told, suffers now from "the absence of volition." That is equally precise. Although "strangely elated" by Birkin's offer of love, Gerald feels "a numbness upon him" (353) because, unable to reciprocate, he also feels guilt, as if betraying Birkin's powerful claim of friendship. Gerald's emotional range is not wide enough to encompass the relationship that Birkin desires. Although Lawrence doesn't imagine well this sort of guilt (perhaps because he doesn't fully understand it), he does perceive that a character like Gerald, defined within "the established world," could feel violated by guilt.

13. I differ from Donaldson, who avers that in *Women in Love* "the basis in nature for the relationship between men is some basis other than sex love," though he concedes that "Lawrence doesn't disclose more of what he means" (54).

14. In Lawrence's draft of the *Blutbrüderschaft* exchange in Chapter 16 (reproduced in Ross, *Composition* 139–41), the narrator records not only Gerald's "curious unwillingness of admission" when Birkin urges commitment but also Gerald's "eyes hot with confusion" and his convulsive clasping of Birkin's hand, "with lips parted, breathing short and fast, his eyes set"—details that appear to gauge Gerald's passion for Birkin as well as his fear of that passion.

What Lawrence's narrator does not reveal is that although Gerald cannot offer his body to Birkin, his spirit does succumb to the pressure of a possible homoerotic bond. "We are mentally, spiritually intimate, therefore we should be more or less physically intimate too," Birkin urges after they wrestle (272). A part of Gerald succumbs to what—physically—would have violated his deepest integrity. It is no surprise that in Chapter 6 Gerald looks over the degenerate Halliday and, with phallic overtones, finds his softness attractive, like the mare's soft thighs: Halliday's "was a soft, warm, corrupt nature, into which one might plunge with gratification" (68).[15] As Weinstein says, although Gerald also "wants something" from Birkin, "the novel refuses to assess, even to identify, what he desires" (215). Instead, Lawrence's narrator blames Gerald's industrial rootedness, calling him "the God of the machine" (223)—an alibi for the deeper psychological truth—and interprets Gerald's failure in a conventional Victorian way, as (for instance) Hardy interprets Angel Clare's, locating failure in a false religious ideal, or as Dickens in *Little Dorrit* traces Mr. Merdle's suicide to a hollow social ideal. Just as Edith encapsulates the tradition of female manipulation for material gain, so does Gerald encapsulate a male version of the same materialistic tendency. For both characters the criticism applied to them is not appropriately psychological but inappropriately social.

Moreover, betrayal works doubly, hastening Gerald's collapse but clarifying Birkin's own guilt. To see Birkin as a traditional seducer, implicated in Gerald's death and coming to great pain, freshly clarifies how Lawrence displaces the seducer's panic to *Aaron's Rod*. In Lawrence's next novel with a male protagonist, composed intermittently from 1918 to 1921, Aaron Sisson reenacts Birkin's role. Deserting his wife and children, he combines as it were Birkin's hidden guilt with his own, falls ill, and, like Carker and Gerald, is then sent to wander abroad. By displacing the true psychological resolution of *Women in Love* to *Aaron's Rod,* Lawrence wrestles artistically with the problem of his sexual ambivalence. One reason he had such difficulty finishing *Aaron's Rod*[16] is, I believe, that as soon as Aaron becomes both ill and a wanderer, expiating himself and his alter ego Birkin, the tension in *Women in Love* is finally resolved. Psychologically, Aaron requires no further resolution.

V

Both Dickens and Lawrence devote extraordinary space to what Lawrence calls the "recoil from things gone dead" (*LCL* 146) and what Wayne Booth

15. It is worth noting that in the novel's suppressed prologue, Birkin similarly "plunged on triumphant into intimacy with Gerald Crich" (493).

16. For example: "My novel jerks one chapter forward now and then" (*Letters* III: 594); "I am still stuck in the middle of *Aaron's Rod*" and "can't end it" (*Letters* III: 608, 626).

calls "uncreated" lives (page 14). Both novelists reject the egotism and bullying of characters like Dombey, Carker, Mr. Harby, Gerald, and Loerke, who cripple the freedom of the females drawn to them. Depending heavily on binary oppositions—selfish/generous, hate/love, cold/hot, snow/fire—both novelists urge spontaneity and openly expressed emotion. A capacity to express feeling helps both Florence and Ursula define themselves against the prison of male power in which they are initially trapped; Alice and Edith, lacking the capacity for free expression, remain imprisoned, victims of abuse.

In this context of recoil from oppression I want, finally, to examine together the problematic endings of *Dombey* and *The Rainbow*. In the English novel a traditional ending mandates marriage (Fielding, Austen, Scott, Thackeray) or occasionally death (Richardson). Both forms of closure often simplify an author's fictional materials, as in both of these novels. Dickens resolves the plot tension in *Dombey* by a death, several returns home, a reformation, and five marriages. Few readers, however, are comfortable with Dombey's long-awaited reformation from tyrant to emotional philanthropist.[17] As Tom Jones reforms in the beneficent light of Sophia's love, so does Dombey's reformation depend on the craven fidelity of his daughter Florence. But her fidelity challenges mimetic truth. Today Florence would be labeled an abused child—deprived of her mother and then her brother, estranged from her father and then (inexplicably) from her stepmother, driven from her home to become an orphan. Feeling guilty, as abused children do ("I somehow provoked that response"), Florence might well seek out her father after his firm collapses, but with feelings of love suffused with anger—troubled, ambivalent feelings that Dickens does not acknowledge. Instead, just as the novel's five marriages simplify its materials, substituting action for exploration, so does Florence's behavior turn her into a stock female nurturer, an Angel in the House for her husband, two children, and now her father.

If Dickens's ending constrains his characters' development, the ending of *The Rainbow* opens out into freedom and release, yet does not fully amplify the richness of Ursula's experience. Ill and depressed by her lover, her job, and her pregnancy, Ursula needs a sign that she may anticipate Birkin in the novel's sequel; hence the rainbow promises her a new earthly "architecture" and "a man created by God" (457). As the flood at Marsh Farm is a natural phenomenon of closure in the first generation, so is the rainbow in the third. But most critics agree that the concluding imagery of the rainbow is strained, an assertion of hope rather than a coherent resolution. John Worthen is representative: "The ending inevitably hangs its rainbow out over a void" as Lawrence diverts the novel "into a new channel—one more passionately

---

17. For a different view of Dombey's reformation, see Tillotson (169–71) and Milner (487).

concerned with society'' (73, 81). Put simply, Lawrence's ending is the imagistic equivalent of marriage in earlier English novels. The man created by God will, in fact, soon become a husband. As marriage connects man and woman, so the rainbow bridges sun and rain. The endings of both novels assert a faith in the future of human relationships that is not fully grounded in the works themselves.

Fielding's dictum that authors must motivate changes in character when ''notorious Rogues'' turn into ''worthy Gentlemen'' (307; bk. 8, ch. 1) is useful here. For both writers, I would argue, the generic expectations set by tradition influence artistic judgment. The five marriages of *Dombey* do not mimetically or artistically follow from Dombey's unsuccessful marriages or from the portrayal of a great many characters—the majority—who are not married. Dickens's optimism rests on a shallow foundation. For Lawrence the problem of closure is less acute, for the image of the rainbow has appeared earlier, in the cathedral arch; and the marriage projected at the novel's close has behind it two earlier portraits of responsible union. Yet Lawrence's assertive rhetoric at the close has the fervor of an apocalyptic vision, less a bridge to a sequel than a way to command optimism and faith. But for both Dombey and Ursula an inner death—of Dombey's pride, of Ursula's unborn child—heralds a new life of ''the unknown, the unexplored, the undiscovered'' (457). Both novelists are alike in recoiling from death by affirming hope.

Lawrence and Dickens, then, can valuably be studied together in the context of the English novel. Although the central axis of constriction and release provides a way of gauging their differing achievements, no simple polarization separates them; for Lawrence, despite his extraordinary honesty, can find the disturbing complexities of the male psyche—of Birkin's or Gerald's—a major artistic challenge; and despite his modernity he can readily follow the generic convention of focusing in *Women in Love* on a pair of unmarried sisters. Paradigms of artistic development shift slowly. The similarities that Lawrence and Dickens share—their fear of assertive women, their methods of caricature, their mistrust of male power, their problematic endings—caution us to regard historical divisions with skepticism. Although Lawrence and Dickens are often held to be the major novelists of their respective eras, their similarities are finally as telling as their differences.

WORKS CITED

Boswell, John. *Christianity, Social Tolerance, and Homosexuality: Gay People in Western Europe from the Beginning of the Christian Era to the Fourteenth Century.* Chicago: U of Chicago P, 1980.

Chatman, Seymour. *Story and Discourse: Narrative Structure in Fiction and Film.* Ithaca: Cornell UP, 1978.

Cowan, James C. "Lawrence and Touch." *D. H. Lawrence Review* 18 (1985–86): 121–37.

Daleski, H. M. *The Forked Flame: A Study of D. H. Lawrence.* 1965. Madison: U of Wisconsin P, 1987.

Delany, Paul. *D. H. Lawrence's Nightmare: The Writer and His Circle in the Years of the Great War.* New York: Basic Books, 1978.

Dickens, Charles. *David Copperfield.* Ed. Trevor Blount. New York: Viking Penguin, 1966.

Dickens, Charles. *Dombey and Son.* Ed. Peter Fairclough. New York: Penguin, 1970.

Donaldson, George. " 'Men in Love'? D. H. Lawrence, Rupert Birkin and Gerald Crich." *D. H. Lawrence: Centenary Essays.* Ed. Mara Kalnins. Bristol: Bristol Classical Press, 1986.

Fielding, Henry. *Tom Jones.* Ed. Sheridan Baker. New York: Norton, 1973.

Foucault, Michel. *Discipline and Punish: The Birth of the Prison.* Trans. Alan Sheridan. New York: Pantheon, 1977.

Gordon, David J. "D. H. Lawrence's Dual Myth of Origin." *Sewanee Review* 89 (1981): 83–94. Rpt. in *Critical Essays on D. H. Lawrence.* Ed. Dennis Jackson and Fleda Brown Jackson. Boston: G. K. Hall, 1988. 238–45.

Green, Martin. *The von Richthofen Sisters: The Triumphant and the Tragic Modes of Love.* New York: Basic Books, 1974.

Humphreys, Anne. "*Dombey and Son:* Carker the Manager." *Nineteenth-Century Fiction* 34 (1980): 397–413.

Jarrett-Kerr, Martin. *D. H. Lawrence and Human Existence.* 1951. New York: Chip's Bookshop, 1971.

Lawrence, D. H. *Lady Chatterley's Lover.* New York: Grove, 1962.

Lawrence, D. H. *The Letters of D. H. Lawrence.* Vol. 1: *September 1901–May 1913.* Ed. James T. Boulton. Cambridge: Cambridge UP, 1979.

Lawrence, D. H. *The Letters of D. H. Lawrence.* Vol. 3: *October 1916–June 1921.* Ed. James T. Boulton and Andrew Robertson. Cambridge: Cambridge UP, 1984.

Lawrence, D. H. *Phoenix: The Posthumous Papers of D. H. Lawrence.* Ed. Edward D. McDonald. 1936. New York: Viking, 1968.

Lawrence, D. H. *The Rainbow.* Ed. Mark Kinkead-Weekes. Cambridge: Cambridge UP, 1989.

Lawrence, D. H. *Study of Thomas Hardy and Other Essays.* Ed. Bruce Steele. Cambridge: Cambridge UP, 1985.

Lawrence, D. H. *Women in Love.* Ed. David Farmer, Lindeth Vasey, and John Worthen. Cambridge: Cambridge UP, 1987.

Lawrence, Frieda. *Frieda Lawrence: The Memoirs and Correspondence*. Ed. E. W. Tedlock, Jr. New York: Knopf, 1964.

Leavis, F. R. *D. H. Lawrence: Novelist*. New York: Knopf, 1956.

Miko, Stephen J. *Toward "Women in Love": The Emergence of a Lawrentian Aesthetic*. New Haven: Yale UP, 1971.

Miller, J. Hillis. *Charles Dickens: The World of His Novels*. Bloomington: Indiana UP, 1958.

Milner, Ian. "The Dickens Drama: Mr. Dombey." *Nineteenth-Century Fiction* 24 (1970): 477–87.

Perloff, Marjorie. "Lawrence's Lyric Theater: *Birds, Beasts and Flowers*." *D. H. Lawrence: A Centenary Consideration*. Ed. Peter Balbert and Phillip L. Marcus. Ithaca: Cornell UP, 1985. 108–29.

Ross, Charles L. *The Composition of "The Rainbow" and "Women in Love": A History*. Charlottesville: UP of Virginia, 1979.

Ross, Charles L. "Homoerotic Feeling in *Women in Love*: Lawrence's 'struggle for verbal consciousness' in the Manuscript." *D. H. Lawrence: The Man Who Lived*. Ed. Robert B. Partlow, Jr., and Harry T. Moore. Carbondale: Southern Illinois UP, 1980. 168–82.

Sagar, Keith. *D. H. Lawrence: Life into Art*. Athens: U of Georgia P, 1985.

Squires, Michael. *The Creation of "Lady Chatterley's Lover."* Baltimore: Johns Hopkins UP, 1983.

Tillotson, Kathleen. *Novels of the Eighteen-Forties*. Oxford: Clarendon, 1954.

Weinstein, Philip M. *The Semantics of Desire: Changing Models of Identity from Dickens to Joyce*. Princeton: Princeton UP, 1984.

Worthen, John. *D. H. Lawrence and the Idea of the Novel*. Totowa, N.J.: Rowman & Littlefield, 1979.

CHAPTER 4

Lawrence and the Edwardian Feminists

JANICE H. HARRIS

Samuel Hynes's *The Edwardian Turn of Mind* (1968) eloquently challenged the nostalgia that had previously colored so many descriptions and reminiscences of the Edwardian era. The garden party, country weekend, motor car, and urbane king were indeed realities, but more noticeable as signs of the time were the heated debates in and out of Parliament about the Liberal government's social agenda, the militant protests and widespread acts of civil disobedience organized by the Suffragettes and the unemployed, the growing fear of war with Germany, and the increasing concern about the possible decline of the British race and thus the British empire. The guns of August 1914 may make the anxieties, demonstrations, and debates of the Edwardians seem tame, but contemporary accounts of the period indicate deep feelings of uncertainty about where British life and culture were heading—and not least with respect to the relations between men and women. As Paul Thompson writes, many Edwardians "believed that Britain faced a social and political crisis of exceptional severity"; moreover, "of all the challenges to authority before 1914, it was possibly feminism which most often made a direct and personal impact" (252–53). In Hynes's view the tensions evoked by the "Woman Question" were such that, for many, "the most moderate move toward liberation seemed a rush toward chaos" (211).

It is within this context of charged debate, especially on the "Woman Question," that I want to examine D. H. Lawrence's challenging contribution to a somewhat anomalous prewar image, the "Modern Girl." Specifically, I want to analyze the ways in which *The Rainbow* can be read as one of a series of Modern Girl novels, in themselves contributors to the complex Edwardian dialogue about modern womanhood. To read *The Rainbow* within the context of this particular subgenre of Edwardian fiction is to understand more fully Lawrence's early ties with the feminist movement in England and to discern more clearly an important aspect of *The Rainbow*'s genesis and ultimate accomplishment.

A word of background. Although Edwardian feminism grew out of the insights and controversies inspired by the nineteenth-century women's movement, it took shape from the infamous New Woman drama and fiction of the 1880s and 1890s.[1] Writers such as Hardy, Gissing, Schreiner, Egerton (Mary Chavelita Dunne), Ibsen, and Shaw posed radical, complex, even scandalous questions about woman's sexual and maternal nature, her appropriate role in the world of work, her special perspective on politics and national policy, and her proper legal rights respecting marriage and divorce. More than in the Halls of Parliament, it was here—on the stage, in the novel—that difficult questions were being aired, by male and female writers alike. Three further points should be emphasized.

First, a consensus was reached on almost none of the feminist issues raised by the writers of the 1880s and 1890s. One could be considered a New Woman writer and argue that women do or do not have sexual desires, that sexual freedom or celibacy is the path toward self-fulfillment, that bearing children is a woman's most sacred calling or an aspect of her degradation, that full participation in the man's world is the goal of any right-thinking woman or, to the contrary, that because the man's world is corrupt, right-thinking women must live apart and find ways to change it.[2] Second, although the range of feminist issues was wide and various, in New Woman writings female sexuality tends to become the dominant concern. As Gail Cunningham writes, when the New Woman came to symbolize "all that was most challenging and dangerous in advanced thinking . . . the crucial factor was, inevitably, sex" (2). And third, the plot of the New Woman play or novel tends to emphasize a deep and abiding sexual antagonism among the characters. Images of loneliness, alienation, and betrayal haunt the narrative. Typically the resolution of the love interest is a murder, suicide, or permanent estrangement.

As the nineties evolved into the Edwardian age, the primary locus of radical inquiry and fierce controversy shifted from fiction and drama to politics. H. G. Wells overstates the case when he says in 1914 that Grant Allen's *The Woman Who Did* (1895) represented "the last wild idea in English fiction" and was, alas, hunted down and killed (281). But Wells's sense of Edwardian fiction as a tame affair was echoed by others, including Ford Madox Ford

1. Excellent work has been done on New Woman writers. See Linda Dowling; Gail Cunningham; Elaine Showalter (ch. 7); Patricia Stubbs; and the journal *Turn-of-the-Century Women*, edited by Margaret Stetz.

2. See Sheila Jeffreys for an important revisionist history of the late nineteenth- and early twentieth-century women's movement in England. Jeffreys indicates the ways current historians have defined the "sexual revolution" of those years solely as the liberation of women into the joys of heterosexuality within a patriarchal society. The counter campaign—to challenge the "normalcy" of aggressive male sexual behavior and the complex power discrepancies that such behavior assumes—has been dismissed as marginal, prudish, retrogressive, man-hating.

when he launched the *English Review* in December 1908. As Elaine Showalter suggests (216–39), the feminists in particular were out on the barricades, engaged for the first time in British history in militant protest against
the government's policies. If they were to be found at their writing desks at
all, they were composing political tracts and social analyses.[3] The issues
raised during the nineties persisted; the genre of discourse had changed.

Nevertheless, radical ideas *can* be found in Edwardian fiction, in Modern
Girl novels of the period such as *A Room with a View* (1908) by E. M. Forster,
Ann Veronica (1909) by H. G. Wells, *Hilda Lessways* (1911) by Arnold
Bennett, and *The Rainbow* (1915).[4] In what follows I want briefly to explore
the Modern Girl novels of Forster, Bennett, and Wells as a way of establishing a context for Lawrence's own thinking as he set out to write *The Rainbow;*[5] to analyze the ways in which Lawrence's novel assumed certain conventions of that subgenre but greatly extended and enriched them; and finally
to explore the extent to which the Modern Girl novel represents an exception
to the general timidity of much Edwardian fiction.

Although the Modern Girl novels of Forster, Wells, and Bennett continued
the nineties' primary interest in female sexuality, the tone had changed—from
minor to major key, from domestic tragedy to domestic comedy. All three
novels share a plot as old as fairy tale. The adventures begin with children—
girl children—fleeing a nest that cannot nurture them. Setting out into the
world, this trio of modern girls suffers an entanglement with Mr. Wrong and
eventually celebrates life and love with Mr. Right. A consensus is reached on
the question of women's sexuality: women do, women have, women are.
Although the emphases and degrees of candor vary, Forster, Wells, and
Bennett clearly believe that women have adult sexual desires that they ignore
at their peril. Far from associating sexual liberation with murder or suicide,
these authors indicate that the suppression of desire causes misery and death.

3. The most interesting nonliterary feminist Edwardian writers include Beatrice Webb, Sylvia
Pankhurst, Margaret Llewelyn Davies, Dora Marsden, and Harriet Weaver.

4. As Hynes notes, one might also look to the period's socialist literature for radical inquiry,
but in vain: "it is a perplexing question why the [Socialist] movement that appealed so strongly
to imaginative minds during the Edwardian period found no major literary expression either in
Wells's work or anywhere else. Surely at that time, if ever, great Socialist literature should have
been written. But it wasn't" (126).

5. An avid reader, Lawrence knew well the work of Forster, Wells, and Bennett—and
continually saw himself surpassing it. In this study I have been interested less in establishing
specific influence than in analyzing the respective contributions each made to the Modern Girl
genre. In Lawrence studies, critics have been especially interested in the question of Lawrence's
influence on Forster and vice versa. See, for example, Frederick P. W. McDowell and Dixie
King. In *D. H. Lawrence and Edward Carpenter: A Study in Edwardian Transition* (London:
Heinemann, 1971), Emile Delavenay also cites certain ideas that suggest a community of thought
shared by Lawrence, Forster, and Carpenter.

Since none of these modern girls—not Lucy Honeychurch, Ann Veronica, or Hilda Lessways—ultimately suppresses her desires, these novels present an optimistic, even dashing image of modern girlhood/womanhood. What has happened to the sexual tensions that haunted the New Woman novels a mere decade before? The tensions are there, but they are neatly contained in the minor characters, Mr. Wrong and the Spinster. Especially in *A Room with a View* and *Ann Veronica,* these two figures present the heroine with a series of negative images and options, most of which suggest that she will deny both her sexuality and her individuality if she marries Mr. Wrong or decides not to marry at all. But whereas the Mr. Right/Mr. Wrong narrative pattern is a familiar one in English fiction,[6] the strategy of using a young unmarried woman as an ominous specter—as a death's head warning the unmarried heroine against a life of celibacy—is new. The fact that she is not only single but often intellectually acute and politically active is of utmost importance, for the malignity associated with her presence—so different from the benign aura surrounding many an earlier maiden sister or aunt—points, one suspects, to the anxiety created by her real-life model, the disaffected, politicized, articulate, and idealistic Suffragette. In any case, given the alternatives of Mr. Wrong and the Spinster, Mr. Right's victory is no surprise.[7]

Apart from the issue of sexuality, the Modern Girl novels increasingly address the role of work in the life of the developing heroine. In *A Room with a View,* as in *Howards End,* Forster's heroine *thinks* about work—captured in the image of "typewriters and latchkeys" and defined as the day-to-day employment that keeps society running—but quickly shies away from the prospect. Wells imagines Ann Veronica sidling up to the world of work by way of her scientific studies. As Wells describes Ann Veronica's student life in the college laboratories, he often emphasizes her excitement in learning, her competence, and the camaraderie and political wrangling she enjoys with her fellow students. But because Capes, her instructor, turns out to be Mr. Right, these moments are fleeting. By contrast, Bennett gives us sustained images of Hilda's longing to work, her joy in the challenge, and her daily sense of freedom as she leaves her mother's dull domesticity to work at the local newspaper office. At the end of the work sequence, as in later sections, Bennett begins to explore the costs implied in Hilda's rebellion—here, the sense of guilt modern daughters often feel in rejecting their mothers' values. But he introduces the idea only to drop it. In *Hilda Lessways,* as in

6. Studies of the two-suitor convention in English fiction include those by Jean E. Kennard and H. M. Daleski.

7. Bennett's novel employs the Mr. Wrong/Spinster pair differently. Nevertheless he controls his novel's tensions with a similar strategy of containment, mainly by giving Hilda no time to reflect. He frequently rushes her on to a new adventure just as she is about to achieve a radical insight into her struggles for freedom in a patriarchal society.

Ann Veronica, the boss turns out to be a key figure in the love plot: George Cannon is a highly intriguing Mr. Wrong. Hilda's pleasure in work quickly becomes associated with her interest in Cannon.

Forster and Bennett in particular were aware of certain problems in their Modern Girl novels as both struggled against the false note implied by their happy endings. Both realized that no Mr. Right and no conventional Edwardian marriage would provide the heroine with permanent bliss. Forster rewrote his ending in a postscript published forty years after *A Room with a View*.[8] In a subsequent volume, *These Twain*, Bennett follows Hilda into her marriage with Edwin Clayhanger, undermining the simplistic joy with which he had ended *Hilda Lessways*.

Nevertheless, the happy ending points to related problems. At the center of each of these Modern Girl novels is a revolutionary who trespasses against several of the major taboos of her time and culture. To focus on such a figure, to introduce the tensions implied in her struggle, to avoid exploring those tensions, and then to imply that a conventional resolution has facilitated her liberation, is to write a novel that falls short of its potential. Whether it is Forster's tone of lyricism and restraint, Bennett's rushed narrative pace, or Wells's continual lapse into condescension and bluffness, each of these Modern Girl novels fails to grapple with its own powerful plot and characters.

Lawrence's *The Rainbow* makes the label "Modern Girl novel" seem quite inadequate. It is therefore worth recalling that Lawrence began "The Sisters" in a flippant mood, like that in *Ann Veronica*.[9] As Mark Kinkead-Weekes and Charles Ross have shown, Lawrence's original intention was to trace the progress of the modern *jeune fille* from childhood, through school, work and the affair with Mr. Wrong, to marriage with Mr. Right. This is the Modern Girl plot. Although Bennett may in 1910 have been cruder in announcing his intentions in *Hilda Lessways*—to "portray the droves of the whole sex . . . it has never been done" (386)—Lawrence's own motives bespeak a similar sweep, as well as a more self-conscious political intent. As he began the first version of "The Sisters," he boasted to his old feminist friend, Sallie Hopkin, "I shall do my work for women, better than the suffrage" (*Letters* I: 490). Several drafts and tentative titles later, his sense of the novel's subject remained clear: "woman becoming individual, self-responsible, taking her own initiative" (*Letters* II: 165).

To examine Ursula's tale alongside the other Modern Girl novels allows us then to see it within one of its literary-historical contexts, but also to expand

8. Forster's postscript is published in *A Room with a View* (London: Arnold, 1977) xvi–xvii.

9. When Lawrence altered the tone of "The Sisters," he did so for many reasons, but it is amusing to read his comment to Edward Garnett, a year before he began the book: "I don't want to be talked about in an *Anne* [sic] *Veronica* fashion" (*Letters* I: 339).

our sense of the genre itself, of what it could accomplish. Rather than finding *The Rainbow* too large to be a Modern Girl novel, one can follow Lawrence's lead and reject a limited definition of the genre.

As Lawrence came to realize, his tale could not begin straightforwardly with his girl-child Ursula fleeing her nest, moving out into the worlds of work and love. His modern girl is not an isolated being, but rather a product of her culture's past and one of its leading shoots. The reader must first know the story of her parents and grandparents before discovering Ursula at work and in love.

Lawrence develops the Brangwen saga along at least two lines important to Ursula's character and eventual fate. First, Anna—herself embedded in Lydia's history—provides Ursula with a context. Each mother embodies choices and potentials available to the daughter, to be rejected or embraced.[10] On this level Tom and Lydia, Will and Anna, give Ursula's rebellion import and intensity. Ursula's grandparents and parents have had their own experiences of love and work. When Ursula turns from them, one feels, as one never does in the other Modern Girl novels, the pain of parents betrayed, the anger of children fighting free. Especially moving, for example, are the miserable fights between Ursula and her father, in which Lawrence dramatizes the deep, personal strains that are inevitable in any social revolution.

But Lydia and Anna, Tom and Will, do more than establish the background for Ursula's rebellion. In a richly innovative way, Lawrence uses the mother and grandmother as indicators of Ursula's future. Two points are important here: in the previous Modern Girl novels, mothers stood unambiguously for worn-out ways, for traditions best discarded; furthermore, the happy ending seemed both unavoidable and unsatisfactory. Lawrence avoids the falsifying denouement to Ursula's adventure partly by implying the quality of Ursula's ongoing venture—beyond this novel, perhaps within some future marriage—through the experiences of her mother and grandmother. At times there are three Modern Girls in this novel: Lydia, Anna, and Ursula.

A tension between images and plot characterizes the treatment of Ursula at work. If we attend solely to plot, we see a vision of women and work not much different from what has gone before: work in the world is something a woman may pass through on her way to love and marriage. Ursula has her fling at financial independence and social responsibility but quickly returns to her real task in life: figuring out how she relates to Skrebensky. Apparently, Lawrence's vision of ''woman becoming . . . self-responsible'' does not include woman working, at least not in a significant way.

But the plot line here does not tell the whole story. Working against the plot's minimizing of Ursula's work experience is an astonishing wealth of

10. Lydia Blanchard explores this neglected topic in Lawrence.

imagery elaborating that experience. In scene after scene, Lawrence gives a range of detail, making the work experience of his heroine come alive. One recalls Ursula's struggle with teaching and the joy she finally feels "getting into the swing of work of a morning, putting forth all her strength, making the thing go. It was for her a strenuous form of exercise" (378). There are her lunches with Maggie Schofield, quiet moments in a hard and busy day, glimpses of modern girls getting through the hours, the weeks. Working, talking, teaching, Maggie and Ursula are defined neither by their sexuality nor by their relations to men. Important here is Lawrence's decision not to include a male perspective in these images of Ursula's workday. Unlike his use of Paul Morel's amorous perspective on Clara Dawes at work in Jordan's factory, Lawrence in *The Rainbow* has no sexually interested male observing Ursula in the classroom. Instead, he portrays Ursula's male supervisor, Mr. Harby, and her colleague, Mr. Brunt, as being uninterested in Ursula as a woman. At one point Ursula tries "to approach [Mr. Harby] as a young bright girl usually approaches a man, expecting a little chivalrous courtesy. But the fact that she was a girl, a woman, was ignored or used as a matter for contempt against her" (351). The lack of sexual empathy troubles Ursula and reinforces Lawrence's depiction of modern teaching and learning as a cold, mechanical clash of wills. But the point still holds: no one finds tantalizing the flush on Ursula's cheek as she reprimands the children; no one remarks the stretch of her body as she writes on the blackboard. The world of work does not blur into the world of love. Without a Paul, Cannon, or Capes, this heroine's sufferings and triumphs as a teacher are conveyed as human sufferings and triumphs: no more, no less. If feminist readings often rightly emphasize Lawrence's tendency to identify with women and the psychological risks this tendency entailed, surely those readings should also emphasize his ability to see women's experiences as simply shareable, part of the common human lot.[11]

Extend the images of daily work to the allied images of women's involvement in political struggle, and again Lawrence's tone is surprisingly supportive. To many writers of the nineties, political activism, like work, held little dramatic interest. Forster and Bennett steer their heroines clear of politics. Wells follows George Egerton, mocking what he saw as sexual frustration at the heart of feminist political activity. By contrast, up to the point of introducing Miss Inger, Lawrence makes political activism a valuable part of Ursula's young womanhood. She and Maggie read books, among them Schreiner's *Woman and Labour;* like Lawrence and his friends, they go to Suffragette demonstrations in Nottingham, and they argue the issues. The

11. For a different view see Faith Pullin; see also Hilary Simpson's valuable study as well as Wayne Booth's discussion of Ursula as a teacher on page 22 of this volume.

vote is not important to Ursula, but, like Maggie, she knows that her culture denies women deep and important freedoms; she will do all she can to gain those freedoms.

In sum, apart from the sections dealing with Miss Inger, the imagery associated with Ursula's intellectual, working, and political life tends to portray the release of human energies and the participation in communal projects so lacking in earlier New Woman or Modern Girl novels. Despite Ursula's disappointment in the university, her encounters with pupils, parents, politics, and books present a far more extensive and solid picture of the modern girl out in the world than Lucy's "typewriters and latchkeys," Hilda's labors in the newspaper office, or Ann Veronica's months in London or even her days in Holloway Prison.

Indeed *The Rainbow* marks a unique moment in Lawrence's own writing. In his earlier fictions on the modern girl—in "Witch à la Mode," "The Shades of Spring," "A Modern Lover," and the Clara Dawes sections of *Sons and Lovers*—the normal, daytime activities of the heroines are either left unmentioned (though the heroes' are sketched in) or treated incoherently. Incoherence is especially apparent in Lawrence's development of Clara Dawes. Although Clara often trenchantly analyzes Paul's character, Lawrence then fails to incorporate her perceptiveness into either her own characterization or Paul's. Given Lawrence's initial emphasis on her political activism and interest in the suffrage movement, it is surprising that Paul and Clara's attendance at Suffragette gatherings receives no authorial commentary. The scene in which Paul bids to be Clara's fighting knight, imagining himself marching under the political banner of the radical Women's Social and Political Union, is typically muddled: it raises intelligent points, retreats into flippancy, and closes with Paul expressing a sudden pity for Clara. Indeed, throughout the Paul-Clara relationship, Lawrence indicates but does not motivate Paul's fluctuating admiration, sympathy, and contempt for her, as a person and as a woman.

In Lawrence's later fictions, material related to Ursula's development as a working, political adult receives cursory or negative treatment. In *The Lost Girl* Alvina Houghton is very much the modern girl in her efforts to escape the parental roof and learn a skill. But the sections that follow her training to become a maternity nurse remain one-dimensional. In *Mr Noon* Lawrence could have explored an intelligent, modern girl twenty years on through the character of Patty Goddard. But the opportunity does not appeal. Forty years old, enfranchised, campaign-scarred, restless, and pensive, Mrs. Goddard blooms briefly, intriguingly, then passes into obscurity as the novel moves on to explore the travesty of modern sexual liberation in Gilbert Noon, silly Emmie, and the Spoon. In the late tale "Mother and Daughter" Lawrence returns specifically to the issue of women and work. The heroine's labors out in the world are depicted as depleting and unnatural—as are similar labors undertaken by heroes.

Love, not work, is of course Lawrence's central topic. His project was not new; rising logically out of the New Woman debates of the nineties, it continued the work of Forster, Bennett, Wells, and others. Yet Lawrence deserves his reputation as the voice of the time proclaiming a woman's liberation through the recognition of her sexual self. Let me begin by asking what is new.

Much has been written on the extraordinary density of the image patterns in *The Rainbow,* particularly the patterns associated with sexuality. What I would emphasize, especially in contrast to the New Woman novels of the nineties, is Lawrence's ability to connect female sexuality, through imagery, to other expressions of physical and sensual life. Typically the New Woman novelist who explored female sexuality depicted it as providing a journey into the self; in *Keynotes* and *Discords* George Egerton carefully details the heroine's sensations, but finally leaves the reader with a sense of the heroine's entrapment in a delicate but isolated body. Lawrence, searching for the fundamental impulses that underlie all creation and destruction—for the "carbon" within diamond or coal—breaks through that sense of isolation by finding the imagery to link female sexuality with a myriad other expressions of desire and energy, human and inhuman. Anna's wooing, honeymoon, and pregnancy, Ursula's miscarriage at the end of the novel, each is associated with growing corn, spinning cosmos, plunging horses. The assertion of connectedness extends in two other directions as well.

In the New Woman's sexual experiences, any expression of boredom or lack of engagement signals a problem with the relationship. In *The Rainbow,* particularly in the experiences of Tom and Lydia or Will and Anna, Lawrence perceives complex and constant connections between the desire for union and the desire to be alone, the desire for intimacy and the desire for social activity. Furthermore, Lawrence conveys this sense of connectedness through time and generations. When Middleton Murry complained that a reader cannot always tell one character from another in Lawrence, he made a valuable observation. Partly through the repetition of imagery, Lawrence conveys the idea that Anna's sexual experiences inevitably parallel aspects of Lydia's, even of Tom's. Ursula's too are inherited from Anna and Lydia, Tom and Will.

With respect to straightforward referential language, it is important to recall that Lawrence inherited a century of evasion and awkwardness in the direct expression of normal sexual emotion. When the plot calls for a kiss, the best writers—Dickens, Thackeray, Trollope, Eliot—seek out an objective correlative or fall into cliché. The worst writers employ a rhetoric of hysterical intensity. Eyes are distended, screams are stifled, swoons overwhelm. Pornographers, then as now, titillate by isolating the sexual encounter from an individual's complex emotion. In the contemporaneous Modern Girl novels, Bennett tends to exaggerate, Wells to hide behind bluffness, and Forster—whose very message is the holiness of the heart's desire—to evade. The lovemaking may occur, but only elsewhere. At his worst, Lawrence can also evade, insist, hide behind banter. But more than the others, he can also—in what one might call plain style—give the reader the scene, the sentence that will convey human warmth and passion. Such a style characterizes many of the early scenes. Here is the scene in which Anna and Will lie in bed on their marriage night, listening to the sounds of the wake outside:

> "It's Dad," she said, in a low voice.
> They were silent, listening.
> "And my father," he said.
> She listened still. But she was sure. She sank down again into bed, into his arms. He held her very close, kissing her. The hymn rambled on outside, all the men singing their best, having forgotten everything else under the spell of the fiddles and the tune. The firelight glowed against the darkness in the room. Anna could hear her father singing with gusto.
> "Aren't they silly?" she whispered.
> And they crept closer, closer together, hearts beating to one another. And even as the hymn rolled on, they ceased to hear it. (133)

The touch is so sure—the style direct, easy in its rhythms, and unclogged with correlatives—that it is easy to forget that Lawrence had no English models for this.

If his imagery may be said to weave new patterns of connectedness, if his referential language may be judged as innovative in its clarity and directness, Lawrence moves his plot in equally new directions when he depicts sexuality. Significantly, one recognizes by the end of *The Rainbow* that Ursula's experiences, although more extensive than her mother's or grandmother's, are not yet as deep. Never mind Skrebensky, her affair with Miss Inger, or even the possibility that Ursula will eventually marry someone suitable. Sexuality, the novel implies, is a long adventure into the unknown. It does not end with youth or the honeymoon—the typical point of closure for the Modern Girl novel—but assumes years of deepening intimacy and exchange, of female growth and male adventure, male growth and female adventure. This in itself is new.

Even more important, sexuality in *The Rainbow* assumes antagonism. As noted above, the issue of sexual antagonism haunts New Woman writings of the 1890s. It is a theme in Ibsen, Hardy, and Gissing, and a continual refrain in Egerton. In Schreiner the antagonism turns in on itself, as Lyndall, in *The Story of an African Farm,* disparages the female lot, longs to be male, and dies in despair after losing her child. In each of these New Woman fictions, the antagonisms lurk, leading to loneliness, hatred, and death. With the exception of *The Rainbow,* the Modern Girl novels examined thus far introduce sexual antagonism only to contain it again through Mr. Wrong and the Spinster.[12] The wrong suitor subplot allows the hero and heroine to declare a dislike of the other based not on personality but on assumptions about the other's maleness or femaleness. Feelings of threat and contempt are stated or implied but then disappear along with Mr. Wrong. The Spinster introduces a different kind of antagonism. Associated with political activism, her character and circumstances imply a new awareness of the link between expressions of sexuality and the sociopolitical construct surrounding them. But the argument behind the implication is simplistic and designed to uphold the status quo. It assumes that what women want is sexual fulfillment as defined by the current social construct; it contends that any political activism that alters the social construct is born of, and will in turn cause, sexual barrenness, frigidity, impotence. But the links between sociopolitical constructs and sexual expression are at least recognized.

At first glance Lawrence seems to retrace the Modern Girl pattern: Skrebensky is the wrong suitor; Winifred Inger raises issues associated with the old maid; and Ursula's vision of a God-created man is the perfect reconciliation. But in fact Lawrence greatly extends and elaborates on the antagonism introduced by Mr. Wrong—allowing the genuine tensions that lurk in the novels of the 1890s to be lived with and not contained—and he deals frankly, though no more positively, with the threat conveyed by the Spinster.

Anna's tale gives especially full expression to the sexual anger, fear, and pain that haunted the earlier novels in the crippling disguise of Mr. Wrong. In the tears, silences, separations, and reconciliations of Will and Anna, Lawrence dramatizes ᵃ vision of love that is far more turbulent, troubled, and yet durable, than recent English fiction had provided. Lawrence repeatedly traces the terror of the self as it feels swallowed up by the other; the misery of having the other turn away, indifferent or repulsed; or the struggle for dominance, which is also a struggle for balancing engagement with independence. Throughout, the reader is asked to recognize that certain aspects of sexual antagonism rest on the deep allure *and* risk that the self may feel in engagement with the other, regardless of political or personal context. The antagonism is resolved, recurs, must be resolved again. This challenge, met

12. One of the few Edwardian novelists to name the antagonism and expose it was Elizabeth Robins in *The Convert* (1907; Old Westbury, N.Y.: Feminist Press, 1980). Robins hoped to force recognition of what quickly became obvious to the imprisoned Suffragettes: that within the male establishment's refusal to grant women the vote was a strain of brutal misogyny; and that within the women's anger and longing for the vote was a similar strain of hatred and disgust. One clear expression of the latter is Christabel Pankhurst's *The Great Scourge and How to End It* (London: N.p., 1913).

by Tom and Lydia, Will and Anna, must also be met by Ursula and her God-created mate.

With respect to the second kind of antagonism, Lawrence refuses to trivialize the complex threat that the independent single woman represented at the time, refuses to depict her as impotent or comic. Winifred Inger is not desiccated, quirky, old, or laughable. Drastically altering the imagery associated with this spinster, Lawrence surrounds her with water images, making her strong and initially attractive. Most important, just where the other novels indicate that the heroine will opt for a lonely, ascetic life if she remains single, Lawrence introduces the possibility of an alternate expression of sexuality. The lesbianism may be immediately denounced by the chapter title "Shame," Winifred may be thoroughly "contained" by Ursula's rejection and by Winifred's marriage to Ursula's uncle, and yet *The Rainbow* has opened its doors to the female separatist's allure much wider than did other Modern Girl novels.

I have argued that if one examines *The Rainbow* within the context of other Edwardian Modern Girl novels, one sees Lawrence begin with the conventions of the genre, then greatly expand them: he broadens the historical and familial scope of the narrative; he creates a sequence of image patterns which newly connect female sexual experiences with other expressions of life and energy; and he so develops the plot to include a range of experiences related to work, love, and sexuality which are finally adequate to the central subject, that is, modern woman becoming individual and self-responsible. Lawrence's novel stands as an extraordinary example of prewar British fiction. But if one now steps back and blurs distinctions, what can one say of these Modern Girl novels as a whole?

I would suggest that any such assessment must take into account the genuine intellectual and political dilemmas these authors faced in writing about feminism: how to take the belief that private sexual revolution must precede human liberation and reconcile that belief with the growing conviction that women must be emancipated from their traditional sphere of "private relationships"; how to reconcile a skepticism about the value of individualism with an awareness that women have yet to enjoy the adventure of Western individualism;[13] how to reconcile a distrust of political activism and marketplace labor with an acknowledgment that women have yet to take their place in the world of politics and commerce. Feminists often seem to be fighting for precisely what the dissenting modern artist finds hollow.[14]

A negative judgment on the Modern Girl novel would argue that in the end none of these writers successfully negotiates the difficulties. None has imag-

13. Roslynn D. Haynes (125) sees this as a plight for Wells in particular.
14. In discussing the modern writer's attraction to fascism, Laurence Lerner (230–35) makes the point in more general terms.

ined a woman who is genuinely "quick" sexually, maternally, politically, and in her work. Less new, less threatening than the New Woman of the nineties, the Modern Girl is, it could be argued, a study in cooption.[15] While the real Edwardian feminists were at the barricades carrying on the work of the movement, these false prophets of liberation were creating novels that only toyed with the radical critiques offered a decade before, that offered insulting solutions to the debates of the current decade. The "woman" is now a "girl," easy to admire and patronize. She may work, complain, rebel for a while, but in the end she lands contentedly at home. Most important, her liberation is accomplished in terms thoroughly gratifying to the hero. Gone is any serious consideration for the claims of the feminist separatist, gone any interest in all-female communities or the alteration of traditional patterns of male-female power. Indeed, it will be half a century before these possibilities are raised again.[16] The Modern Girl finds her apotheosis in, and only in, a monogamous heterosexual relationship. Obviously she is the creation of males, for males. What is modern about this?

On the other hand, still keeping in mind the often anguished and sometimes morbid novels of the New Woman writers, one can see the Modern Girl novel as a study in assimilation rather than cooption. Major compromises have been reached, but they are compromises that lead to images of energy, intelligence, love, desire, victory, humor, and survival. If Lucy, Ann Veronica, Hilda, and Ursula have not convinced their culture or their creators that they have a permanent role to play in the work of the world, they have, with the exception of Lucy, made an entry into that world. In the debate over women's liberated sexuality, they have firmly decided the issue in favor of recognizing desire. Their sexuality is celebrated: it leads not to murder, suicide, exile, or self-absorption, but to something more obvious—sexual relationships. Admittedly the emphasis falls on heterosexual desire within the framework of fairly traditional patterns of dominance. But again, the main fight of the time was between those who would venerate woman's supposedly nonsexual, angelic nature and those who would recognize her sexuality. The debate between richer and narrower definitions of sexual desire would fall to a later age, a different feminism, one that could further refine and enrich the culture's understanding of desire, male and female.[17] Finally, one could argue that these Modern Girls, in their rapprochement with men, possess more potential for altering men's lives than did the disaffected New Women. Certainly

15. Cunningham makes this point in her conclusion.

16. Carol Gilligan is among several current feminists reviving certain of the separatists' ideas.

17. T. H. Adamowski closes his comparison of Lawrence and Sartre with a fine awareness of Lawrence's inability to rise above gender, "to pursue bisexually the will-o'-the-wisp of natural consciousness" (55).

Forster, through George Emerson, and Lawrence, through Tom and Will, carry on the complex project of feminizing the hero, making the sexual revolution—that longest of long revolutions—one that alters all lives, male and female.

WORKS CITED

Adamowski, T. H. "The Natural Flowering of Life: The Ego, Sex, and Existentialism." *D. H. Lawrence's "Lady": A New Look at "Lady Chatterley's Lover."* Ed. Michael Squires and Dennis Jackson. Athens: U of Georgia P, 1985. 36–57.

Bennett, Arnold. *The Journals of Arnold Bennett.* Ed. Newman Flower. London: Cassell, 1932.

Blanchard, Lydia. "Mothers and Daughters in D. H. Lawrence: *The Rainbow* and Selected Shorter Works." *Lawrence and Women.* Ed. Anne Smith. London: Vision, 1978. 75–100.

Cunningham, Gail. *The New Woman and the Victorian Novel.* London: Macmillan, 1978.

Daleski, H. M. *The Divided Heroine: A Recurrent Pattern in Six English Novels.* New York: Holmes & Meier, 1984.

Dowling, Linda. "The Decadent and the New Woman in the 1890's." *Nineteenth-Century Fiction* 33 (1979): 434–53.

Egerton, George. *Keynotes* and *Discords.* 1893, 1894. London: Virago, 1983.

Gilligan, Carol. *In a Different Voice.* Cambridge: Harvard UP, 1982.

Haynes, Roslynn D. *H. G. Wells: Discoverer of the Future.* London: Macmillan, 1980.

Hynes, Samuel. *The Edwardian Turn of Mind.* Princeton: Princeton UP, 1968.

Jeffreys, Sheila. *The Spinster and Her Enemies: Feminism and Sexuality, 1880–1930.* London: Pandora, 1985.

Kennard, Jean E. *Victims of Convention.* Hamden, Conn.: Archon, 1978.

King, Dixie. "The Influence of Forster's *Maurice* on *Lady Chatterley's Lover.*" *Contemporary Literature* 23 (1982): 65–82.

Kinkead-Weekes, Mark. "The Marble and the Statue: The Exploratory Imagination in D. H. Lawrence." *Imagined Worlds.* Ed. Maynard Mack and Ian Gregor. London: Methuen, 1968. 371–418.

Kinkead-Weekes, Mark. " 'This Old Maid': Jane Austen Replies to Charlotte Brontë and D. H. Lawrence." *Nineteenth-Century Fiction* 30 (1975): 399–419.

Lawrence, D. H. *The Letters of D. H. Lawrence.* Vol. 1: *September 1901–May 1913.* Ed. James T. Boulton. Cambridge: Cambridge UP, 1979.

Lawrence, D. H. *The Letters of D. H. Lawrence.* Vol. 2: *June 1913–October 1916.* Ed. George J. Zytaruk and James T. Boulton. Cambridge: Cambridge UP, 1981.

Lawrence, D. H. *The Rainbow.* Ed. Mark Kinkead-Weekes. Cambridge: Cambridge UP, 1989.

Lerner, Laurence. *The Truthtellers: Jane Austen, George Eliot, D. H. Lawrence*. New York: Schocken, 1967.

McDowell, Frederick P. W. " 'Moments of Emergence and of a New Splendor': D. H. Lawrence and E. M. Forster in Their Fiction." *D. H. Lawrence's "Lady": A New Look at "Lady Chatterley's Lover."* Ed. Michael Squires and Dennis Jackson. Athens: U of Georgia P, 1985. 58–90.

Pullin, Faith. "Lawrence's Treatment of Women in *Sons and Lovers*." *Lawrence and Women*. Ed. Anne Smith. London: Vision, 1978. 49–74.

Ross, Charles L. *The Composition of "The Rainbow" and "Women in Love": A History*. Charlottesville: UP of Virginia, 1979.

Showalter, Elaine. *A Literature of Their Own*. Princeton: Princeton UP, 1977.

Simpson, Hilary. *D. H. Lawrence and Feminism*. DeKalb: Northern Illinois UP, 1982.

Stubbs, Patricia. *Women and Fiction: Feminism and the Novel, 1880–1920*. London: Methuen, 1981.

Thompson, Paul. *The Edwardians: The Remaking of British Society*. Bloomington: Indiana UP, 1975.

Wells, H. G. *The Wife of Sir Isaac Harman*. New York: Scribner's, 1926.

CHAPTER 5

Lawrence and the Decline of the Industrial Spirit

PAUL DELANY

In Galsworthy's *The Silver Spoon* the aristocratic beauty Marjorie Ferrar begins an expensive lawsuit against Fleur Mont, then finds herself five thousand pounds in debt. The only escape from her difficulties, she decides, is to get married. When her grandfather, the Marquess of Shropshire, learns of her engagement he invites her to breakfast. His hobbyhorse is electrification, so he is delighted to hear that Marjorie's fiancé, an industrialist M.P., is "dead keen on electricity" (242). The conversation then comes around to wedding presents, and Shropshire asks Marjorie if she would like some of his antique lace:

"Oh! no, please, dear. Nobody's wearing lace."
With his head on one side, the marquess looked at her. "I can't get that lace off," he seemed to say.
"Perhaps you'd like a Colliery. Electrified, it would pay in no time."
Marjorie Ferrar laughed. "I know you're hard up, grandfather; but I'd rather not have a Colliery, thanks. They're so expensive. Just give me your blessing." (245)

The breakfast takes place in January 1925, fifteen months before the General Strike; but Marjorie looks her gift colliery in the mouth because she knows that the industry is already in a bad way. The Germans must sell coal abroad in order to make their reparation payments, and British mine owners want to cut wages to remain competitive. Marjorie's joke shows that the aristocracy has lost faith in coal and would rather put its capital somewhere else. She is in fact a shrewd prophet, for what lies ahead is sixty years of decline for British mining. Whether it is lace or mines, she has no wish to be stuck with something that is out of fashion.

It is a far cry from Marjorie Ferrar's offhand joke to D. H. Lawrence's deep involvement with mining and miners; but careless and thoughtless people may sometimes be closer to the truth than experts. I want to argue that Lawrence's

77

personal experience caused him to assume that mining was as central to British culture generally as it was to him individually, and to overestimate the political and industrial power of the mine-owning classes. It is true that mining has long held a special place in the British cultural imagination; but that is because mining, more than any other industry, is "known" in terms of myth (which exists, in part, because practically no one except the miners themselves has ever been down a mine). Myth and economic necessity have always been opposed; at certain crucial moments they have been brought into bitter confrontation—notably in the great strikes of 1926 and 1984, and in the nationalization of 1945.

By the myth of mining I mean a cluster of popular responses: about the danger of mining, the solidarity of the workers, the insularity of their communities, their fondness for singing, and the like. Part of the myth, indeed, is the miner's sensitive son who becomes a teacher or writer. And most of the myth is grounded on social fact. It is mythical not because it is untrue, but because it is incomplete: it obscures the profound changes in the industry over the past century, and it makes mining into an archetype that is not necessarily relevant to British industry as a whole. Furthermore, the industrial myth does not live independently, but as the counterpart to something older and more powerful: the myth of Britain as it was before industry came to change it.

Let us call this rival idea the "rural myth." It has recently been the subject of a seminal book by Martin Wiener, *English Culture and the Decline of the Industrial Spirit, 1850–1980.* "The leading problem of modern British history," Wiener begins, "is the explanation of economic decline" (3). In Britain, he argues, the industrial revolution was crippled just when it was being wholeheartedly exploited by Germany, the United States, and Japan. During the first half of the nineteenth century there was a national enthusiasm for the British industrialist and engineer, culminating in the Great Exhibition of 1851 at the Crystal Palace. But the advance of industry also provoked strong opposition from traditionalist interest groups. This opposition prevailed, and it bears the final responsibility for Britain's long and notorious economic crisis. The present condition of Britain has not been determined by the loss of empire or the strains of the two world wars. It has older and deeper roots, visible in the dominance of landed and financial interests over industrial ones, of the rentier over the manager, of the South over the North.[1] Nominally Britain is ruled by either the Conservative or the Labour Party; effectively, it is ruled by the Garden Party.

From Cobbett and Blake onward, those sages who pronounced on the

---

1. Wiener focuses on the complex two-sided opposition between these forces; however, a comprehensive treatment of the issue would include the three elements of South, North, and the "Celtic fringe" (Scotland, Wales, and Ulster).

"condition of England" spoke with one voice on the issue of industry, regardless of whether they were right or left politically. Their common ideal was the "organic" rural community, devoted to spiritual rather than material values. They established the Rural Myth as the country's most important received idea, the uncontested premise of most cultural production. "England's green and pleasant land" must be saved, over and over again, from "those dark satanic mills." The "red rust" of semidetached housing—and all that goes with it—creeps from *Howards End* to Eliot's Waste Land to Orwell's "Lower Binfield" in *Coming Up for Air*. Liberal, reactionary, or socialist, all unite in a mystified love of Olde Englande and in contempt for whatever is new.

It is assumed by the Rural Myth that industry and urbanization have no moral basis; they express only a materialism without aim or limit. "High wages are not an end in themselves," said Arnold Toynbee, a leading disciple of Ruskin. "No one wants high wages in order that working men may indulge in mere sensual gratification" (qtd. in Wiener 82). Sixty years later, G. M. Trevelyan lamented the decline of rural England in his lifetime. "Agriculture is not merely one industry among many," he wrote, "but is a way of life, unique and irreplaceable in its human and spiritual values" (Wiener 87). Toynbee and his followers (such as the Hammonds) established certain axioms in cultural history: that traditional rural societies were better than their successors, that modernity represented the triumph of "gross materialism" over spiritual ideals, and that the industrial revolution was "a period as disastrous and as terrible as any through which a nation ever passed" (Wiener 82).

The demonology of the Rural Myth lumps together the factory and the town. "I am always haunted by the awfulness of London," went one lament in 1891, "by the great appalling fact of these millions cast down, as it would appear by hazard, on the banks of this noble stream. . . . [London is a] tumour, an elephantiasis sucking into its gorged system half the life and the blood and the bone of the rural districts" (Wiener 106). This was not some rustic sage speaking, but Lord Rosebery, who had just completed his term as the first chairman of the London County Council. Leonard Bast's trajectory in *Howards End*—from rural Wiltshire origins to a job as an insurance clerk to parasitic unemployment—made the point, for E. M. Forster, that the English race has degenerated in moving from the open field to the factory or office.

If we accept Wiener's definition of what is particularly English about English culture, it follows that D. H. Lawrence is not such an outsider and iconoclast as he has commonly been painted. Rather, he has his place in the great stream of anti-industrial sentiment that runs continuously from Blake to Orwell. F. W. Bateson described English Romanticism as "the shortest way out of Manchester"; for Lawrence, the shortest way out of Eastwood was the road to Felley Mill farm. His family, after all, had its roots and its fortunes in industry. His maternal grandfather was an engineer in the naval dockyard at Sheerness, his father a miner and skillful amateur mechanic, and his elder brother George a manager of an engineering company in Nottingham. Yet Lawrence, as an adult, made a virtue of his incompetence to deal with a car or a typewriter. His youthful letters say almost nothing about technology, and his first major literary project was a pastoral idyll, *The White Peacock*. His cultural formation alienated him from the industrial society of the Midlands long before he physically left it, on his long pilgrimage in search of an ideal South.

In his youth Lawrence could afford to take industry for granted because it was in a phase of relatively untroubled expansion. Between 1885 and 1913 production of coal in Britain rose by about 60 percent. Almost all coal was still cut by hand and seams were getting more inaccessible; as a result, employment in mining more than doubled, from half a million to over a million men.[2] The Nottinghamshire coalfield was more modern and productive than most, and its workers less militant than those farther north or in Wales.[3] They were influenced by being closer to London and living more intermingled with the middle classes (exemplified, of course, in Lawrence's own divided family). *Sons and Lovers* leaves us with the impression that Morel has been steadily degenerating both personally and socially. But a walk around Eastwood shows that the Lawrence family had a better house each time they moved, as Arthur Lawrence shared in the general prosperity of the mining industry.

Lawrence himself wanted to move much farther than just up the hill from "The Breach." But he also had a lifelong need to return and re-create the world of his youth, beginning with *Sons and Lovers*. The depiction of industry there is primal—what would be taken in by the eyes of a mother-fixated child who himself never went "down pit." In contrast with agricultural or artisan societies, industry brought about a complete separation of work between the sexes. Before, they worked at different tasks in the same place; now one sex worked at home, the other in the factory or mine. So Morel is not shown in his work, but only as a brutal domestic intruder. Each sex makes the rules for its own territory and resists intrusion by the other: men have the pit and the pub, women the house and the chapel. The fundamental opposition is one sex against the other, rather than people against machinery. In this novel, then, Lawrence has not yet established a polarity between the sensual and the mechanical. By sharing a physical task, the miners can affirm their sensuality

2. See M. W. Kirby (6–7). Employment peaked at one and a quarter million in 1920; currently (1988) it is about one-tenth of that.

3. In 1984–85 the Nottinghamshire miners generally refused to join the national strike (as they had also refused in 1926); a majority voted in October 1985 to secede from the National Union of Mineworkers.

together; but they are sensually alienated from their spiritual and moralistic womenfolk.[4]

When Paul Morel writes his first letter of application, the narrator calls him "already . . . a prisoner of industrialism" (89). But the novel as a whole does not show industry as closing off the development of those who take part in it. It is surely significant that Lawrence extended his three months at Haywood's in 1901 into a fictional stay at "Jordan's" that covers ten years of his life, up to his mother's death in 1911. His emotional development as student and teacher during this period is mapped onto the life of a factory clerk, with no obvious difficulty of fit. Despite his occupation, Paul Morel preserves his dignity and sensitivity, and is the credible hero of one of the major *Bildungsromane* in English.[5] As with Lawrence himself, Paul's hostility to industry derives from cultural tradition rather than from direct perception of its malignancy.

In his early work, then, Lawrence followed the middle road of the anti-industrial tradition; he showed preference for rural settings, a measured distaste for factories and towns, and an escapist or romantic attitude toward sex. His inclusion in the earlier volumes of *Georgian Poetry* marked his acceptance as a relatively orthodox Edwardian writer. Between 1912 and 1916, however, he shifted to a much more radical view of the industrial question. This shift was motivated by upheavals in his personal life rather than by working through the traditional debate over the "condition of England." Lawrence's anti-industrial vision was the product of his lived experience of sexual liberation, economic independence, exile, and war. This was its strength; but this strength came at the cost of dissociation from the everyday concerns and perspectives of most of his countrymen.

By eloping with Frieda, Lawrence chose also to be a writer rather than a teacher, and to live among peasants rather than on the fringes of London. The sexual fulfillment that he enjoyed in Germany and Italy led him to situate his phallic and sensual ideals within the peasant way of life instead of within the masculine comradeship of the mines. Having abandoned or even annihilated his personal past, he liked to imagine how the society he had left behind might literally be destroyed; and the outbreak of war promised to turn his projective fantasy into sober truth. This vision—we might call it Lawrence's industrial

4. At Jordan's warehouse, the sexes have correspondingly different attitudes to factory work: "The man was the work and the work was the man, one thing, for the time being. It was different with the girls. The real woman never seemed to be there at the task, but as if left out, waiting" (*SL* 155). See also Marko Modiano.

5. However, there is a sense in which Jordan's has only one foot in the camp of industry—because, for Paul at least, it is still part of the woman's realm and his important relations there are with women. An exclusively male work environment would be much more threatening to him, as is indicated in the scene where he goes to pick up his father's pay.

apocalypse—is expressed in one of his most powerful poems, "The North Country":

> In another country, black poplars shake themselves over a
>   pond,
> And rooks and the rising smoke-waves scatter and wheel
>   from the works beyond:
> The air is dark with north and with sulphur, the grass is
>   a darker green,
> And people darkly invested with purple move palpable
>   through the scene.
>
> Soundlessly down across the counties, out of the resonant
>   gloom
> That wraps the north in stupor and purple travels the deep,
>   slow boom
> Of the man-life north imprisoned, shut in the hum of the
>   purpled steel
> As it spins to sleep on its motion, drugged dense in the
>   sleep of the wheel.
>
> Out of the sleep, from the gloom of motion, soundlessly,
>   somnambule
> Moans and booms the soul of a people imprisoned, asleep
>   in the rule
> Of the strong machine that runs mesmeric, booming the
>   spell of its word
> Upon them and moving them helpless, mechanic, their will
>   to its will deferred.
>
> Yet all the while comes the droning inaudible, out of the
>   violet air,
> The moaning of sleep-bound beings in travail that toil and
>   are will-less there
> In the spellbound north, convulsive now with a dream near
>   morning, strong
> With violent achings heaving to burst the sleep that is now
>   not long.

(CP 148–49)[6]

Lawrence's anti-industrialism was born in exile; it was a set of emotions and fantasies that never amounted to a serious program, except during his

---

6. The poem was probably drafted at Croydon, then put into its published form at Porthcothan in early 1916, when two other poems—"In Church" and "At the Front"— were split off from it. See Carol Ferrier.

association with Bertrand Russell in 1915.[7] Contemporaries like Ford, Belloc, Forster, or Galsworthy made a careful study of how English rural life could be revived, though each looked to different groups to take the lead: "small producers," the Catholic church, liberal intellectuals, or the country gentry. *Sons and Lovers,* however, shows no real concern for the economics or social viability of Felley Mill farm. The Leivers are ineffectual dreamers, and it is taken for granted that they will in due course go bankrupt. For Lawrence, what matters about the country is its spiritual opposition to industry and the city. Indeed, this opposition can only be spiritual because the rural way of life cannot and will not defend itself against the profound wish of modern man "to create the great unliving creators, the machines, out of the active forces of nature that existed before flesh" (*Twilight* 60). When Lawrence awoke to the power of industry, he tended to see it as the only real force in civil society—something demonic and overwhelming that would expand, without effective resistance, until it reached a destructive consummation. "Anything that *triumphs,* perishes," he wrote in "The Crown"; but the industrial juggernaut must drive on until it *has* triumphed (*Phoenix II* 373).

Lawrence's impassioned elegy for Garsington, in 1915, assumes that everything the house stands for is obsolete and therefore doomed:

this house of the Ottolines—It is England—my God, it breaks my soul—this England, these shafted windows, the elm-trees, the blue distance—the past, the great past, crumbling down, breaking down. . . . So vivid a vision, everything so visually poignant, it is like that concentrated moment when a drowning man sees all his past crystallised into one jewel of recollection. (*Letters* II: 431, 459)

The actual instrument of this doom is left vague; but in *John Thomas and Lady Jane* Lawrence makes the conflict between old and new England into a moralized tableau:

The great houses, "stately homes of England," still loom and make good photographs. But they are dead. . . . The mines were blotting out the halls. It was inevitable. When the great landowners started the mines, and made new fortunes, they started also their own obliteration. . . . The old England was doomed to be blotted out, with a terrifying absoluteness, by a new and gruesome England. (153–54)

"Stateliness is on its last legs," observes Gerald Barlow in *Touch and Go,* explaining how his colliery has taken an abandoned eighteenth-century hall and made it into offices.[8] His former mistress Anabel Wrath and his sister

---

7. For the failure of Lawrence's political collaboration with Russell, see my *D. H. Lawrence's Nightmare* (chs. 3 and 4).

8. See Wiener (149) for an instructive account of the fate of Winnington Hall. When a giant chemical complex grew up around this Tudor manor house, it was preserved by I.C.I. as an exclusive club for its executives.

Winifred are both appalled by Gerald's boundless ambitions:

WINIFRED: . . . if Gerald was a bit different, he'd be really nice. Now he's so *managing*. It's sickening. Do you dislike managing people, Anabel?

ANABEL: I dislike them extremely, Winifred.

WINIFRED: They're such a bore.

ANABEL: What does Gerald manage?

WINIFRED: Everything. You know he's revolutionized the collieries and the whole Company. He's made a whole new thing out of it, so *modern*. . . . [He] adores electricity. (365, 334)

The argument of these passages is that when the landed gentry collaborated with the rise of industry, they signed their own death warrant as a class. Modern historians would see this as a simplistic view of English culture. In fact, the landed interests shifted much of their wealth into British (and later foreign) industry, but without radically changing their way of life or losing their cultural hegemony. Within Lawrence's own circle, Lady Ottoline Morrell was a good example of how wealth derived from coal could be devoted to artistic enterprises and ambitions. The Bell family history shows the actual shift away from industry toward a more prestigious style of life. William Heward Bell made his fortune as a colliery owner and mining engineer in Wales. He then established his family in mock-Jacobean splendor in Wiltshire, went by the name of "Squire Bell" among the local rustics, and made sure that his tenants joined him at Anglican services though he was privately an atheist (Spalding 67–71). His son Clive made the final step into the bohemian intelligentsia. In this family the hall blotted out the mines, rather than the other way around!

Lawrence fails to appreciate the flexibility of the landed gentry and to understand how they are more visible as a caste than as a class. Their traditional manners are preserved, while the actual management of their wealth is carried on first by the financial interests of the City of London, then, at second hand, by the industrial managers and technicians who have never, in Britain, achieved parity of status and power with the traditional owning (and ruling) classes. One of the chief concerns of this system is to make its own workings invisible. So Lawrence responded to the dynamism of Midlands industry as he had observed it in his youth, but failed to see how, in the long run, Britain was not imbued with the "industrial spirit."[9] On Lawrence's own ground, the last two mines in Eastwood closed down in the year of his centennial.

---

9. It would perhaps be more accurate to say that Britain preserved the industrial spirit—so long as the industry was overseas. The City of London gathered together the country's capital and invested it largely in the expanding economies of Britain's colonies, or rivals. The distaste for "trade" and the cult of the "private income" were sustained by massive foreign investments. The moral complications of this system are examined in Forster's *Howards End*; see my " 'Islands of Money.' " It is a weakness of Wiener's book that he neglects the complicity between the Rural Myth and the export of capital from Britain.

Lawrence felt keenly, of course, the general crisis of British industry in the twenties. But he still took the primacy of industry for granted and focused on the internal struggle between management and labor rather than on the place of industry in British society as a whole. Gerald Barlow in *Touch and Go,* Gerald Crich in *Women in Love,* and Clifford Chatterley are demonic magnates, examples of "the human soul worshipping at the mystery of Matter" (*JTLJ* 335). Their interest in machinery is shown as a compensation for some essential flaw, such as a death wish in Crich or paralysis in Chatterley. At the managerial level, Ursula's uncle Thomas Brangwen in *The Rainbow* reveals his unhealthiness by his affinity with the lesbian Miss Inger. Those who have lost contact with the "Body Electric" become obsessed with the electrified colliery and must follow out that obsession to its limit—which is some form of psychic death. Industrial modernization and expansion are thus reduced to modes of sexual pathology, and Lawrence ceases to be a social novelist, that is, one who works within Britain's complex dialectic of class and regional interests.[10]

How might my argument affect Lawrence's status as writer or thinker? Wiener's study puts forward two propositions: that the central fact of modern British history is the country's decline relative to other developed nations; and that the cause of this decline is not narrowly economic but rather a pervasive *cultural* hostility to the "industrial spirit."[11] Literature, Wiener argues, has helped disseminate this hostility, and insofar as economic performance is the measure of a country's success, literature bears a large share of the responsibility for Britain's failure. British intellectuals, said C. P. Snow in 1959, are "natural Luddites."[12]

A number of polls taken in the seventies found that *The Rainbow* was the novel most widely read and admired by British students. Can it be that Lawrence had ceased to be a heretical author; or was his message, as I have tried to show, never too far removed from the crucial pieties of his culture? How much of *The Rainbow*'s popularity, we may ask, derived from its nos-

10. For example, Lawrence makes a passion for the machine, or for making money, equivalent expressions of the sterile, materialist character. However, the crucial opposition in the British economy is between industry and finance; the latter is less "materialistic" but more "sterile." It is also the economic base of the southern rentier class, whose mentality is brilliantly allegorized in "The Rocking-Horse Winner."

11. The impressive performance of the British economy over the past four years (1984–88) may, if continued, lead to a revision of the Wiener thesis. However, British industrial production is still lower than in 1979, the year Thatcher was elected; and industrial employment is substantially lower. On the subordination of industry to finance, see Perry Anderson and Geoffrey Ingham.

12. *The Two Cultures and the Scientific Revolution* (Cambridge: Cambridge UP, 1959). Snow's main adversary in the ensuing debate was Britain's leading Lawrence critic, F. R. Leavis.

talgic view of social evolution; from its pastoral bias, its hostility to large-scale organization; or from the vision of deindustrialization with which it ends? Did these features appeal especially to that generation of youth, or do they permeate all levels of British culture? How far does Lawrence's popularity depend on the anti-industrial sentiments of teachers as a class? What are the social responsibilities of novelists and poets, and are they the same for each kind of writer?

One might begin to answer these questions by recognizing that there are two traditions of anti-industrial literature in modern Britain: the "soft" and the "hard." The soft version centers on Bloomsbury but also includes novelists like Ford, Galsworthy, and Evelyn Waugh. Its worldview is that of the southern rentier class, oriented toward some version of the country house (or country cottage) ideal.[13] The hard version alternates between nostalgia for antique or primitive societies and dystopian visions of modernity. Its leaders include Lawrence, Eliot, Pound, Yeats, Orwell. In their works, a debased contemporary world is often starkly opposed to an innocent nature: Birkin's fantasy of a world swept clean of people, Winston and Julia escaping from the London of Big Brother into a sexualized landscape.

Writers who choose the "soft" option tend to have substantial or sentimental ties with the dominant financial and landed classes; they retain these ties even as they deplore what Britain is coming to. They are the insiders of the anti-industrial tradition. The outsiders, less compromising and compromised, either never belonged to the English upper classes or, like Orwell, resigned from them. The former group tend to be "little Englanders" by politics and temperament; the latter see England from a European, or even a global, perspective. The insiders work over the classic "middle ground" of the English novel; the outsiders are mythmakers, religious revivalists, or primitivists.

I would argue that Lawrence began as a traditional "soft" pastoralist, became a "hard" primitivist in his middle period, and tried to reconcile the two modes in *Lady Chatterley's Lover*. *The White Peacock* and *Sons and Lovers* are faithful to the Edwardian "country cottage" ideal, which also contributes to Will and Anna's life at Cossethay in *The Rainbow*. These earlier novels incorporate the standard dialectic of the Rural Myth: traditional values are pitted against the encroachments of modernity, but the struggle is conducted within gradualist and indigenously English terms. In early 1915,

---

13. Lawrence entertained both ideals at times: one was represented by Garsington, the other by his occasional fantasies of living obscurely in a cottage with his mother, Louie Burrows, or even Frieda. He recognized, however, that the latter style of life could never accommodate artistic ambitions on the level that he set himself. (During the war he was obliged to live in country cottages, but he resisted the traditional ideals of village life—what Orwell called the cult of "beer and cricket.")

when Lawrence debated postwar reconstruction with Bertrand Russell, he proclaimed a far more radical opposition to the modern industrial system. "But we shall smash the frame," he told Russell. "The land, the industries, the means of communication and the public amusements shall all be nationalised. . . . Then, and then only, shall we be able to *begin* living. Then we shall be able to *begin* to work. . . . Till then, we are fast within the hard, unliving, impervious shell" (*Letters* II: 286). From these new convictions Lawrence made a new, apocalyptic conclusion to *The Rainbow,* showing industry and urbanization as "a dry, brittle, terrible corruption spreading over the face of the land" (458).

The traditionalists viewed the Great War as a defense of the English "unofficial rose" against Prussian mechanized destruction. Lawrence did not believe in such limited rules of engagement. Either the war would bring about the end of the machine age in Europe, or else Moloch would reign and Lawrence himself would have to flee into a primitive exile. Whatever the outcome, his novels from 1915 on would assume the "smashing of the frame": he would abandon the classic middle ground of the English novel and embrace the Savage God. The Second World War inspired a corresponding move in Orwell's fiction from mimesis to fable in *Animal Farm* and *Nineteen Eighty-Four.*

Lawrence and Orwell courted similar dangers in making this shift. Assuming a radical opposition between the "human" (pastoral) and industrial worlds, they ruled out any evolving mediation between the realms of nature and technique. But in Britain, I have argued, the industrial revolution was hedged around by powerful countervailing social interests. The northern manufacturing classes never achieved a cultural hegemony over the existing landed, commercial, or financial elites; rather, they tried to acquire the social prestige of these older classes by aping their style of life. When Lawrence returned to the "condition of England" novel in *Lady Chatterley's Lover,* he was still strongly committed to the apocalyptic and symbolic modes that he had deployed in the fiction of his middle period. Clifford Chatterley thus becomes an overdetermined embodiment of war, industry, and sexual inadequacy, complete with mechanical wheelchair. If Clifford Chatterley is postwar England personified, then Connie and Mellors have no viable social agenda; they can only plot their escape to the virgin forests of British Columbia. In *Sons and Lovers* the Leivers farm represents a complete and credible alternative to the industrialism of Bestwood; but in *Lady Chatterley* the alternative has shrunk to the cramped and vulnerable space of the gamekeeper's hut. Somewhere along the way, Lawrence has charged sex with the exclusive responsibility for confronting the modernist juggernaut. John Thomas and Lady Jane, fragile redeemers of an age of iron, are the sole positive terms in Lawrence's final politics of cultural despair.

WORKS CITED

Anderson, Perry. "The Figures of Descent." *New Left Review* Jan./Feb. 1987: 20–77.

Delany, Paul. *D. H. Lawrence's Nightmare: The Writer and His Circle in the Years of the Great War.* New York: Basic Books, 1978.

Delany, Paul. " 'Islands of Money': Rentier Culture in E. M. Forster's *Howards End.*" *English Literature in Transition: 1880–1920* 31 (1988): 285–96.

Ferrier, Carol. "D. H. Lawrence's Pre-1920 Poetry: A Descriptive Bibliography of Manuscripts, Typescripts, and Proofs." *D. H. Lawrence Review* 6 (1973): 333–59.

Galsworthy, John. *The Silver Spoon.* New York: Scribner's, 1926.

Ingham, Geoffrey. *Capitalism Divided? The City and Industry in British Social Development.* London: Macmillan, 1984.

Kirby, M. W. *The British Coalmining Industry 1870–1946.* London: Macmillan, 1977.

Lawrence, D. H. *The Complete Poems of D. H. Lawrence.* Ed. Vivian de Sola Pinto and F. Warren Roberts. New York: Viking, 1971.

Lawrence, D. H. *John Thomas and Lady Jane.* London: Heinemann, 1972.

Lawrence, D. H. *The Letters of D. H. Lawrence.* Vol. 2: *June 1913–October 1916.* Ed. George J. Zytaruk and James T. Boulton. Cambridge: Cambridge UP, 1981.

Lawrence, D. H. *Phoenix II: Uncollected, Unpublished and Other Prose Works by D. H. Lawrence.* Ed. Warren Roberts and Harry T. Moore. New York: Viking, 1968.

Lawrence, D. H. *The Rainbow.* Ed. Mark Kinkead-Weekes. Cambridge: Cambridge UP, 1989.

Lawrence, D. H. *Sons and Lovers.* Ed. Keith Sagar. New York: Penguin, 1981.

Lawrence, D. H. *Touch and Go. The Complete Plays of D. H. Lawrence.* New York: Viking, 1966. 321–86.

Lawrence, D. H. *Twilight in Italy.* Harmondsworth, Eng.: Penguin, 1960.

Modiano, Marko. *Domestic Disharmony and Industrialization in D. H. Lawrence's Early Fiction.* Uppsala: Acta Univ. Uppsaliense, 1987.

Spalding, Frances. *Vanessa Bell.* London: Weidenfeld & Nicolson, 1983.

Wiener, Martin. *English Culture and the Decline of the Industrial Spirit, 1850–1980.* Cambridge: Cambridge UP, 1981.

CHAPTER 6

Out on Strike: The Language and Power of the Working Class in Lawrence's Fiction

ROBERT KIELY

The industrial problem arises from the base forcing of all human energy into a competition of mere acquisition.

D. H. Lawrence, "Nottingham and the Mining Countryside"

At the culmination of the historical effort of a society to refuse to recognize that it has any function other than the utilitarian one. . . . [The resulting] subjective impasses [include] a demand for commitment, expressing the impotence of a pure consciousness to master any situation; a voyeuristic-sadistic idealization of the sexual relation; a personality that realizes itself only in suicide; a consciousness of the other that can be satisfied only by Hegelian murder.

Jacques Lacan, "The Mirror Stage"

In D. H. Lawrence's short story "Fanny and Annie," a young woman returns home to marry her first beau, a foundry worker named Harry. As she steps off the train, Harry greets her in dialect: "Tha's come, has ter?" (*CSS* 458). He means the words as a cheerful welcome, but she has been a lady's maid and regards herself as superior. She finds his accent repulsive and is disheartened by her future mother-in-law, who "fairly hated the sound of correct English" (463). Since Fanny finds Harry physically attractive, her struggle is not with sexual inhibition but with her hard-earned veneer of class prejudice. The story touches on disappointment, jealousy, and aroused feeling, but all of these are framed by a highly particularized social context and dominated by a language

89

derived from region, work, and socioeconomic rank rather than by the exigencies of love. Sexuality is always a central factor in the behavior and speech of Lawrence's characters. More problematic is the depth, durability, and importance of class origin.

Lawrence's attitude toward the working class, inseparable from his feelings about his father, was unstable, ambivalent, and crucial to his sense of himself and his work as a writer. At times he appeared to deny any connection with mines and miners and to want to become assimilated into the society of artists and their well-to-do patrons. But in other moods, he regretted his social-climbing tendencies and looked back on the lives of colliers with an almost romantic nostalgia. His respect for any kind of skill, including that of the manual laborer, conflicted with his persistent, often explosive impulse to repudiate existing social mechanisms through a refusal to submit human energy to the demands of an impersonal system. His efforts to imagine a future in which labor would be restructured were polarized political fantasies alternating between visions of a classless, propertyless preindustrial utopia and an authoritarian hierarchical state. At one extreme he argued for a benign anarchy: rustic and noncompetitive, made up of loosely organized communities in which people would work according to talent and mood, wear colorful clothing, and have plenty of time for singing and dancing; at the other extreme, he seemed to long for a dictatorship organized according to a strict division of labor, rank, and gender; cultic, solemn, formal, suggestive of the ambition of a Coriolanus rather than the dream of the Faerie Queene.[1]

The language associated with the first vision is song, whereas that of the second (as in *The Plumed Serpent*) is ritual incantation. Lawrence could be both lyrical and repetitious, but the primary mode of his fiction is dialogue. Dealing with the present or the immediate past rather than with an ideal future, he explored the exercise of power in terms of spoken language, the medium of day-to-day exchange. In attempting to understand the role of the working class in his fiction, one turns to the dialogics of speech, to the dynamics of cooperation and conflict rather than to an imaginary and static solution beyond story-telling. How do workers "classify" themselves through their speech and behavior? And to what extent do their collective expressions of self come into conflict with the classification imposed on them by society? Relying on postindustrial terminology, Lawrence usually excludes from the category of "worker," or member of the "proletariat," farmers or

1. Lawrence's efforts to imagine alternatives to the political system of his time appear sporadically throughout his writing. In addition to the attention given to politics in *Aaron's Rod, Kangaroo,* and *The Plumed Serpent,* intriguing reflections on the subject can be found in various essays in the *Phoenix* collection, especially "Nottingham and the Mining Countryside" and "Democracy," as well as in Lawrence's letters, particularly those written in 1915 to Bertrand Russell and Lady Cynthia Asquith.

artisans, especially those who own property, however modest, and who work either for themselves or for a loosely defined clan or community.

For Lawrence, as for Marx, the worker is, by the economic and social standard of the time, one who is not his own master. He is not in control of the conditions, duration, or rewards of his labor, and the product of his effort is not primarily or proportionately related to his own needs or pleasure. The worker belongs to industry and is indispensable to its functioning, but his indispensability is generic, not particular. As an easily replaceable part, the worker, in terms of his ontological status within the industrial system, is cut off from his individuality. Within the production structure he is valued as a type. The particulars of personality matter only as they interfere with his functioning according to classification.

For Lawrence, these associations with the postindustrial worker are indistinguishable from the lot of the coal miner. Though he did not work in the mines himself, his knowledge of them, of their mark on the landscape and the human beings who were tied to them, was as intimate and durable as any imprint left on his imagination as he was growing up. If Lawrence was to some extent influenced by what Paul Delany calls the ''myth of mining'' (see the preceding essay), he also brought to that myth a direct emotional and perceptual involvement that survives his sporadic disavowals and breaks through his daydreams. He was unable to dissociate the subterranean world created by the demands of industry from the social, domestic, and sexual life which, though aboveground, nonetheless seemed under the sway of the omnipotent Company. Although he was clearly aware of the importance of the division of labor according to gender, Lawrence was unable to see the conditions of the working class except as they affected both sexes in all aspects of life. Furthermore, insofar as he was conscious of the alienation of personality from worker function within the industrial system, he was sensitive to gender classification and its ramifications for the typology of labor and its alienating consequences. Whether one thinks of early stories like ''Strike-Pay'' and ''A Sick Collier'' (both 1913) or a great novel of his maturity, *Women in Love,* it is impossible to find a worker in the foreground without being led to consider the character's sexuality and the relationship between class and gender. This is the case generally in Lawrence's fiction.

The pattern established in *Sons and Lovers* in the marriage of Paul Morel's parents is one of the most persistent paradigms in Lawrence's writing of the relationship between class and gender. Mr. Morel's masculinity is seen by his son to be, if not indistinguishable from his class, at least deeply rooted in it. He is an instinctive, passionate, sensual creature, graceful and spontaneous at best; crude, stupid, and violent at worst. Mrs. Morel appears as the feminization of bourgeois ambition and indirection. She is intelligent, sensitive, refined; she can appear touchingly fragile and ethereal or cold, willful, and neurotically possessive. Lawrence returned to this pattern again and again. It is included in "Red-Herring," a bitter autobiographical poem written late in his life and printed in *Pansies* (1929):

> My father was a working man
>   and a collier was he,
> at six in the morning they turned him down
>   and they turned him up for tea.
>
> My mother was a superior soul
>   a superior soul was she,
> cut out to play a superior rôle
>   in the god-damn bourgeoisie.

(CP 490)

The novel and the poem both provoke considerations of a merging of gender and class or, at the very least, a metaphorical reading in which the attributes associated with class somehow stand for sexual traits and, more specifically, for the embattled relationship between male and female. The female as worker's wife, insofar as she is a manager of the household and its finances, more dependent on wit than brawn, seen by the worker as one for whom he is obliged to work, appears like the female personification of the company. The class struggle for power and the outbursts of resistance that reveal themselves sporadically in strikes and individual acts of insubordination in the mines are paralleled by a conflict of will and potency between wife and husband.[2]

I would like to suggest—without denying the importance of this pattern in Lawrence—that other forces in his fiction operate in opposition to it, disrupt and dislocate its structural symmetry. I would also like to argue that these forces emerge not late in Lawrence's career but as early in his fiction as the familiar conflict between worker-male and bourgeois-female. In "A Sick Collier," for example, a young collier, a "good worker," marries a cook who people say is "too good for him," suggesting that though she is not middle class, she is a cut above him in the socioeconomic system. That those who voice this opinion are themselves from the working class, with the difference in education and economic standing slight, seems to parody the distinctions applied more broadly and destructively in the world at large. Yet the couple are happy together until the husband is injured in a mining

---

2. For a discussion of class and marital conflict in *Sons and Lovers*, see Scott Sanders (32–42). Sanders refers to Mr. Morel as "Marx's classic laborer, owner of nothing but his body." But he goes on to argue that Lawrence's concentration on individual psychology overshadows considerations of class. My view is that the personal and the collective are interlocked.

accident and is driven almost mad by pain. Since the accident affects his bladder and since the muscular, energetic collier is confined to his bed, there is a large temptation—seemingly offered by the text on a platter—to read this accident metaphorically as a form of castration resulting from marriage to a superior female who is as determined to deprive the male of his self-sufficiency and power as the industrial magnates are. In an outburst of agony, the young husband turns on his wife, screaming "It's 'er fault. . . . Kill her, kill her!" (*CSS* 272).

Had the story ended here, the metaphorical reading would be difficult to challenge. But the husband regains his senses and apologizes. He and his wife and the female neighbor who had come to help all weep over the misfortune that has fallen not just on the male but on the couple. In other words, the text presents the metaphorical paradigm of gender and class hostility in a particularly bold and obvious form, and then shows it to be a futile and pathetic misreading. The wife is not responsible for her husband's injury; it is an industrial accident that is as wounding to her as to him. They are both victims of a system that conceals its authors and encourages false projections of blame on those of both sexes who are enslaved by it.

Though male workers may frequently confuse their wives with their industrial masters, both the men and women of this class are subject to "the base forcing of all human energy into a competition of mere acquisition" (*Phoenix* 138). In the language of the industrial utilitarian machine, women "labor" to produce children in order to provide replenishment of the work force. The sexual energies of males also fall within the metaphorical grip of the competitive and acquisitive machine. In the story "Strike-Pay," a young worker is given an increase in his weekly allowance because "he had twins a-Monday night" and is told by another collier, "Get thy money, Sam, tha's earned it" (*CSS* 46). Ephraim, who has recently married, is chided by his fellow workers for having lost his strength because being married "ta'es a bit o' keepin' up" (*CSS* 47). Whether referred to in common puns and jokes or through melodrama and pathos, the signal is clear. Sexual and especially marital relations are so dominated by the exigencies of the capitalist-industrial system as to seem indistinguishable from its values and vocabulary. Intercourse and childbearing are forms of work, performances of duty to a machine with an insatiable need. The return pay is a currency so modest and neutral as to be a humiliation. Though it appears to signify power, it is, in fact, so sparingly bestowed as to ensure minimum survival and therefore continued servitude. Sexuality and gender are not the primary realities for which class struggle is the image. On the contrary, what is fundamental is the endless round of labor for an invisible, resented, imperfectly understood other. The marital relationship is sometimes seen as a caged parody, a frail image or shadow of this reality, in which love, pleasure, beauty, and the particulars of gender are obliterated by a supply and demand system which has no use for them.[3]

Even as Lawrence's fiction constructs in linguistic terms this systematic repetition of parallels and substitutions, it provides a complex instrumentation for breaking the hermeneutical circle it delineates.[4] When the internal logic and efficiency of a structure made up of transferable parts appear to increase in direct opposition to the value and significance of the structure as a whole, the best tactic for the victim is not to attack the self-contained economy of the system, but to remove an essential part and bring the system to a halt. In warfare, this would mean sabotage rather than massive assault. In the dimension of class struggle, it means to "go on strike." In sexual terms, it means a refusal to submit gender to the demands of acquisition and competition. In narrative terms, it means to dislocate the metaphorical link, with its appearance of finality and coherence, and to replace it with the looser, vaguer juxtapositions of metonymy.[5] Virtually all of Lawrence's fictions about the working class reveal a sense in which the text establishes a system of linguistic, economic, and sexual exchange, then "goes on strike" against it.

The idea of language as a smoothly functioning tool for the exchange of practical and useful information is disrupted in a rich variety of ways in Lawrence's fiction, but where the working class is concerned the device readiest at hand is dialect. Most colliers in Lawrence's world turn dialect on and off at will; they play it like a musical instrument. It is a means of communication tuned to the mood of the moment rather than to the needs of an unreachable future. Its sounds, images, and rhythms establish harmonics that often thwart and mock the speech forms of those who are anxious about unambiguous meaning.

In the dialectics of the Morel family in *Sons and Lovers,* it is the mother in both her feminine and her bourgeois roles who, as a speaker of standard English, interprets and verifies the children's narrated experience: "No one told [the father] anything. The children, alone with their mother, told her all about the day's happenings, everything. Nothing had really taken place in them until it was told to their mother" (101–2). Mrs. Morel validates and completes their half-finished sentences and adventures in her own heart. As a

3. Variations on this theme can be found in "The White Stocking," "Odour of Chrysanthemums," and the early chapters of *Aaron's Rod.*

4. Some of Lawrence's most explicit and satirical references to the closed circularity of the capitalist system and its effect on all aspects of life appear in his poetry. Two lines from a poem entitled "Wages" are representative: "The work-cash-want circle is the viciousest circle / that ever turned men into fiends" (*CP* 521).

5. My use of the term *metonymy* is influenced in part by Jacques Lacan's essay "The Agency of the Letter in the Unconscious," *Écrits* 146–78.

member of the bourgeoisie, she also, when the children grow older, translates their experiences into ambitions for education, a higher status, a better life.

Despite fits of drunkenness and rage, Mr. Morel rarely interferes with this closed family and linguistic circle. Occasionally, when things need fixing, Morel, "the good workman," sets happily about his task, singing and gathering his children around him for stories:

> "Tell us about down pit, daddy."
> This Morel loved to do.
> "Well, there's one little 'oss—we call 'im Taffy," he would begin. "An' he's a fawce 'un!"
> Morel had a warm way of telling a story. He made one feel Taffy's cunning.
> "He's a brown 'un," he would answer, "an' not very high. Well, he comes i' th' stall wi' a rattle, an' then yo' 'ear 'im sneeze."
> " 'Ello, Taff,' you say, 'what art sneezin' for? Bin ta'ein' some snuff?' " (103–4)

Such stories, we are told, could go on "interminably." They have no conclusion and no point. They do not invite interpretation or translation. Mrs. Morel never seems present during their telling and Mr. Morel's terms of affection—"my beauty," "my darlin' "—are directed at his children. Morel's stories in dialect are not presented as direct challenges to his wife's authority over him or their children. They are part of a verbal and emotional world apart, a language of noncooperation, a whimsical refusal to join the discourse of practical sense. It is affective and playful language, not in the service of work (as defined by industry) yet unmistakably the language of the "good worker" since the text tells us that "these happy evenings could not take place unless Morel had some job to do." What is dislocated, then, is not Morel's identity as a laborer, but his function in an industrial mechanism and class structure that dominate his marriage and his life.

In "Strike-Pay" the dialect of the striking men shows the influence of the economic system while they are being paid, but they quickly leave this influence and banter playfully with one another. They do not simply break the work cycle of being "turned down to the pit" at six in the morning and "turned up again for tea"; they temporarily remove themselves from the linguistic and material obligations of competition and acquisition. They decide to attend a competition very different from the kind that binds their lives, a football match, a game, much like their own discourse, with no productive purpose. Young Ephraim loses his pay while riding a pony, and the other workers willingly share their own with him. But when he returns home, his mother-in-law demands his money and berates him for wasting his time. She speaks in standard English and he replies in dialect, "sticking to his broad Derbyshire" (*CSS* 51), and deliberately using not just an argument but a kind of language to defend himself.

The striking worker refuses to be assimilated into the obligatory round of exchanges in which his energy is dissipated in return for verbal and monetary tokens of a system that enslaves him. His quarrel with his mother-in-law is as much one of class as gender; it is a reminder to her, through his refusal to turn off his dialect, that they are both of the same breed and speak the same language. When the woman is at last riled by the young worker's resistance, she too breaks into dialect:

"If tha dares ter swear at me, I'll lay thee flat."
"Are yer—goin' ter—gi'e me—any blasted, rotten, còssed, blòody tèa?" he bawled, in a fury, accenting every other word deliberately. (53)

Since it is the tea that is grammatically the object of the collier's curses and the mother-in-law who exits, a strict metaphorical reading is comically displaced. The relationship between class and gender is similarly inexact, accidental, and superficial. It is based on contiguity, not phenomenological resemblance, and it is easily exploded by a language that refuses to empty itself of personality and emotion in the interest of efficiency.

When the mother-in-law leaves the house in a fury, husband and wife address each other softly and peacefully in dialect, demonstrating a tentative assertion of a discourse and relationship outside the utilitarian industrial network. Dialect, which at first had seemed a peculiarly male form of speech, is, in fact, a class language with a capacity not only to bond male laborers but also to unite males and females of the working class in a discourse that resists the intrusions of the middle-class language of dispassionate bargaining.

The workers' dialect does not derive its power from physical force or wealth. Obviously, it would not have a chance against the machine and the bank. Even Ephraim's mother-in-law is bigger and wealthier than he is. Dialect derives its power from its direct relation to the mood and circumstance at hand. It does not seek strength, like the bartering language of the bourgeoisie, on assumptions about accumulating wealth and storing up treasure for the future. Whether the occasion is a holiday with fellow workers or a family quarrel, the images, puns, accents, and rhythms are spontaneously and deftly tuned to the moment. Dialect is very much like Lawrence's definition of the "poetry of the present" in his introduction to the American edition of *New Poems* (1918): "the poetry of that which is at hand: the immediate present. In the immediate present there is no perfection, no consummation, nothing finished" (*CP* 182). Workers may be too poor to boast about the past or plan for the future, but unlike the nostalgic and anxious bourgeoisie, they are able to break through and make vital contact with the here and now.

Dispossessed from the language of economic power and the contingent power (or appearance of power) that such a language gives over past and future, Lawrence's workers become by default the poets of the present. Although they are dispossessed from the land, their relationship to place is similarly privileged as a direct result of their underprivileged socioeconomic status. The colliers, of course, do not own the land on which they live and work. Yet in his essay "Nottingham and the Mining Countryside" and throughout his fiction, Lawrence stresses the unique and intimate relationship between the workers and the earth. Though, economically, they "belong" to the Company, their external mark of uniformity is not a regulation working costume, but a natural imprint. One of the unmistakable signs of the collier is the grime and pit dust with which he is covered at the end of each working day.

As with dialect, the miner's blackened torso appears at first to signal a gender as well as a class distinction. A tableau repeated many times in Lawrence's work is that of a woman, half repelled, half fascinated, watching a blackened collier eating a meal or washing himself. The sexual implications have been frequently discussed and, in any case, are usually underlined in the text: the confrontation with a mysterious other and the insistence on the earthbound nature of the sexual relationship. There are unquestionably moments when Lawrence seems to identify the male with the demonic underworld and the female with the enlightened, more social and articulate world above ground. But there are also important indications that rootedness in the dark earth is not an exclusively male phenomenon. In his introduction to *Pansies,* Lawrence says that "the fairest thing in nature, a flower, still has its roots in earth and manure . . . the black of the corrosive humus. . . . So it is: we all have our roots in earth" (*CP* 417–18). The male worker is not the owner of the underworld, though by virtue of his class and gender as defined by the social structure of the time, he may be its messenger.

In "Daughters of the Vicar," when Louisa, a woman of the middle class, visits Alfred Durant's house and watches the young miner eating without having washed, her first reactions are more indicative of her social rank than her gender. "His black face and arms were uncouth, he was foreign" (*CSS* 169). When old Mrs. Durant asks Louisa to wash her son's back, once again the girl categorizes the task in class terms and thinks of the mother and son less as individuals than as members of a large mass to which she does not belong: "It was all so common, so like herding. . . . After all, there was a difference between her and the common people" (170). However, when she does touch the man's dirty flesh, "her feelings of separateness passed away" (171). In other words, the true difference in gender overcomes the false difference in class. If the female has been excluded from contact with the earth, it is not because of some inherent reticence or incapacity associated with her sex, but rather because of the constraints imposed by class. Later in the story when the couple come together in a passionate embrace, Alfred is once again necessarily and significantly unwashed:

"Your face is black," she said.
He laughed.
"Yours is a bit smudged," he said. (182)

Though the scene has some of the same ingredients as a decadent bourgeois melodrama in which a character from the upper or middle class goes slumming, the effect is the exact opposite. The episode does not reflect sexual debasement, a brutalizing or lowering of some approved standard, but a kind of coming home. The "smudge" is not a synonym for "stain," a metaphor for sin, but a sign of self-discovery through another. In expressing her female sexuality, Louisa crosses a class barrier and finds herself, like Alfred, not in possession of the earth but part of it.

Impurity of language and body appears to be the distinctive property of the disinherited worker. But in Lawrence's logic, impurity and disinheritance are not negatives, nor are they really peculiar to one class or gender. They are aspects of a natural human condition denied and distorted by the class system of a competitive industrial economy. For Lawrence, no one is free from the generative and limiting power of the earth, and one only does harm by pretending to be. It also seemed to him that no one really owned the earth or any part of it and that the private ownership of property was both a great evil and a "false" fiction.[6]

In Lawrence's "truthful" fiction, the claim to ownership or possession of people and land, with its constituent functions of manipulation and oversight, and the indirect gratification derived through the effort of laborers are socio-economic neuroses, a counterpart to voyeurism. Industrialists and their agents, under the illusion that they possess the land and the laborers who work on it, create for themselves a role of anxious watchfulness over a process on which their attention is relentlessly fixed but in which, by structural definition, they must not participate.

As a fascinated but uninvolved observer of the blackened collier, Louisa in "Daughters of the Vicar" is a true representative of her class. When she touches the man's flesh and the grime that covers it, she gives up her illusory control over the scene and enters into it, not as a privileged and invisible overseer but as a participant, a co-worker as it were, willing to get her hands dirty. That the scene depicts a sexual encounter is obvious. But it is equally important to notice that the scene is about the crossing of class boundaries and, furthermore, that the class differentiation is not part of a simple metaphorical

6. For some of Lawrence's most unequivocal condemnations of private ownership, see poems like "Why—?" (*CP* 451), "O! Start a Revolution" (*CP* 453), and "Property and No-Property" (*CP* 663); and letters, including one to Mary Cannan, 24 February 1915 (*Letters* II: 292–93), and another of equal importance to Lady Cynthia Asquith, 3 August 1915, in which he says, "Owners and owned, they are like the two sides of a ghastly disease" (*Letters* II: 375–76).

equation with gender. In abandoning the inhibited and voyeuristic tendencies of her class, the bourgeois woman does not abandon her sex but finds a common ground with the male in which both can flourish.

No single work of Lawrence's deals more fully with the issues we have been exploring than *Women in Love*. I would like to focus on a chapter that contains one of the most memorable and vivid scenes in Lawrence's fiction: that of Gerald Crich forcing a terrified mare to stop at a railroad crossing while a train rumbles past. The sexual ramifications of the scene have been elaborately noted, but what is frequently forgotten is that this violent moment is the relatively short beginning of a chapter entitled "Coal-Dust," concerned with the industrial landscape and the lives of miners.

If one reads the chapter metaphorically, taking the first episode as the key to the code, virtually everything in it can be translated into sexual terms, specifically of rape, in which the distress of the two sisters, the ruin of the landscape, and the debasement of the workers and their families are all variants on a theme of violation by a phallic force uncontrollably dominated by an urge to possess and destroy. Without denying the logic of this way of reading the chapter, I would like, as in my earlier examples, to argue for another approach which is less eager to find a conversion table for the sexual and socioeconomic, but which permits both to command a privileged status. Surely, the entire chapter, though it begins with a forced connection, "the heterogeneous . . . yoked by violence together," is also filled with instances of displacement, of what Lacan calls "that veering off of signification that we see in metonymy" (160). The structure of the chapter makes the reader continually aware of odd juxtapositions and missed connections, of disturbing divisions and distances.

There is not a character who is not presented as part of a curiously matched pair. Neither opposites nor doubles, they appear irrevocably linked and alike yet somehow split, reminders of "the self's radical ex-centricity to itself" (Lacan 172). Gudrun and Ursula are united by family, gender, and class, yet their reaction to Gerald's behavior differs sharply; similarly the two workmen who watch the sisters and, later in the chapter, Gudrun and her friend Palmer are "two units" with odd points of resemblance. Even Gerald and the mare are not quite opposites; they are both thoroughbreds, and her torment is proleptic of his self-destruction. In short, these pairings, whether of gender, class, or accidental proximity, provoke comparison but resist transference and consolidation.

The divisions within and between individual characters are extended to those between the sexes and social classes. Not only is every character vaguely doubled, but every action is presented as observed by someone at a distance. The voyeuristic elements in the opening and closing scenes of the chapter have much in common, but there are also subtle shifts in perspective and in the relationship between demand and desire. In both sections, Gudrun is almost paralyzed by feelings of contempt and attraction; she is drawn toward what she hates. She is fixated and tantalized by her own alienation, capable, like an ingenious bureaucrat, of endlessly multiplying the distance between herself and the action with which she is obsessed. Though the physical details—Gerald's thighs, the mare's blood—call attention to sexual attraction and an apparent closing of the gap between observer and observed, there are repeated reminders of a separation which is not exclusively spatial. As the last car of the train approaches, Gudrun notices the guard looking out his window: "And, through the man in the closed wagon Gudrun could see the whole scene spectacularly, isolated and momentary, like a vision isolated in eternity" (*WL* 112). In a double displacement, Gudrun disconnects the event from a temporal continuum and therefore presumably from her own life story, and detaches herself from a direct line of sight through the agency of an observer who is literally her opposite, a male worker in motion looking at the scene from the other side. There is no reason to believe that Gudrun's momentary shift of perspective is the result of an empathetic impulse. We are never told what the worker thinks or sees or that Gudrun cares. He provides a moving vantage point for a "veering off of signification."

The chapter ends with Gudrun taking pleasure in watching the bodies of the blackened miners and listening to their "broad dialect." With her friend Palmer, an earnest mine electrician "with a passion for sociology" (117), she goes slumming on Friday nights among the workers, feeling a nostalgia to be near the masses of common people. The idea of Gudrun, well dressed, analytical, observant, fitting into the scene at the workers' market is, of course, absurd. Her immersing herself into the midst of the human stream only accentuates her alienation and a desire which is unclear in everything except its incapacity to be fulfilled.

And what do the working classes make of this? "Streams of humanity" do not speak, but two colliers standing on the other side of the tracks do. Backing up a few pages to the center of this chapter, we return to these workers watching the two sisters as they "seemed to glitter . . . in motion across a hot world silted with coal-dust." This time it is the two workers who are motionless while the women, not the train, "drew near . . . passed, and . . . receded." The older worker shows himself a product of the system:

"What price that, eh? She'll do, won't she?"
"Which?" asked the young man, eagerly, with a laugh.
"Her with the red stockings. —What d' you say? —I'd give my week's wages for five minutes;—what!—just for five minutes." (114)

It is a vulgar parodic replay of the paradigm of metaphoric interchange between sexuality and the economics of competition and acquisition. It is a paradigm that the text repeatedly proposes and undermines. Gerald owns the purebred Arab mare; he can destroy her, but he cannot possess her. Gudrun confuses her sexual restlessness with a daringly decadent interest in the working class, but the rate of exchange is nonexistent. The introduction of the market system into the sexual relationship causes nothing but pain and frustration, and is a disastrous sign of its unsuitability to human interaction.

The young workers' reaction to his companion's hypothetical bid for Gudrun seems unobtrusive in a chapter that begins so violently, but I would argue that it is central to the text and to Lawrence's view of the power of the working class: "No," he says. "It's not worth that to me" (115). Like some of the workers in the early stories about mining, he is, in his own way, "on strike." He refuses to compete and acquire, even in fantasy. In this chapter so filled with feverish efforts to dominate, his words have an extraordinary dignity and serenity. Once they are spoken, the blackened landscape is miraculously touched with beauty:

The heavy gold glamour of approaching sunset lay over all the colliery district. . . . On the roads silted with black dust, the rich light fell more warmly, more heavily; over all the amorphous squalor a kind of magic was cast, from the glowing close of day. (115)

The worker's refusal, like the dialect and coal dust associated with his class, is not a static or negative sign, but a metonymic escape from a metaphoric trap. It is not a rejection of the female but of the acquisitive system. It does not deny distance or try to manipulate it through a voyeuristic and illusory exchange of gratification for vicarious participation. By virtue of not forcing connections, it has a mysteriously transforming power, and a rapport with a beauty it does not own nor wish to.

In "Nottingham and the Mining Countryside," Lawrence recalls and recreates those moments when the workingmen of his youth, including his own father, seemed in perfect harmony with nature:

I've seen many a collier stand in his back garden looking down at a flower with that odd, remote sort of contemplation which shows a *real* awareness of the presence of beauty. It would not even be admiration, or joy, or delight, or any of those things which so often have a root in the possessive instinct. It would be a sort of contemplation: which shows the incipient artist. (*Phoenix* 137)

The language of this passage is too careful and restrained to be dismissed as mere nostalgia. Here we discover not only a crucial distinction between voyeurism and aesthetic contemplation, but also a key to what may be Lawrence's deepest identification with the working class. Capable of an existence outside "the competition of mere acquisition," dispossessed, at rest, or on strike, the workingman is redeemed from brutality and reinstated as the father of the artist. Though in some moods Lawrence seemed to want to disown his background, an equally strong and more passionate tendency was toward identification:

> Ah the people, the people!
> surely they are flesh of my flesh!

("The People," *CP* 585)

WORKS CITED

Lacan, Jacques. *Écrits: A Selection*. Trans. Alan Sheridan. New York: Norton, 1977.

Lawrence, D. H. *The Complete Poems of D. H. Lawrence*. Ed. Vivian de Sola Pinto and F. Warren Roberts. New York: Viking, 1971.

Lawrence, D. H. *The Complete Short Stories of D. H. Lawrence*. 3 vols. New York: Viking, 1961.

Lawrence, D. H. *Phoenix: The Posthumous Papers of D. H. Lawrence*. Ed. Edward D. McDonald. 1936. New York: Viking, 1968.

Lawrence, D. H. *Sons and Lovers*. Ed. Keith Sagar. New York: Viking, 1981.

Lawrence, D. H. *Women in Love*. Ed. David Farmer, Lindeth Vasey, and John Worthen. Cambridge: Cambridge UP, 1987.

Sanders, Scott. *D. H. Lawrence: The World of the Five Major Novels*. New York: Viking, 1974.

Lawrence, D. H. *The Letters of D. H. Lawrence*. Vol. 2: *June 1913–October 1916*. Ed. George J. Zytaruk and James T. Boulton. Cambridge: Cambridge UP, 1981.

CHAPTER 7

The Circling Hawk: Philosophy of Knowledge in Polanyi and Lawrence

M. ELIZABETH WALLACE

D. H. Lawrence rarely shied away from exact, forceful expression of his thought or feelings at any particular moment, so proving him inconsistent, at least superficially, is easy. A critic who wishes to discuss Lawrence as a serious thinker therefore faces immediate problems. The first is Lawrence's memorable statement about his "belief in the blood, the flesh, as being wiser than the intellect" (*Letters* I: 503), written a few months after his elopement with Frieda. This passage must somehow be squared with the late poem "Thought" (from *More Pansies,* written in 1919):

> Thought, I love thought.
> But not the jiggling and twisting of already existent ideas . . .
> Thought is gazing on to the face of life, and reading what can be read,
> Thought is pondering over experience, and coming to a conclusion . . .
> Thought is a man in his wholeness wholly attending.
>
> (*CP* 673)

No simple progression—from the young Lawrence discovering the full beauty of the flesh, to the dying Lawrence rediscovering the more profound powers of the mind—can explain the contradiction. Bert Lawrence of Eastwood, devourer of books, first in all England and Wales in the 1904 King's Scholarship examination (Moore 65), pronounced "well-read, scholarly, and refined" by his teaching supervisor in 1908 (Moore 84), and commended by his Croydon headmaster for his teaching of biology (Nehls 86), cannot be called a despiser of intellect. Nor can one point to the last novels, *The Man Who Died* and *Lady Chatterley's Lover,* to illustrate Lawrence's failing appreciation of "the marvellous piercing transcendence" of physical desire (*EC* 57).

Ever since T. S. Eliot proclaimed Lawrence incapable of "what we ordinarily call thinking" (58), critics have concentrated more on one side of this

103

tension than on the other. The cliché of Lawrence as enemy of intellect, as a disorganized, illogical thinker, has been pervasive. Even Wayne Booth in *Modern Dogma and the Rhetoric of Assent* mentions "Lawrentian men of passion" (19), "the irrationalist D. H. Lawrence" (45), and finally "Lawrence's attacks on the murderous intellect in the name of the darker gods" (98). When Booth writes of Lawrence at length (as he does in this volume), Lawrence benefits from the attention; but the cliché of the genius who consistently preferred sex to sense still flourishes.

However, if we focus on Lawrence's thoughts *about* thought, particularly in the context of modern theories of knowledge, we can see how he attempted to revise our notions of "what we ordinarily call thinking": our valuing of skepticism and doubt over sympathy and commitment, our preference for impersonal, bodiless thought or "objectivity." If he succeeded, then the very terms of the argument may need to change. We must not discount Lawrence's thought because our own theories of knowledge are inadequate.

Lawrence's critiques of certain epistemological biases are often misread as simple disapproval of knowledge and intellect. He consistently damns mechanical intellectual activity and challenges empirical and positivist assumptions about knowledge—from the early *Study of Thomas Hardy* and "Education of the People" to the psychology books and the portrayal of Clifford in *Lady Chatterley*. However, these works and many others also reveal Lawrence's continuing interest in theories of knowledge, in how people learn, how knowledge is created/discovered, and especially how "art-speech" can work to build and reveal truth.[1]

Of particular importance in this respect is the seminal work of Hungarian-born philosopher Michael Polanyi (1891–1976). Although Lawrence could not have read Polanyi's work in epistemology (begun in 1939) and although Polanyi was not influenced by Lawrence's writings, significant parallels in their thought need to be explored. F. R. Leavis began this work in *Thought, Words and Creativity: Art and Thought in Lawrence* (1976), but it is by no means finished. A study of Polanyi can help us read Lawrence more accurately, recognizing not only his powerfully articulated philosophy of knowledge but his disciplined, lifelong commitment to "art-speech" as a workshop for constructing, exploring, testing, and discovering reality.

I. POLANYI AND SCIENCE

A widely published and respected physical chemist, Polanyi turned to philosophy in mid-career to challenge assumptions about how scientists work. In

---

1. For instance, see Michael Squires's discussion of the education theme in *Lady Chatterley's Lover* (94–115).

the process he articulated an epistemology with profound implications for other disciplines. His ideas, most fully expressed in his major work *Personal Knowledge* (1958) and in *The Study of Man* (1959) and *The Tacit Dimension* (1966), have been discussed not only by other scientists and philosophers but by mathematicians, psychologists, theologians, art historians, educators, poets, doctors, novelists (Saul Bellow, Andrew Greeley), and teachers of writing and literature (Peter Elbow, Janet Emig, James Britton, Sam Watson, Wayne Booth, Frank Kermode, F. R. Leavis).[2]

Polanyi found it inexcusable that philosophers of science should try to account for scientific work without adequately accounting for the paradigmatic moment of scientific discovery. Because such moments rarely follow the strict rules of scientific inquiry or experimental proof, philosophers of science have tended to ignore them. Polanyi's analysis of the central role of discovery in the advancement of science led him to distinguish, as Lawrence does, between the routine manipulation of explicit knowledge ("the jiggling and twisting of already existent ideas") and the passionate, creative plunges "by which we gain a foothold at another shore of reality" and on which the scientist must stake "his entire professional life" (*Personal Knowledge* 123). Polanyi's phrasing resembles Lawrence's discussion of knowing and being in the *Study of Thomas Hardy:*

I wish we were all like kindled bonfires on the edge of space, marking out the advance-posts. What is the aim of self-preservation, but to carry us right out to the firing line, where what *is* is in contact with what is not. . . . He who would save his life must lose it. . . . When he reaches the shore, when he has traversed his known and come to the beach to meet the unknown, he must strip himself naked and plunge in, and pass out: if he dare. (18–19)

In *Personal Knowledge,* Polanyi challenges three common criteria for real knowledge—first, that it be impersonal; second, that it rely on no unexamined assumptions but only on fact or proof; and third, that it be explicit, capable of

2. See particularly Elbow's *Writing Without Teachers* (1973), *Writing with Power* (1981), and *Embracing Contraries* (1986), all published by Oxford University Press; Janet Emig's *The Web of Meaning* (Montclair, N.J.: Boynton/Cook, 1983); James Britton's *Language and Learning* (New York: Penguin, 1970) and *Prospect and Retrospect* (Montclair, N.J.: Boynton/Cook, 1982); Sam Watson's essay "Breakfast in the Tacit Tradition" in the special issue of *PRE/TEXT* Watson edited on Polanyi and rhetoric, 2 (1981): 9–31; Wayne Booth's *Modern Dogma and the Rhetoric of Assent*; Frank Kermode's *The Art of Telling* (Cambridge: Harvard UP, 1983); F. R. Leavis's *Nor Shall My Sword* (London: Chatto & Windus, 1972), *The Living Principle: English as a Discipline of Thought* (New York: Oxford UP, 1975), and *Thought, Words, and Creativity: Art and Thought in Lawrence* (London: Chatto & Windus, 1976). See also M. Elizabeth Wallace, "Literature as Knowledge: Polanyi's Influence on F. R. Leavis and Wayne Booth," *Tradition and Discovery* 15 (1988): 12–20; and Pamela A. Rooks, "D. H. Lawrence and Michael Polanyi: Redefining Objectivity and Subjectivity," *Tradition and Discovery* 15 (1988): 20–26.

being stated. He argues, instead, that all knowing is a skill that can never be fully detached from the person performing it, that relies on unexamined assumptions and beliefs, and that can never be fully accounted for in words or formulae alone.

According to Polanyi, the personal coefficient in our knowledge is no imperfection to be eliminated, but the inescapable condition of all knowledge. Not only do the intellectual passions of scientists determine what problems they choose to explore, but these passions also sustain their attention, uphold rigorous standards of verification, and then help them persuade others that their discoveries are true and important (3–17).

Polanyi's second claim, that science depends on unexamined assumptions, leads him to argue that we can never examine all of these assumptions because without them we would be unable to think. Consider how acritically we dwell in language. A belief in the stability of objects influences the way we learn our native tongue; still other beliefs result from our habit of naming and categorizing—our distinguishing, for example, between health and sickness, good and evil. To acquire a language is to accept a whole framework of beliefs about the nature of reality. Of course, we can question any part of this framework and change it, but we must rely on most of the framework un-questioningly in order to do so. This is, in fact, how scientists rely on a tradition of accepted scientific beliefs in the hope of changing one part of it through their discoveries (59, 69–131).

Third, according to Polanyi much of our knowledge can never be articu-lated. Our nineteenth-century epistemological heritage would have us believe that true knowledge can be explicitly stated. But Polanyi argues that knowing is a skill that cannot always be passed along through documents and equa-tions, but often only directly from master to apprentice. The formula for riding a bike—"you adjust the curvature of your bicycle's path in proportion to the ratio of your unbalance over the square of your speed" (50)—never reaches six-year-olds. To learn a skill, one must temporarily submit to an authority, a master who passes on those rules of his art which even he can't specify. We know much more than we can say, from recognizing a face to reading x-rays to applying old words to new situations (*Personal Knowledge* 49–65; *Tacit Dimension* 204–9). In "Education of the People," Lawrence's passage on learning to solder a kettle explores the same distinction between explicit and tacit forms of knowledge (*Phoenix* 653).

In all three claims, Polanyi, like Lawrence, emphasizes the bodily roots of knowledge. Scientific research, Polanyi argues, is a skill like that exercised by a blind man using a stick to explore a cave. As he touches the walls or floor, he can picture the uneven terrain. However, he focuses not on the probe where it touches his palm, but on the tip of the probe as it describes the cave to him. The probe becomes an extension of his body: he pours himself into it to discover something beyond it (*Tacit Dimension* 12–13; *Personal Knowledge* 55–56). We might think here of Lawrence's idea in "Why the Novel Matters" of a hand that learns and knows and thinks as it "meets all the strange universe, in touch" (*STH* 193).

We extend our bodies in the world through such intellectual tools, and all our knowledge has this *from-to* structure. We attend *from* certain details close to us *to* something further which we want to discover and which we think will meaningfully organize those details (*Personal Knowledge* 55–63). Whether scientist or humanist, we rely on intellectual tools and probes, our interpretive frameworks, to make discoveries about ourselves and our world, thus relying on prior *tacit* knowledge for the construction/discovery of all our *explicit* knowledge.

The actual moment of discovery or insight cannot be logically accounted for. Mathematicians, trying to teach the unspecifiable skill of problem solving, of playing tricks on one's perception to reorganize a problem so that one can suddenly see its solution, have advised students to "Look at the unknown. Look at the conclusion." In other words, focus not on the particulars of the problem, but dwell in them, as in a probe, to focus on the whole solution that could contain and explain them; envision the parts of a problem as "clues to the unknown; as pointers to it and parts of it" (*Personal Knowledge* 127–28).

Thus for Polanyi, human beings, motivated and sustained by intellectual passions and relying on assumptions about reality built into the very language they speak, practice the unspecifiable skill of knowing. The explicit knowledge that scientists discover is validated by them, but it is not therefore subjective. A scientist does not make up his conclusions at will, but states them to be true to his data, his theory, and reality. His knowledge is based on a tension between personal passion and impersonal truth, and he claims universal validity for it (*Personal Knowledge* ix–xiii, 63–65, 321–24).

Because all explorers share a responsibility to reality, Polanyi argues that the sciences and the humanities exist on a continuum. In some sciences the value of precision must be weighed against the value of scientific interest since there are many uninteresting subjects about which science can be exact, and many fascinating subjects—such as the study of living organisms—about which science cannot be exact. Nevertheless, the study of living organisms has scientific value at least equal to that of the more precise study of physics. Thus the fields of history, literature, religion, and philosophy, for instance, make up for their relative lack of precision by their extraordinary human interest (*Study of Man* 71–99; *Personal Knowledge* 134–39).

II. LAWRENCE AND THE GAY SCIENCE

Polanyi's epistemology helps reveal the common thread in Lawrence's writings about consciousness and discovery. Lawrence excels at portraying char-

acters on the verge of discovery and at making articulate—as far as possible—
the tacit elements in their struggle for understanding. Usually these discoveries concern a character's relation to family, lover, friend, God, or
death—as in "Odour of Chrysanthemums"—but they occasionally touch on
science or philosophy—as in Ursula's puzzlement over her professor's mechanical view of biology or in Birkin's philosophizing about dissolution. And
it would be difficult to imagine two English novels that offer a finer study of
the creation/discovery of knowledge, a surer rendering of young people reading, studying, and assimilating their heritage, than *Sons and Lovers* and *The
Rainbow*.

Lawrence would have agreed with Polanyi that "tacit knowing is more
fundamental than explicit knowing: we can know more than we can tell"
(*Personal Knowledge* x). In the *Study of Thomas Hardy,* however, Lawrence
couched the distinction more in terms of knowing (close to Polanyi's "explicit" knowing) and being (close to Polanyi's "tacit" awareness or indwelling), and saw the adventure in consciousness as furthering the movement of
life—or of being—itself.

It seems as if the great aim and purpose in human life were to bring all life into the
human consciousness. . . . But the bringing of life into human consciousness is not an
aim in itself, it is only a necessary condition of the progress of life itself. Man is
himself the vivid body of life. . . . Altogether devoid of knowledge and conscious
motive is he when he is heaving into uncreated space, when he is actually living,
becoming himself.
    And yet, that he may go on, may proceed with his living, it is necessary that his
mind, his consciousness, should extend behind him. . . . And this *knowing* . . . is a
force active in the immediate rear of life, and the greater its activity, the greater the
forward, unknown movement ahead of it. (41–42)

Furthermore, Lawrence's developing epistemology closely parallels Polanyi's three claims—that knowledge is personal, is based on unexamined
assumptions, and is an unspecifiable skill involving risk and commitment, the
extension of our bodies into the world. Like Polanyi, Lawrence emphasized
the bodily roots of knowledge ("a true thought . . . comes as much from the
heart and the genitals as from the head" ["Introduction to *Pansies,*" *CP*
417]), the creative nature of perception, and the need for fierce, steady attention to unknown solutions—an attention that acknowledges one's responsibility to discover what one *must* rather than what one would like. As
Lawrence wrote in "Books" in 1924,

There are, in the consciousness of man, two bodies of knowledge: the things he tells
himself, and the things he finds out. . . . Man is a thought-adventurer. But by thought
we mean, of course, discovery. We don't mean this telling himself stale facts and
drawing false deductions, which usually passes as thought. (*Phoenix* 732)

From the Hardy *Study* to "Introduction to *Memoirs of the Foreign Legion*" to "Books" to the last poems, Lawrence emphasized the venture into consciousness. In "The Future of the Novel" he argues for the reuniting of fiction and philosophy in this venture, to make fiction less precious and philosophy more concrete, less detached from its roots in the body of life. Lawrence beautifully states his insistence on examining ideas in their physical context, one idea against another, in "Art and Morality," "Morality and the Novel," "Why the Novel Matters," and "The Novel and the Feelings"—all from 1925—as well as in the earlier *Studies in Classic American Literature*. In "Morality and the Novel" Lawrence's statement that "the novel is the highest complex of subtle inter-relatedness that man has discovered. Everything is true in its own time, place, circumstance, and untrue outside of its own place, time, circumstance" (*STH* 172) fleshes out his famous remark in *Studies in Classic American Literature* that "Art-speech is the only truth" (8). But a letter of 1914 to Gordon Campbell anticipates both formulations: "All vital truth contains the memory of all that for which it is not true" (*Letters* II: 247). Lawrence early understood the precision necessary to narrative. As he wrote to Blanche Jennings in 1909, "all mysteries and possibilities lie in things and happenings, so give us the things and happenings, and try just to show the flush of mystery in them, but don't begin with a mystery and end with a foolish concrete thing" (*Letters* I: 107).

Even in his nonfiction, Lawrence often proceeds with the detail, the contextuality, and the oppositions that characterize the embodied thought—the "art-speech"—of his fiction. In the introduction to Verga's *Cavalleria Rusticana,* for instance, he describes the workings of the mind with a rhythmic detail that perfectly embodies the hawklike, sustained attention that focuses one's whole being on a problem in a desire for its solution:

The mind makes curious swoops and circles. It touches the point of pain or interest, then sweeps away again in a cycle, coils round and approaches again the point of pain or interest. There is a curious spiral rhythm, and the mind approaches again and again the point of concern, repeats itself, goes back, destroys the time-sequence entirely, so that time ceases to exist, as the mind stoops to the quarry, then leaves it without striking, soars, hovers, turns, swoops, stoops again, still does not strike, yet is nearer, nearer, reels away again, wheels off into the air, even forgets, quite forgets, yet again turns, bends, circles slowly, swoops and stoops again, until at last there is the closing-in, and the clutch of a decision or a resolve. (*Phoenix* 249–50)

This passage, though similar to Polanyi's discussion of a mind in pursuit of discovery, is unlike anything in Polanyi's writing. The stylistic difference may explain why Lawrence's theories of knowledge are often misunderstood. Lawrence frequently used the techniques of fiction in his essays, a practice that makes much of his best nonfiction disconcerting. Writing about Lawrence's stories, Weldon Thornton argues that Lawrence's originality lies in his refusal to keep an objective distance from his characters. Lawrence dwells in his characters with an intense energy that frequently misleads critics; they assume that he is stating his own point of view as omniscient narrator, when— as Wayne Booth shows (pages 16–21 of this volume)—he is presenting one character's point of view, a view to be challenged elsewhere in the story by an opposing statement or action presented with equally misleading energy on behalf of a different character. These contradictory statements must be weighed against each other before the critic can glimpse the complete thought the story is meant to be.

Lawrence uses the same method to present ideas in his nonfiction. He enters into an idea as he enters into a character—to learn something, holding nothing back. He states that idea as convincingly as he can, with all his energy.[3] Then, a few paragraphs later, Lawrence discovers another idea that discloses all the inadequacies and imperfections of the first. He may suddenly attack the first idea, or he may enter wholeheartedly into the new idea and dwell in it as he did in the first, trying to see the world from a new perspective. When he goes on to another discussion altogether, he may leave behind two contradictory statements, each equally convincing. This procedure makes Lawrence easy to quote out of context, but it illustrates the heuristic value of what Polanyi refers to as "indwelling" (*Personal Knowledge* 58–65). Lawrence's belief that sympathy is a more effective heuristic tool than doubt (a belief most novelists share) finds confirmation in Polanyi's systematic critique of doubt (269–98).

In his best nonfiction Lawrence develops these oppositions within the piece itself. But Lawrence can also shoot off a lively essay under the influence of one thought, so we often need to set one essay against another in order to get an accurate picture of Lawrence's mind. Usually, however, this setting of one idea or character or even word against another serves him well (think of Lawrence's frequent use of oxymoron). He uses such dichotomies and antitheses as a discipline forcing him to apprehend new realities. He recognizes tensions as aids to perception, then strives to discover a whole that can account for and include without reduction the oppositions he presents.

This attempt to bring the intellectual powers of art-speech into nonfiction prose is striking in the *Study of Thomas Hardy,* in which Lawrence worked out his own epistemology as a way of evaluating Hardy's. Significantly, Lawrence's original title for this piece, visible on the typed manuscript, was "Le Gai Savaire," the gay science or skill, a phrase medieval troubadours

---

3. Such a methodology is called phenomenology in the psychology of perception and the history of religions and is often the only way to understand an alien worldview. Cf. Maurice Merleau-Ponty.

used to describe their poetic craft.[4] This linking of knowledge and poetry underscores Lawrence's interest in the theory of knowledge that shaped Hardy's art.

By increasing the tension between equally strong but opposed forces— self-preservation and self-expression, stillness and activity, knowing and being, Christianity and Judaism, male and female—Lawrence leads the reader into a fuller understanding of related conflicts between and within Hardy's characters, surprising us with his shifts of sympathy. For instance, after vigorously appreciating Jude's true education through Arabella and Sue—as opposed to Jude's passion for "mere academics" (*STH* 107)—Lawrence suddenly adopts Sue's point of view, defends her special nature, and condemns Jude for violating it.

Lawrence understood Hardy's love/hate relationship with Sue Bridehead, through whom Hardy struggled with the scientific and philosophic ideas that troubled him. In his close reading of Hardy—Lawrence read at least fourteen novels, *The Dynasts,* and some stories—Lawrence realized that he would need to confront the nineteenth-century positivist philosophies of knowledge that influenced Hardy in order to understand characters like Clym, Angel, and Jude who struggled to accumulate ideas and impart them to others.[5] Lawrence, who appreciated Hardy's rendering of the impasse of vigorous minds caught in a mechanical concept, argued that Clym, Angel, and Jude struggled with knowledge that did not pertain to them and struggled in the wrong way, to no purpose (*STH* 23–30, 43–44).

Positivism denied the imaginative power of scientific theory: theories were simply descriptions of observed phenomena, not probes into unknown territory. Thus the imaginative power of art to uncover or create knowledge was also denied, a denial Hardy felt keenly. The *Study of Thomas Hardy* attempts to understand the kind of knowledge fiction can create and to proclaim its value. The chapters that fail to mention Hardy are not digressions but necessary groundwork where Lawrence develops his theories of knowing and being, of perception, of mind and body in order to deal more fruitfully with the epistemological biases in Hardy's work.

The *Study* has received serious attention ever since H. M. Daleski established its significance in *The Forked Flame* (1965), but it is still possible for

4. See Bruce Steele's comments in his edition of *Study of Thomas Hardy* (xxiii, xxxv–xxxvi, 255, n. 7). See also Howard Mills's suggested translation, "the cheerful wisdom," in David Ellis and Howard Mills, *D. H. Lawrence's Non-Fiction* (Cambridge: Cambridge UP, 1988) 11.

5. For the influence of nineteenth-century philosophy of science on Hardy's thought, see M. Elizabeth Wallace (213–47). Hardy's close reading of Comte and his lifelong interest in and argument with positivism are documented in Robert Gittings's *Young Thomas Hardy* (Boston: Little, Brown, 1975) and *Thomas Hardy's Later Years* (Boston: Little, Brown, 1978), and in Michael Millgate's *Thomas Hardy: A Biography* (New York: Random House, 1982).

critics as fine as Keith Sagar to refer to the *Study*'s "strident tone and un-controlled form" and to find much of it "tedious, turgid, or incomprehensi-ble" (Sagar 76, 61). Actually its structure repays detailed scrutiny, especially if, following the clue of the typescript title, we approach it as an early statement of Lawrence's theory of knowledge, a theory that grew naturally out of his profound engagement with Hardy's work. Through the power of art-speech, tensing one idea against another, Lawrence used the *Study* to under-stand Hardy's achievement and to ground his own.

III. STORY AS THOUGHT

If a cogent theory of discovery and knowledge emerges from Lawrence's work—a theory often parallel to Polanyi's systematic analysis of personal knowledge and tacit knowing—the question remains: How does this affect our reading of Lawrence's fiction?

We will, of course, better appreciate certain aspects of Lawrence's art, especially his skill at portraying the growth of consciousness in inarticulate men and women, which now reveals his profound sensitivity to the priority of tacit forms of knowledge. As Michael Squires says, Lawrence differentiates characters "by their capacity to verbalize" (108); the "most original and insightful theme" of *Lady Chatterley's Lover,* he argues, is "the value of emotional intelligence expressed in nonverbal ways" (114). Novelists, who live by words, find it difficult to dwell fully in characters who do not; and no writer surpasses Lawrence at this kind of indwelling. In "Education of the People" Lawrence writes:

Those whose souls are alive and strong but whose voices are unmodulated, and whose thoughts unformed and slow, these constitute the great base of all peoples at all times. . . . For the creative soul is for ever charged with the potency of still unborn speech, still unknown thoughts. (*Phoenix* 608)

In stories like "The Horse-Dealer's Daughter," "The Blind Man," and "You Touched Me," Lawrence excels at giving these "alive, strong souls" a voice.

More significantly, we might now assume Lawrence's philosophical so-phistication rather than his naïveté, thus reshaping our discussions of, say, *The Rainbow* and *Women in Love* as powerful examinations of nineteenth- and twentieth-century thought. When the distinction is made early in *The Rainbow* between the men who look toward the back of the farm, toward animals and harvest, and the women who look toward the village "and the world be-yond," Lawrence assesses the Brangwen women's desire in terms of con-flicting theories of knowledge:

She strained her eyes to see what man had done in fighting outwards to knowledge, . . . her deepest desire hung on the battle that she heard, far off, being waged on the edge of the unknown. She also wanted to know. . . .

It was this, this education, this higher form of being, that the mother wished to give to her children, so that they too could live the supreme life on earth. . . . Ah, it was something very desirable to know, this touch of the wonderful men who had the power of thought and comprehension. (11–13)

This passage begins the novel's complex testing of competing philosophies of knowledge: the primitive, pagan, Edenic state of consciousness; Anna's rationalism and Will's mysticism; Will and Anna's unsettling, intense responses to religious art; and Ursula's confrontations with Christian theology and ritual, with Benthamism, with educational theory and practice, with mechanistic scientific theories, and with the rationalist/religious dilemma she inherits from her parents. As the novel closes, Ursula's task is not to rest in the knowledge of those who preceded her, but "to create a new knowledge of Eternity in the flux of Time" (456).

By the time Ursula marries Birkin in *Women in Love,* Lawrence has tested an even wider range of contemporary ideas about how knowledge is created and discovered. From Gerald's expertise in the mines to Hermione's at Breadalby, from Gudrun's animal carvings to the African statuette, from Birkin's drawing of a Chinese goose to Loerke's sculptural interpretation of industry, we encounter trenchant presentations of alternative forms of knowledge and gain a rich sense of the possibilities and dangers of each mode of discovery.

However, we can do more than claim Lawrence's skillful, sophisticated incorporation of contradictory philosophies into his novels. His true work was not merely understanding, presenting, and testing the ideas of others, but building his own complex, embodied thoughts—his novels, stories, poems, and plays. "Thought" is not something to be extracted from a story; rather a reader dwells in the story's every word to discover the entire thought. The reader's indwelling parallels the adventure of the artist, who similarly dwells in confusing and disparate particulars in order to discover their possible relations to each other. Lawrence believed that the true artist was an explorer "sent forth from a great body of people to open out new lands for their occupation" (*Letters* II: 283) and that on the way an explorer "should go to the extremity of any experience" ("Education of the People," *Phoenix* 653).

Lawrence's exploration of unoccupied territory can best be illustrated by three of his most abstract works, whose approach to parable is implied in their titles: "The Woman Who Rode Away" (composed in 1924), "The Man Who Loved Islands" (composed in 1926), and *The Man Who Died* (composed as *The Escaped Cock* in 1927–28). Only the middle piece has consistently been viewed as a testing of ideas that appealed to Lawrence. "The Man Who Loved Islands" challenges dreams of isolation from humankind and absorption into nature. The tale reveals an unmistakable sympathy for Cathcart in spite of nature's final judgment on his absolute solitude. Lawrence admired explorers in realms where he could not go: he had a horror of extreme cold, for instance, and he needed interaction with a variety of people, as the sheer number of his letters proves. But through his characters he could go to the "extremity of experience" and test there the "perfect" solutions to life's problems. "The Man Who Loved Islands" sets Cathcart's intense pleasure in discovering a new mode of existence against the final frozen outcome of that existence; the reader forgets neither the death nor the pure appeal of the complete thought.

Another "perfect" solution to which Lawrence was repeatedly drawn was the abandonment of conscious thought altogether, the return to the primitive. Although Lawrence treated this problem in *The Plumed Serpent,* the novel's realism made it difficult for him to draw Kate Leslie convincingly into the worship of Quetzalcoatl. In the summer before he finished the novel, Lawrence tried to build the thought more simply in "The Woman Who Rode Away," using a woman who said almost nothing, who felt dead even before she began her journey toward the Chilchui Indians. We never know her first name, only that she considers herself a modern woman, is stultified by her marriage, and leaves on her adventure under the influence of "a foolish romanticism" (*CSS* 549).

By stripping away details of her personality, Lawrence draws us into a profound experience of another person's consciousness. It is a dim, altered consciousness, where drugs enable the woman to hear "the little dog conceive, in her tiny womb, and begin to be complex, with young"; to hear "the vast sound of the earth going round, like some immense arrow-string booming"; and to hear "the snow on a cold, cloudy day twittering and faintly whistling in the sky" (568, 572). Her concentration on sounds emphasizes the nonmental reality she has entered. The success of the tale depends on the skill with which we are drawn into this consciousness; we must dwell in the woman's nonrational, muted mind if the deadly prophecy of the Indians and her eventual willingness to participate in it are to make sense.

"The Woman Who Rode Away" is one of Lawrence's most perfect creations; rarely do we have a sense of the narrator's intruding voice. The two points where critics have located the narrator's voice (in Part II, page 569, where "her kind of womanhood . . . was to be obliterated again" and in the last line of the story) do not imply that the author approves of cutting out the hearts of modern women. Both passages use a remote, summarizing language to articulate something of what the increasingly inarticulate and dazed woman must sense about her fate. She cannot meditate clearly on the wider significance of the primitive rite, on the meaning of the sacrifice from the Indians' point of view, without destroying the stilled, elemental mind Lawrence has succeeded in giving her. In her infrequent conversations with the young Indian, Lawrence is careful to keep her questions from penetrating to the explicit facts: even her unspoken thoughts and questions are kept distant from graphic reality.

Indeed, these two "intrusive" passages reveal the tale's central conflict. Although critics have usually focused on the sexual implications of the story[6] (after all, a woman is sacrificed, in a cave, lying prone, with a sunlit, phallic shaft of ice dominating the scene as a male priest raises his knife), Lawrence's main interest is in the irreducible conflict between two modes of consciousness, primitive and modern. The Indians' myth condemns white *men* as much as it condemns white *women:* the sacrifice is intended to emasculate white men by stealing their power over the sun. Although Lawrence sacrifices a human being to the Indian gods, he manages to do so only by obliterating her personality long before she faces a knife. The novella—the complete thought— immerses us in a dissolving mind. We experience the great power of the primitive, but know finally that it can persuade only if the adventure into consciousness is abandoned. The result of that abandonment is death.

Of course, readers of *Studies in Classic American Literature* or "Indians and an Englishman" already knew where the weight would fall. Lawrence felt the profound pull of the dark gods, but could never turn his back on the responsibilities of consciousness:

We can't go back to the savages: not a stride. We can be in sympathy with them. We can take a great curve in their direction, onwards. But we cannot turn the current of our life backwards. . . . Not for a moment. If we do it for a moment, it makes us sick. (*SCAL* 145)

The drug that stripped normal consciousness from the woman also made her vomit, even as it gave her luxurious relaxation. Similarly, Kate Leslie cannot stomach total immersion in Quetzalcoatl's mesmerizing ritual, although she takes "a great curve" in the direction of primitive religion and consciousness while yet moving "onwards." Lawrence's going to the "extremity of experience" in the shorter tale influenced the final version of *The Plumed Serpent*, making extreme forms of acquiescence no longer possible for Kate. Lawrence had seen too clearly what they looked like.

The third fable, *The Man Who Died,* dares the most. Although not as successful artistically as "The Woman Who Rode Away," it reveals more clearly the obstacles encountered when an abstract idea is tested and extended by incarnation, when explicit statement takes on the unpredictable flesh of art. Unlike the two earlier fables, *The Man Who Died* attempts to test an idea

---

6. See Kate Millett (285–93) and David Cavitch (163–69). Cavitch also points to Lawrence's fear of male brutality and power in Indian and Mexican culture.

that gives life, not death. Neither the isolation of the individual in lone supremacy nor the sacrifice of the individual consciousness to the community prevails; instead, Lawrence offers an image of a profound and fruitful balance between self and other. Indeed, he offers an alternative religion or at least challenges and enriches an existing one. In *The Plumed Serpent* Lawrence tried to create a religion, with rituals, hymns, myths, traditions, even a trinity of gods; he failed. But in *The Man Who Died,* working within his own religious tradition, he nearly succeeds. Dissatisfied with the Protestant emphasis on the crucifixion (which left the resurrection a pale fact and most of the Christian year bland and gray), Lawrence built his own resurrection narrative.

Lawrence makes thinkable his idea about the resurrection by imagining a cross-fertilization between Christian and pagan traditions. Christianity's uncertain valuation of the body is transformed in the tale by a more ancient tradition that celebrates fertility goddesses, gods that die and are resurrected each spring, and sacred marriages between the two that ensure the world's fruitfulness. In this older tradition one celibate, male god would seem an inadequate image for the life of humanity, but Lawrence did not want to dismiss Christianity. His artistic solution was to extend and complicate it, to include it without reduction in a larger context with another religious tradition.

He had used this method earlier in the *Study of Thomas Hardy,* discovering fruitful relationships between concepts that contradicted each other. In *The Man Who Died* these very contradictions and juxtapositions—especially of body and spirit, male and female—disrupt our old ways of thinking. Readers of Lawrence's tale are shocked by its "disturbing connection of godhead with sexuality" (Steinberg 26)[7] and by the presence of a woman as priestess, a woman as powerful in serving her goddess as the man in serving his god. In this resurrection account, woman is not follower, mourner, observer, but equal—a virgin in the ancient sense of singleness and devotion to a calling. The priestess serves a fertility goddess whose religion can easily incorporate, as Osiris, the hitherto sterile man-who-died. On the deepest level the priestess impregnates the man, making potent and fruitful his barren religion, previously blind to the profound mystery of body, creation, and physical communion.

The sheer audacity of dwelling in this reversal, exposing it to the test of incarnation, giving a face and voice to the woman the thought requires, reveals Lawrence's commitment to the risks of exploratory thinking, to the truths only art-speech could uncover. As Polanyi puts it, "Things which we

7. In his controversial study of the emphasis on Christ's genitals in Renaissance art, Leo Steinberg finds the erection/resurrection motif not only in Renaissance paintings but in a long tradition from Osiris worship to Mediterranean mystery cults to Boccaccio's *Decameron* (Third Day, Tenth Tale) to the love poetry of the sixteenth and seventeenth centuries; for Steinberg, however, Christ's sexuality is always understood to be "potency under check" (17).

can tell, we know by observing them; those that we cannot tell, we know by dwelling in them'' (*Personal Knowledge* x).

The technical problems of this particular indwelling are enormous, determined by preexisting intense feeling or potential hilarity in the audience. The delicate handling of language and tone, the archaisms and biblical rhythms, the detached impersonality of the conversations between the nameless ''man who had died'' and the ''woman of the pure search'' (*EC* 47) could serve either to excite ridicule or to disarm accusations of obscene sacrilege. Lawrence chose to write primarily for those within the Christian tradition, often using the exact words attributed to Christ but putting them in audacious puns or other new settings that reverse or complicate their meaning.[8] ''On this rock I build my life'' (instead of church), ''My hour is upon me, I am taken unawares,'' and the echoes of Christ's words on the cross—''Father! . . . Why did you hide this from me?''—all culminate in the suggestion of Christ's passion, the implied pun of the entire scene in the temple of Isis (*EC* 57–58). Not every reader is moved when the man proclaims ''I am risen!'' in his climactic moment with Isis, but between those who are offended and those who are amused are those for whom the words of the Judeo-Christian tradition are irreversibly complicated. In this sense *The Man Who Died* works best for those it shocks the most.

A novelist's ability to create sympathetic, believing readers serves a heuristic purpose: only when we have consented to enter the story (suspended our disbelief, willingly submitted to someone else's authority for a time) can our powers of imagination be disciplined and extended to share the author's complete thought. We withhold sympathy from authors for many different reasons, from their technical incompetence or incomprehensible complexity to our own fixed biases and beliefs. Though *The Man Who Died* faces serious problems of the latter sort in creating sympathetic readers, the struggle to become one repays the effort.

All science and all art depend on our ability to take risks, to dwell in new ideas and believe the hitherto unbelievable. Science and art are built by the strength and flexibility of our imaginations, our ability to attend to the unknown and discover/create meaningful wholes that make sense of the disparate particulars of our existence. An alert reader of Lawrence's best work turns away with an imagination strengthened, altered, and empowered for such attending to life.

In his novels and stories, then, Lawrence embodies the intense concentration of discovery. It was both his true subject and his method. In *Etruscan Places* he writes:

---

8. On the altered biblical allusions in *The Man Who Died*, cf. James C. Cowan.

An act of pure attention, if you are capable of it, will bring its own answer. And you choose that object to concentrate upon which will best focus your consciousness. Every real discovery made, every serious and significant decision ever reached, was reached and made by divination. The soul stirs, and makes an act of pure attention, and that is a discovery. (153)

Polanyi describes a similarly impassioned concentration in the lives of great scientists like Einstein and Kepler, who wrote passionately of moments of insight before experiments or calculations ever substantiated their theories (*Personal Knowledge* 6–17). Lawrence, the successful biology teacher at the Davidson Road School, continued all his life to appreciate the methods of creative scientists. As he wrote in "Introduction to These Paintings":

Any creative act occupies the whole consciousness of a man. This is true of the great discoveries of science as well as of art. The truly great discoveries of science and real works of art are made by the whole consciousness of man working together in unison and oneness: instinct, intuition, mind, intellect all fused into one complete consciousness. . . . (*Phoenix* 573–74)[9]

Though not a scientist, Lawrence understood the similarities between science and art. He too brought his powers of concentration to bear on his self-assigned task of "gazing on to the face of life and reading what can be read." Like Polanyi, he accepted that the knowledge he articulated had its roots in his flesh, in an imprecise and unpredictable language, and in tacit forms of understanding he could never fully express. And like most great artists and scientists, he was often wrong; not every theory or experiment led to success. At every turn the opportunity to discover truth and establish knowledge involved the risk of error.

In the course of his work, Lawrence articulated a coherent epistemology, a philosophy of knowledge and discovery that was less an attempt to dictate a system than a way to understand his own vocation as a novelist. He claimed, as Polanyi did later, that art was a difficult, complex form of knowledge, giving reports on reality as real and important as those of physics and, like physics, building dwelling places for the human mind—theories, stories— capable of changing irreversibly the way we enter and explore what remains unknown. If "what we ordinarily call thinking" ever excluded this achievement, Polanyi's work of redefinition now requires us to acknowledge it, to recognize the intelligence of Lawrence's commitment to "art-speech" as a form of truth. Furthermore, Lawrence's puzzling oxymorons—"thinking blood," "blood consciousness"—can never again contribute to the cliché of the genius who couldn't think; for in the light of Polanyi's own oxymoron,

9. In "Hymns in a Man's Life" Lawrence describes the real scientist as one who "works in the sense of wonder" (*Phoenix II* 599).

"personal knowledge," we have discovered that they mean the same thing as "man in his wholeness, wholly attending."

WORKS CITED

Booth, Wayne C. *Modern Dogma and the Rhetoric of Assent*. Chicago: U of Chicago P, 1974.

Cavitch, David. *D. H. Lawrence and the New World*. New York: Oxford UP, 1969.

Cowan, James C. "Allusions and Symbols in *The Escaped Cock*." *Critical Essays on D. H. Lawrence*. Ed. Dennis Jackson and Fleda Brown Jackson. Boston: G. K. Hall, 1988. 174–88.

Eliot, T. S. *After Strange Gods: A Primer of Modern Heresy*. New York: Faber & Faber, 1934.

Lawrence, D. H. *The Complete Poems of D. H. Lawrence*. Ed. Vivian de Sola Pinto and F. Warren Roberts. New York: Viking, 1971.

Lawrence, D. H. *The Complete Short Stories of D. H. Lawrence*. Vol. 2. London: Heinemann, 1955.

Lawrence, D. H. *The Escaped Cock*. Originally published as *The Man Who Died*. 1928. Ed. Gerald M. Lacy. Los Angeles: Black Sparrow, 1973.

Lawrence, D. H. *Etruscan Places*. *Mornings in Mexico* and *Etruscan Places*. Harmondsworth, Eng.: Penguin, 1971. 95–215.

Lawrence, D. H. *The Letters of D. H. Lawrence*. Vol. 1: *September 1901–May 1913*. Ed. James T. Boulton. Cambridge: Cambridge UP, 1979.

Lawrence, D. H. *The Letters of D. H. Lawrence*. Vol. 2: *June 1913–October 1916*. Ed. George J. Zytaruk and James T. Boulton. Cambridge: Cambridge UP, 1981.

Lawrence, D. H. *Phoenix: The Posthumous Papers of D. H. Lawrence*. Ed. Edward D. McDonald. 1936. New York: Viking, 1968.

Lawrence, D. H. *Phoenix II: Uncollected, Unpublished and Other Prose Works by D. H. Lawrence*. Ed. Warren Roberts and Harry T. Moore. New York: Viking, 1968.

Lawrence, D. H. *The Rainbow*. Ed. Mark Kinkead-Weekes. Cambridge: Cambridge UP, 1989.

Lawrence, D. H. *Studies in Classic American Literature*. Harmondsworth, Eng.: Penguin, 1983.

Lawrence, D. H. *Study of Thomas Hardy and Other Essays*. Ed. Bruce Steele. Cambridge: Cambridge UP, 1985.

Merleau-Ponty, Maurice. *Phenomenology of Perception*. London: Routledge & Kegan Paul, 1962.

Millett, Kate. *Sexual Politics*. Garden City, N.Y.: Doubleday, 1970.

Moore, Harry T. *The Priest of Love: A Life of D. H. Lawrence*. Rev. ed. New York: Farrar, Straus & Giroux, 1974.

Nehls, Edward, ed. *D. H. Lawrence: A Composite Biography*. Vol. 1. Madison: U of Wisconsin P, 1957.

Polanyi, Michael. *Personal Knowledge*. New York: Harper & Row, 1964.

Polanyi, Michael. *The Study of Man*. London: Routledge & Kegan Paul, 1959.

Polanyi, Michael. *The Tacit Dimension*. New York: Anchor- Doubleday, 1967.

Sagar, Keith. *The Life of D. H. Lawrence*. New York: Pantheon, 1980.

Squires, Michael. *The Creation of "Lady Chatterley's Lover."* Baltimore: Johns Hopkins UP, 1983.

Steinberg, Leo. *The Sexuality of Christ in Renaissance Art and in Modern Oblivion*. New York: Pantheon, 1983.

Thornton, Weldon. "The Originality of Lawrence's Short Stories." *The English Short Story, 1880–1945*. Ed. Joseph Flora. Boston: G. K. Hall, 1985. 39–56.

Wallace, M. Elizabeth. "*Study of Thomas Hardy*: D. H. Lawrence's Art-Speech in the Light of Polanyi's *Personal Knowledge*." Diss. U of Kent, Canterbury, 1974.

CHAPTER 8

Repetition, Consummation, and "This Eternal Unrelief"

JOHN N. SWIFT

To his 1919 foreword to *Women in Love,* Lawrence appended a response to a charge—or at least an observation—that's still made by many of his readers, a charge of stylistic repetitiveness:

In point of style, fault is often found with the continual, slightly modified repetition. The only answer is that it is natural to the author: and that every natural crisis in emotion or passion or understanding comes from this pulsing, frictional to-and-fro, which works up to culmination. (486)

Lawrence saw his repetitions as "natural," creativity in language duplicating the structures of creativity in nature. He analogized writing and sexual activity, and found in the building rhythms of intercourse an appealing model for the rhythms of his own prose (and the rhythms of his political thought, the main subject matter of the *Women in Love* foreword): a pulsing interplay of opposites works toward orgasmic consummation, transformation, a lapsing out and a new birth. The results were, on the one hand, what one critic calls the "sexualization of style" in *Women in Love* (Gordon 366); on the other, Lawrence's increasingly clear articulation of theories of art, politics, and psychology against the paradigm of repetition leading to culmination, in works such as the *Study of Thomas Hardy,* "The Reality of Peace," and eventually the two *Unconscious* books.

Simple instances of verbal repetition are everywhere in Lawrence's work. In *Women in Love* itself they most typically occur in the representing of characters' thoughts, as in this passage from near the novel's end:

Oh, why wasn't somebody kind to her? Why wasn't there somebody who would take her in their arms, and hold her to their breast, and give her rest, pure, deep, healing rest. Oh why wasn't there somebody to take her in their arms and fold her safe and perfect, for sleep. She wanted so much this perfect enfolded sleep. She lay always so

121

unsheathed in sleep. She would lie always unsheathed in sleep, unrelieved, unsaved. Oh how could she bear it, this endless unrelief, this eternal unrelief. (465)

"Continual, slightly modified repetition": this kind of slow ticking over, submergence and reemergence, of a few words and phrases is the most distinctive among various Lawrentian repetitive strategies. Here Gudrun muses on the barren close of her relation with Gerald, and to some extent the repetition maps the circular process of her thought. But it's not atypical of Lawrence's style elsewhere in the novel; at one time or another similar language invests all of the major characters.

The rhythm may be natural or sexual, but it plainly subverts Lawrence's understanding of repetition as prelude to consummation: Gudrun's "frictional to-and-fro" *doesn't* move to any thematic or formal "culmination," but to what looks like its opposite, an inconclusive "eternal unrelief," a repetition of a statement of frustration. After this passage, Gudrun's thoughts and Lawrence's language wind through several stylistically similar paragraphs, describing Gerald himself as a monstrous repetitive machine, to peter out in exhausted uncertainty: "But oh heavens, what weariness! What weariness, God above! . . . So many wheels to count and consider and calculate! Enough, enough—there was an end to man's capacity for complications, even. Or perhaps there was no end" (466). Repetition in fact seems to be one necessary effect of an inability to conclude. Moreover, this pattern of endless, unconsummated repeating isn't restricted to individual words describing *Women in Love*'s most narcissistically limited characters, Gudrun and Gerald: in a sense a dissatisfied repetition provides the novel's entire structure, from the sisters' stuttering conversation of the opening pages to Birkin's final refusal to accept the closure of his achieved "star-equilibrium" with Ursula. At every opportunity in his assault on "culmination," Lawrence obstinately insists on one word more: the result is a recurrence of words and patterns, a stammer in the text. And these frustrated repetitions produce a corresponding frustration in the reader, who is likely to ask impatiently (and rather in the posture of Ursula listening to Birkin's professions of love): Why doesn't he just say it and have done with it?

Lawrence doesn't say it because he *can't* say it, because it can't be said; but perhaps his failure says it eloquently enough after all. I will continue by sketching a psychoanalytic elaboration of this paradoxical proposition, because Freudian analysis directed itself at exactly the symptomatic gesture that simultaneously occludes and reveals its own sense, its own origin—and because the ceremonial of repetition was the staging point for the production of the symptom. The classic Freudian symptom marks itself off from "normal" behavior in two ways: by its inutility or senselessness, and by its self-replicating energy. Early in his work, Freud understood compulsive repetition of a senseless act as the neurotic's alternative to articulated memory, a partial way of saying things that couldn't be said: "The patient does not *remember* anything of what he has forgotten and repressed, but *acts* it out. He reproduces it not as a memory but as an action; he *repeats* it, without, of course, knowing that he is repeating it" ("Remembering" 150). What can't be remembered can be—in fact must be—repeated as an apparently incomprehensible action. The symptom, like a dream, attempts the symbolic satisfaction of a repudiated wish, marking desire's persistence in subverting and speaking through the forces of repression. For example, in Freud's experience of the analytic transference, a repressed and unresolved hostility toward parents finds an object and a language: "The patient does not say that he remembers that he used to be defiant and critical toward his parents' authority; instead, he behaves in that way to the doctor" ("Remembering" 150). Thus the symptomatic gesture can be decoded by realigning it with the repressed context in which it once had meaning, articulating openly a forgotten wish.

Does this formula of the psychogenic symptom help in understanding Lawrence's repetitive habit? Not very much: for Freud—initially at least—it's the signifying content of the repeated action that's symptomatic, not the act of repetition itself. Repetition is simply the formal by-product of repression, a manifestation of continuing pressure from untranslated, inarticulate desire: "a thing which has not been understood inevitably reappears; like an unlaid ghost, it cannot rest until the mystery has been solved and the spell broken" ("Analysis of a Phobia" 122). But repetition in *Women in Love* is a general expressive condition, not displaying any single or even localizable content. It's not as if, for example (and as we might expect), Lawrence repeats only the frustrating elements of his childhood's Oedipal catastrophe. These kinds of recurrences, such as the Magna Mater theme, have an important part in the novel; but he also repeats references to plants, animals, and objects of all kinds; references to qualities of things, to states of mind, to abstract structures—including the structure of repetition itself. In short, his repetitions are so varied in content that if we were fully to accept the art-symptom analogue, to read repeated gestures as the disguised returns of repressed desires, we would be forced to the troubling position that virtually every experience of object-relation was for Lawrence a potential trauma. This may not actually be so frivolous a possibility as it sounds; to make it meaningful, though, requires more consideration of repetition itself as symptom, separate from its referential content. The pervasive repetitions of Lawrence's style function finally to sever words from their reference, suggesting that what's being worked over is not a single traumatic event, but the production of language in general.

Freud began the consideration of repetition as symptom in the years after World War I, in his essay "The Uncanny" and most ambitiously in *Beyond the Pleasure Principle,* in which he set forth the most controversial of his paradigms: a primary death instinct deduced—in a much-debated logical leap—from its manifestations in a compulsion to repeat. In his preliminary discussions of repeated activities Freud arrived at two related understandings of the purpose of repetition. First, using the example of a child's repeated game of throwing away and retrieving a toy, he understood repetition as the mastery of a loss through the production of controllable representations; the repeater counters his helplessness in object-reality by demonstrating his power to make representations appear and disappear at will. Second, he proposed that repetition might be the psyche's belated struggle to prepare itself for a trauma that's already occurred, by developing the anxious readiness retrospectively whose lack initially permitted a breach in its defenses: a kind of desperate attempt to bar the doors after the thieves have entered. In essence, Freud by 1920 saw one of repetition's functions as the shaky affirmation of the threatened ego's powers to compensate for a loss or to bind a wound.

This double task of repetition seems explicit enough in the thoughts of Gudrun that I've quoted. The passage resolves itself into two basic statements: "Why wasn't there somebody?" and "She would lie always unsheathed"— statements of loss and vulnerability. Some of the novel's other repetitions apparently derive their energy from even more manifest perceptions of loss and subjective threat, such as Birkin's contemplation of Gerald's corpse:

He felt chiefly disgust at the inert body lying there. It was so inert, so coldly dead, a carcase, Birkin's bowels seemed to turn to ice. He had to stand and look at the frozen dead body that had been Gerald.

It was the frozen carcase of a dead male. . . .

He reached and touched the dead face. And the sharp, heavy bruise of ice bruised his living bowels. He wondered if he himself were freezing too, freezing from the inside. . . . His brain was beginning to freeze, his blood was turning to ice-water. So cold, so cold, a heavy, bruising cold pressing on his arms from outside, and a heavier cold congealing within him, in his heart and in his bowels. (*WL* 477–78)

A loved one's loss intimates the stealthy incursion of one's own death: it's tempting with evidence like this to engage the entire Freudian machinery of narcissistic compensation as explanatory construct. Facing object-loss, the energy of desire turns inward, investing the ego and its projective representations; confronted by the immanence of the ego's dissolution, the psyche frantically repeats—as a denial of death—its one genuinely masterful activity, its capacity for producing representations of language. Repetition, in effect, constructs itself over a real emptiness, fueled by an ungratifiable desire for permanence of the world and of the self. Thus it's fated to trail off in "eternal unrelief." A persistently destabilizing murmur infects even those moments of *Women in Love* when "culmination" seems most complete, as in Birkin's first passionate satisfaction with Ursula:

Far away, far away, there seemed to be a small lament in the darkness. But what did it matter? What did it matter, what did anything matter save this ultimate and triumphant experience of physical passion, that had blazed up anew like a new spell of life. "I was becoming quite dead-alive, nothing but a word-bag," he said in triumph, scorning his other self. Yet somewhere far off and small, the other hovered. (188)

Death, then, is the mother of repetition. Perhaps: such a reading invokes a general (and classical) tragic theory of art-language as a pained response to the betrayal of human mortality. On the other hand, it leads specifically with the Lawrence who wrote *Women in Love* to consideration of biographical elements, a cataloguing of the historical losses and threats of the war years: Lawrence's uprooted homelessness in England, his poverty, the suppression of *The Rainbow*, the forming and dissolving of friendships, his failure to produce children with Frieda, the war itself; behind these the still-open wound of his loss of Lydia Lawrence (still open, despite the groping self-therapy of *Sons and Lovers*, because no reconstruction or re-presentation can be more than a substitute satisfaction); behind all of these, the ominous recurrence of his "seediness," the "wintry inflammations" that punctuated the trajectory of his descent toward death. Against this history the work busies itself with a futile healing energy, reconstructing a failing world and a dying self: systematizing, totalizing, mythologizing, in the narcissistic manner suggested by Samuel Weber: "The pursuit of meaning; the activity of construction, synthesis, unification . . . all this indicates the struggle of the ego to establish and to maintain an identity" (13–14). In the process Lawrence's voice acquires those characteristics that critics have found "shrill," "didactic," "prophetic"—acquires, appropriately, the "Salvator Mundi touch," one of whose hallmarks is stylistic repetition.

To reach this understanding of Lawrence's art is to push the Freudian interpretive system to its limits and perhaps beyond them; to push it, in fact, as far as Freud himself did in considering repetition, "beyond the pleasure principle" of gratification in life to a privileging of death (or death-awareness) as origin and end of all mental behavior. The argument is morbidly attractive in its explanatory powers. With Lawrence it foregrounds the growing intensity and transformation of repetitive energy in his other works, from an early self-insistence—"I, I am royally here! / I am here! I am here!" ("The Wild Common," *CP* 34)—to the chiasmatic defensive structure that Michael Squires has identified as the "loop" in *Lady Chatterley's Lover* (159–73), or to a final repeated desire to stop repeating, to give in: "Do you think it is easy to change? / Ah, it is very hard to change and be different. / It means passing through the waters of oblivion" ("Change," *CP* 727). In Lawrence's work the defense against death follows the self-subverting logic of all defenses: the ego guards itself most energetically against the psyche's most powerful and unacceptable drives, and death's repudiation eventually collapses into and becomes indistinguishable from a drive toward or desire for death. Jacques Lacan presumably has the primacy of this defense or desire in mind in his relatively early formulation of the origin of speech: "When we wish to attain in the subject what was before the serial articulations of speech, and what is primordial to the birth of symbols, we find it in death, from which his existence takes on all the meaning it has. It is in effect as a desire for death that he affirms himself for others" ("Function and Field" 105).

As psychoanalytic speculation, a primary death-awareness is a poetically evocative hypothesis; as the ground of literary interpretation, though, it isn't finally entirely satisfactory. Identifying death as the origin of representation and repetition (and by extension of artistic creativity in general) seems no less reductive than other more colorfully crude Freudian approaches that indicate a single event or trauma as the cause of expressive activity. Its reductio ad absurdum is that we speak (beyond the necessities of communication) because we are going to die. Furthermore, to treat the artwork as purely symptomatic, as the necessary result of unconscious conflict, allows us to ignore one obvious fact: repetition in *Women in Love* and Lawrence's work in general may well reflect his unacknowledged admission of his own death, but the novel is also clearly and consciously *about* repetition and death: about mechanical repetition that leads to a stasis, a death-in-life, and about biological death or oblivion as an escape from that repetition. In fact, Lawrence's thought during the war often oddly anticipates, even interprets and diagnoses, the Freudian text of 1920 that I've used as an interpretive instrument: "We long most of all to belong to life. . . . And corresponding with this desire for absolute life, immediately consequent is the desire for death. This we will never admit. . . . This is the root of all confusion, this inability for man to admit, 'Now I am single in my desire for destructive death'" ("Reality of Peace" 40). The production of art, though it surely involves the working-over of unconscious determinants, is vastly more complex, more self-aware, than the recurrence of a dream or a child's game with a toy.

I want to conclude, then, by keeping in the foreground the linkage of repetition and death, adjusting the hypothesis that I've been developing of repetition as a response to death. Its inversion seems more immediately plausible, both for Lawrence and for Freud: that death, as a conceptual and textual presence, emerges from the contemplation of repetition. I do not intend another reductive absurdity—that we die because we speak—but rather that our speech, looked at closely enough, teaches us of loss, provides us with the structure in which to apprehend our own extinction. The acknowledgment of repetition is *prior to* the awareness of death: this is the rhetorical pattern of *Beyond the Pleasure Principle,* of Lawrence's thought, and of this essay itself.

Lawrence was from the beginning a writer for the ear, a celebrant of the possibilities of symmetry and rhythm in art-language. His poetry's open debt to Whitman, his lifelong love of hymns and the rhythms of the King James Bible, and his later fascination with hieratic gesture and ritual—all mark him as a poet aware of the power of formal order in expression. Like other poets and musicians, he found repetition with variation the essential structure of his art. But Lawrence was also (like Freud) an attentive student of the signifying properties of language, of the process of representation. As a result, perhaps more fully than most writers, he developed a love-hate relationship with his medium: even while exploiting the rhetorical and euphonic possibilities of repetition (as he did in the poetry and claimed to do in the foreword to *Women in Love*), he saw that ultimately language is *only* repetition and can never be more than more of itself, the permutations of constant elements in the enclosed, finite space of grammar and lexicon. Every word, every letter, must be a repetition of a prior appearance in order for public meaning to exist.

Thus nothing new, unique, or primary can come of language; thus expression is limited and falsified in its vehicle from the very beginning. "How could he say 'I,'" wonders Birkin, "when he was something new and unknown, not himself at all? This I, this old formula of the ego, was a dead letter" (*WL* 369). Lawrence here dramatizes what Lacan has insisted upon in his revision of Freudian theory: that the speaking subject's self-construction in language irrevocably produces in him a radical alienation of himself *from* himself. What is the relation of language's "I" to the subject who claims it by uttering it? How can that subject be uniquely "I", if "I" is a token in an impersonal repeating system? But what is the subject if *not* "I"? Language offers what Lawrence elsewhere calls a "strange split" or "interval" (*WL* 140) between subjective feeling and words. And awareness of this split—a necessary consequence of self's inscription in language—challenges the integrity of identity, threatening the extinction that Lacan identifies as *aphanisis:* language's "lethal" appropriation of the self, an act in which it "petrif[ies] the subject in the same movement in which it calls the subject to function, to speak, as subject" (*Four Fundamental Concepts* 207).

Hence my inversion, the proposition that death as a textual emblem arises from repetition. Like *Beyond the Pleasure Principle*, Lawrence's work in general and *Women in Love* specifically are in a way meditations on the alienating and destructive necessities of language. An anxiety over language manifests itself in two paired ideas of death in *Women in Love:* the "deadalive word-bag" state of the subject obliterated in its submission to repetition, and the oblivion of biological death—the desired death that ends all repetition and restores the self paradoxically to itself: "Better die," thinks Ursula, "than live mechanically a life that is a repetition of repetitions" (192).

I claim for Lawrence an understanding of language that is both profound and unsettling, suggesting and often anticipating the most disturbing speculations of twentieth-century psychoanalytic thought. If his repetitive style sometimes sounds strange and excessive to the modernist ear, that is because we are conditioned in the schools of Joyce and early Eliot, of "scrupulous meanness" and excision as the necessary characteristics of serious art. But repetition is not an incidental awkwardness in Lawrence's work, not the mark of amateurish technique or sloppy thought. Rather, the pushing of language to its repetitive extremes is the *essential* of his technique: the heuristic action whereby he discovered, confronted, and described—more immediately than other great modernists—not only human experience, but also the crippling wounds and dislocations that threaten that experience as it attempts to find a voice.

WORKS CITED

Freud, Sigmund. "Analysis of a Phobia in a Five-Year-Old Boy." 1909. *The Standard Edition of the Complete Psychological Works of Sigmund Freud.* Vol. 10. London: Hogarth, 1955. 1–149.

Freud, Sigmund. "Remembering, Repeating and Working-Through." 1914. *The Standard Edition of the Complete Psychological Works of Sigmund Freud.* Vol. 12. London: Hogarth, 1958. 145–56.

Freud, Sigmund. *Beyond the Pleasure Principle.* 1920. *The Standard Edition of the Complete Psychological Works of Sigmund Freud.* Vol. 18. London: Hogarth, 1955. 3–64.

Gordon, David. "Sex and Language in D. H. Lawrence." *Twentieth Century Literature* 27 (1981): 362–75.

Lacan, Jacques. *The Four Fundamental Concepts of Psycho-Analysis.* Ed. Jacques-Alain Miller. Trans. Alan Sheridan. New York: Norton, 1978.

Lacan, Jacques. "The Function and Field of Speech and Language in Psychoanalysis." *Écrits: A Selection.* Trans. Alan Sheridan. New York: Norton, 1977.

Lawrence, D. H. *The Complete Poems of D. H. Lawrence.* Ed. Vivian de Sola Pinto and F. Warren Roberts. New York: Viking, 1971.

Lawrence, D. H. "The Reality of Peace." *Reflections on the Death of a Porcupine and Other Essays.* Ed. Michael Herbert. Cambridge: Cambridge UP, 1988. 25–52.

Lawrence, D. H. *Women in Love.* Ed. David Farmer, Lindeth Vasey, and John Worthen. Cambridge: Cambridge UP, 1987.

Squires, Michael. *The Creation of "Lady Chatterley's Lover."* Baltimore: Johns Hopkins UP, 1983.

Weber, Samuel. *The Legend of Freud.* Minneapolis: U of Minnesota P, 1982.

CHAPTER 9

The Familial Isotopy in The Fox

JANE A. NELSON

I

The presence of the Father, I would claim at the beginning of this reading of *The Fox,* is indicated in the text by his absence. To argue the point is, of course, to reintroduce the issue of the Oedipus into readings of this problematic tale[1] by constructing out of certain textual elements a level of coherence I will refer to somewhat loosely and metaphorically as the "familial isotopy."[2] Such a construction depends principally on identifying and associating several foregrounded details of the text that readers will recognize as signifying the relationships and patterns of behavior of the classical Western family.

In constructing and interpreting this isotopy, I will also acknowledge the relevance of Jacques Lacan's arguments, specifically, that the language of culture preexists the individual's arrival in this world and provides the developing child with an already established structure of social and sexual roles. Unfortunately, the acquisition of language, of what Lacan calls the Symbolic Order, requires that the child must at the same time accept the preexistent authority of this Other that he or she encounters. In Lacan's view such acceptance constitutes for the subject an inevitable alienation, for by entering into the entangling network of social roles and relations of the Symbolic, the subject is henceforth defined by the discourse of the Other and distanced from desire. Granted, the compensations for this alienation are considerable since

---

1. For Jacques Lacan, the absent Father is the primary impulse behind narrative. See an introduction to this view in Davis (3). A review of the issue of the Oedipus in criticism of *The Fox* may be found in Ruderman, "*The Fox* and the 'Devouring Mother.'" Ruderman's identification of the pre-Oedipal elements in the tale, although different from mine, is important to my argument and is developed further in her *D. H. Lawrence and the Devouring Mother* (48–70).

2. *Isotopy* refers to a single autonomous "content level" of the text. It is identified by the reader's knowledge of cultural conventions. An isotopy does, of course, interact with other isotopies. For explanations of the history and current meanings of the term, see Eco (ch. 6).

through language the subject assumes the enviable power of the Symbolic and acquires the means by which to locate *almost* acceptable substitutes for unacceptable presymbolic sexual demands on the biological parents. Nevertheless, in a patriarchal culture, the very acquisition of verbal language requires us all to submit to the inescapable Law of the Father.[3]

But in such elements as the representation of the languages of the body, *The Fox* also identifies a resistance against the symbolic power and the tyranny of patriarchal Law. This imagery we may identify both with Lacan's preverbal register of the Imaginary and with—even more important—a feminine ''semiotic''[4] of preverbal communication that excludes the Father. This semiotic—established between the human infant and its mother—enters into an especially crucial opposition to patriarchal authority as it is represented in the tale by the symbolic requirements of established social and sexual identities.

II

The familial isotopy that structures the text's opposition to the Symbolic operates in all the important categories by which we organize our textual experiences, including those of setting, character, and story. Consider, briefly, the details usually used to develop the category *setting* and the elements of the initial situation of the story as these direct the reader to construct unexpected as well as conventional familial arrangements. A fair number of the details, for example, indicate that Bailey Farm, to which the boy returns from Canada and from the war, is in effect a return home, although in the final version of *The Fox* the farm is a home he shared not with his parents but with his grandfather. Nevertheless, in the patterns such details direct the reader to construct, the boy's arrival at the farm is figuratively the return home of the son who ran away.[5]

Such information can, of course, serve in various interpretations as a mo-

3. A helpful introduction to the difficult and controversial arguments of Lacan may be found in Rifflet-Lemaire and in the more recent work of Ragland-Sullivan. On the Lacanian view of the child's experience in the acquisition of language, see Ragland-Sullivan (55) and Lacan (67).

4. The argument for the existence of a feminine semiotic that challenges Lacan's Symbolic has been advanced by Julia Kristeva (133). Jane Gallop (124–25) argues the ''danger'' that this semiotic cannot be distinguished from Lacan's Imaginary.

5. Ruderman points out that in an earlier version the boy's father, not his grandfather, is indicated. This fact strengthens my view that the boy's return is a figurative homecoming and that a displacement of parental authority occurs in the text. As a result of such displacement the ''death'' of the ''father'' also becomes more acceptable. Such evidence would be important to any further development of my argument, especially if one were concerned with Lawrence's creative processes. Here I am interested in a reading of the data of the final version of the text available to most readers. References to the names and details of characterization as well as page references to passages quoted are to those found in the text of the Viking edition of 1965.

tivation for the boy's arrival at Bailey Farm. But it would not be necessary to these interpretations. It would in fact be possible for Lawrence to offer more appropriate motivations for the boy's arrival were the text narrowly conceived as a realistic tale about an adult love triangle. However, the details of this homecoming seem peculiarly relevant to those readings of *The Fox* that recognize the important pre-Oedipal relationships developed between the boy and the women now living on the farm (Ruderman, "*Fox*"). Such interpretations would appear to be reinforced by the recognition of a synthesized family structure at Bailey Farm.

Information about the boy's presumed parental home, or indeed about his parents, is nowhere provided by the text. This missing generation may not immediately strike a reader as a lack, a gap, a violation of a convention, or indeed, if we look at the commentary on the tale, as anything that attracts much attention at all. But it cannot fail to become important in relation to the numerous other details from which readers are inevitably directed to construct—in our culture—the presence of family. In these constructions the boy's father becomes conspicuous by his absence. Equally important, the father's paternal authority had been displaced onto a now-dead grandfather (if we ignore the substitute figure of the boy's ineffective captain). And this grandfather, from whose demands the boy once fled, is not the only significant grandfather at the beginning of *The Fox*. Banford's grandfather is also pointedly dead. Indeed, such repetition reinforces the significant figurative familial relationships we are encouraged to synthesize. Lawrence's murderous little tale offers us an excess of two dead grandfathers at the same time that it emphasizes everywhere the displacement of male parental authority onto aged or ineffective figures.

We should notice what is missing in relation to what is given. We have no information at all about March's family, yet in this most economical of structures, Banford is provided with both a father and a mother as well as with one of the dead grandfathers. Her parents are curiously present at the scene of her murder, but their attendance at this event is poorly motivated by realistic conventions.[6] Moreover the response of Banford's father to her death becomes almost as important as that of March, yet the response of her mother goes unmentioned. Twice, just before the boy fells the tree that kills her, Banford's similarity to her father is specified. At the most important moment in the preparation for the murder, for example, she is provoked into rejecting the boy's warning: " 'Who, me, mind myself?' she cried, her father's jeering tone in her voice" (173). A few passages earlier, this coalescence of the two

6. Ruderman observes that Banford's father was missing from the first version of *The Fox* altogether, and that Cecily Lambert, the prototype for Banford, resented what she perceived as Lawrence's hostility toward her father being transferred to her ("Prototypes" 84).

figures is achieved by establishing that the father's complaints of "rheumatics in his shoulder" are identical to those of his daughter.

But numerous foregrounded details have already led the reader to associate Banford with the roles and functions of a middle-class "father" before she is murdered by the boy, by the presumed Henry Grenfel of the text. This is the case even though at the beginning Lawrence shifts the binaries of male and female signifiers between the two figures. March, dressed as the phallic girl, appears at first to play the man about Bailey Farm, but her figure comes to be identified increasingly with the sexual and maternal feminine. On the other hand, Banford's frailty and nerves at first direct us to construct a character with what are conventionally perceived as feminine, not masculine, characteristics. Yet it is she who is most firmly fixed in the familial, economic, and class structures of patriarchal society. Her money (through her father) finances the undertaking at Bailey Farm, and her objections to the marriage echo those of an insecure paterfamilias disturbed by March's decision to "throw herself away" on a "beastly labourer" and thereby drag Banford herself down to the "level" of the people in the village (144).

The identification of Banford with her father at the time of the murder provides these details with a significance difficult to overlook. In addition, throughout the development of the relationships which textual details constrain us to construct, Banford slowly hardens, loses the conventional softnesses of femininity, and most important, *ages*. The signifiers that enable us to construct this figure gradually begin to function in a relentless opposition between age and youth—an opposition we perceive as one of the most important binaries structuring the text.

Within the context of the familial isotopy, the murder assumes an unmistakably Oedipal significance. In formulaic terms, the way to the mother is through the death of the father. The murder weapon itself is described in terms we associate with phallic significance. It stands, an aged, dead fir tree, protected—the point is carefully made—by the Law. March (in figurative collusion with the boy against the Father) chops away at its base, but is unable herself to bring it down. It continues to stand "with a great yawning gap in his base, perched, as it were, on one sinew, and ready to fall. But he did not fall" (168) until the boy appears and fells it in his destruction of Banford. The anomaly of the pronoun in Lawrence's text reinforces our recognition of the castration image. Moreover it is the head of the Banford that is smashed when the boy destroys her, identifying unmistakably in the classical terms of psychoanalysis the sexual meanings of this murder: "The back of the neck and head was a mass of blood, of horror" (174).

In this crucial scene, moreover, the anomalous use of the term *boy* for the figure of Henry Grenfel underscores further the Oedipal role he plays. From the beginning of *The Fox*, the narrator's use of *boy* or *youth* calls attention to the difference in age between March and Henry and provides as well an important detail in the construction, by both reader and text, of the familial isotopy. In fact, March's reminder to the boy at the time of his proposal that she is old enough to be his mother (132) should be read in relation to the naming of Henry. For *naming* remains, as critics have noted, an important problem in this tale.

III

In the final version of *The Fox,* Lawrence's choice of the term *youth* in roughly the first half of the tale yields to his use of the term *boy* in the second half. Consequently, readers construct a figure that does not—cannot—properly mature. The important name *Henry* (ruler of the enclosure) appears throughout the text, for example, less frequently than the designation *boy*. The family name *Grenfel* scarcely appears at all. In the context of Lacan's arguments, such a resistance to naming would indicate a disturbance with respect to the Symbolic as important as that noted by various critics in the use of the last names *March* and *Banford* for the "girls."[7]

Much of this disturbance is reflected in commentary on the tale, for the choice of names that a critic makes in talking about the characters often moves his or her construction of these characters closer to various realistic conventions. Such choices will suggest that a character is more or less masculine or feminine. They will repress certain elements and concentrate on others that are actually played down in the text. Finally, especially in the case of the boy, they will change familial and social roles. In fact, critics generally seem to prefer the term *youth* or *Henry* as a designation, shying away from the term *boy* and ignoring altogether the frequency of its use.

Lacan, it is useful to recall, recognized the profound consequences for the human subject that result from the act of naming, from the assumption of those proper names representing the name of the Father, and from the functions of those pronouns that serve to anchor the subject in the Symbolic.[8] The text's resistance to the naming of Henry Grenfel serves to mark that figure's

7. Ruderman believes that in choosing the last names *March* and *Banford* for his characters, Lawrence was influenced by the fact that his prototypes for *The Fox* were known by their surnames, and that Monroe Engel "goes too far" in suggesting that the use of the girls' surnames implies a disorder in the text ("Prototypes" 80). In naturalizing the names of the characters, however, Ruderman chooses to use the first names of the girls and the full or last name of Henry Grenfel. These choices repress certain meanings generated by the elements of the names.

8. See Jameson's useful summary of the importance of the naming function of language for Lacan (362–63).

ambivalence with respect to the system of social relations within which he is caught, much as the fox is caught in the sound of the dogs "making a noise like a fence of sound, like the network of English hedges netting the view" (146). Refusing the name of the Father is to refuse the Father as Lawgiver, to refuse phallocentric Law.

It is the boy's entry—or his failure to enter—into this Symbolic, into the cultural traditions, the modes of expression, the linguistic symbolism, the social organizations he confronts, that is at stake in *The Fox* and that is revealed by the failure of naming. In the imagery of the text, moreover, the opposition of the boy's animal nature to the culture here represented manifests part of this struggle in that the traits he shares with the fox are those we conventionally, according to certain codes, associate with Nature as opposed to Culture.

But as readers we are conditioned to repress some of the details structuring this opposition in *The Fox* in order to create characters that for interpretive purposes are presumed to have depth and human boundaries. For such constructions we often need little more than stick figures in our explanatory space, and the instability of the characters in this tale may be evaded or explained away by several strategies. Nevertheless, binaries generated by textual details in *The Fox* continually threaten such constructions, a point any review of the commentaries would support. The "boy," for example, is not a separate entity with recognizable human boundaries. His sharp yap of laughter, his face with its "glisten of fine whitish hairs on the ruddy cheek-bones" (121), his odor and behavior deliberately and inevitably signal the animal, the fox, for readers. He enters the human world—the world of patriarchal culture, of names, classes, relationships, roles—from outside a human enclosure, from outside the "netted" structure of the English island, even from outside the order of Law, for he has just returned from war. March finds the stroke of his heart "like something from beyond, something awful from outside, signalling to her" (160). His face is out of place in the farm's parlor like a "piece of the out-of-doors come indoors: as holly-berries do" (155–56). March responds in kind to this animality by becoming "still and soft in her corner like a passive creature in its cave" (125).

Working within the tradition that constructs characters as if they were individual entities, commentators frequently locate this identification of boy and fox in the mind of March as a symbol of her sexual vulnerability. Certainly many details of the text encourage this explanatory strategy—to a point. But the boy-fox identity is also sustained by the omniscient voice inscribed in the text. This voice describes the boy as sending a "faint but distinct odour into the room, indefinable, but something like a wild creature" (125). Far from being a neutral transparency, the narrator's "consciousness" unfailingly represents the boy in animal terms, distinguishing him in various ways from those figures identified with human culture. He is represented as sly and subtle like the fox, for example, marked (again in the narrator's voice) by the habit of walking "about the fields and along the hedges alone in the dark at night, prowling with a queer instinct for the night, and listening to the wild sounds" (135). In fact, the narrative voice serves to underscore a failure to fix in the text on a *verbal* continuum the boy-youth-Henry-Grenfel figure—a continuum that might very well be said to begin with *fox*. It is not necessary to speak metaphorically of a deep structure in which this symbolism occurs. The details that signify the animal may be seen on the surface of the text juxtaposed with those details that register and foreground Culture.

Other characters that readers construct from textual elements in *The Fox* are equally unstable since the details from which they must construct the principal figures are by and large congeries of conventional oppositions, whereas minor figures function in important relationships to these oppositions. In addition, details that function in the construction of characters also enter into binary relationships with the other categories of literary analysis such as setting. One might even describe the action of the text as a process that attempts to locate or appropriately *name* the human in order to fix it in some stable, mediating term between culture and nature, male and female, child and adult, child and parent. March, for example, is a highly unstable combination of such polarities, both at the beginning of the text, as I have suggested, in her maternal roles and male roles, and at the end in her reduction to weeping child after the Oedipal murder.

In her landgirl's uniform March the phallus girl performs activities about the farm that are both "masculine" and "feminine" in significance. She is the carpenter who endlessly repairs the farm buildings and mends the fence that separates Bailey Farm from the unformed Nature but one field away. In the evening she paints swans or crochets.[9] We associate such activities with Culture, and we understand them accordingly. But she is also a creature of Nature (still and soft in her cave) as the meanings generated by her name and by other details indicate. She is the figure of spring (March in a soft green dress) and of forward, "marching" movement in opposition to the "forbidding of crossing" signified by the syllables of Banford's name.

In the Banford, moreover, is eventually focused all the power and authority of patriarchal culture as it is encountered and attacked by the boy. At first she, too, is perceived in the narrator's voice as feminine, frail, protective, sis-

9. Ruderman points out that in the 1921 version the shift of this activity from Banford to March may have been to show "even more conclusively that March . . . 'was a creature of odd whims and unsatisfied tendencies'" ("Prototypes" 81 n. 9). The shift surely marks the instability of characterization in the text.

terly—a split of the maternal figure the human infant first perceives as both
mother and father, male and female. But she becomes especially important as
the representative of the Father—of ''culture'' and social hierarchies as well
as of the figure who forbids access to the mother. She resents the boy's
appearing in shirtsleeves at tea and squirms when he drinks his tea noisily. In
opposition to the music of desire sung by the fox, she skillfully plays shallow
popular tunes on her piano. She cherishes the fashionable improvements she
has made in the farm's parlor and resents the boy's ''lower-class'' intrusions.
In addition, she is sensitive to the voice of the village inhabitants, having
established herself as their social superior.

Even before the Oedipal murder giving him forbidden access to the
''mother'' represented by March in the familial isotopy, the boy refuses
insertion into the Symbolic, refuses, that is, to be constituted in the language
of the Other. In an important scene that echoes (and may be circularly interpreted by) the primal scene of classical psychoanalytic theory, he steals down
the hall at night to overhear the ''girls'' in bed:

> He got stealthily out of bed and stood by his door. He could hear no more than
> before. Very, very carefully he began to lift the door latch. After quite a time he had
> his door open. Then he stepped stealthily out into the passage. The old oak planks were
> cold under his feet, and they creaked preposterously. He crept very, very gently up the
> one step, and along by the wall, till he stood outside their door. And there he held his
> breath and listened. (143–44)

The boy has been drawn from the sounds of the quiet and frosty night—the
yap of a fox and the barking response of distant dogs—toward the human
sounds in that most intimate of spaces in human enclosures, the parental
bedroom. Outside the door, listening to the words of the Banford, he sees
himself defined by the rage of this figurative Father while March soothes
Banford and mitigates the judgments she delivers. But Banford delivers the
judgments of a society which the boy feels is threatening the fox everywhere
by its hedges, its ''netted'' structures:

> ''He's just a good-for-nothing, who doesn't want to work, and who thinks he'll live
> on us. But he won't live on me. If you're such a fool, then it's your own look-out.
> Mrs. Burgess knew him all the time he was here. And the old man could never get him
> to do any steady work. He was off with the gun on every occasion, just as he is now.''
> (144)

It is at this point, too, that the boy also hears himself labeled a hateful,
red-faced boy, a beastly laborer who will pull the Banford down. His response
is an angry withdrawal to the world of Nature outside the fences of Bailey
Farm. When he returns, he counters the power of verbal authority with the

language of gesture: he presents the fox he has finally killed as phallus, as the object of desire, to March.[10]

IV

Traces of the languages of gesture, of images, of sound—of all forms of nonverbal communication—are everywhere entangled in the linguistic structures of *The Fox*. They may well constitute that "infinitely supple conceptual category" Lacan calls the Imaginary and lead us to question whether language is the "agent of interhuman dialogue" we think it is (Rifflet-Lemaire 60–61). Most pertinently, Julia Kristeva raises another issue when she argues that the preverbal semiotic established between infant and mother continues to challenge the authority of the Symbolic by a significant (and disruptive) presence in the rhythms, tones, and other "nonrepresentative" elements of a text.[11] Whether we recognize in our readings of *The Fox* a Lacanian Imaginary or Kristeva's feminine "semiotic," these elements appear to function in the familial isotopy of this text by steadily opposing the symbolic register of language. In addition, empirical research into early infant-maternal behavior would support theoretical arguments that the more significantly foregrounded representations of preverbal behavior function in *The Fox* as the expression of a pre-Oedipal relationship between mother and child. The presence of these signifiers in fact moves readers to construct the familial isotopy I have been outlining.

Gaze behavior as it is represented in *The Fox* is one of the most important of these manifestations of a "different" relationship between mother and child, between March and the boy of the text. Such pre-Oedipal elements bear out Ruderman's observation that Lawrence's tale is "closely associated with [his] intuitions about the nature of the mother-child relationship" ("*Fox*" 254). Of course the language of eyes in *The Fox* has not gone unnoticed by commentators, but its significance is usually read as sexual, to be interpreted in terms of symbols of penetration and vulnerability.[12] As long

10. An examination of the complex function of the "phallus" (which is not identical with the penis in Lacanian arguments) and its role in the relationship between mother and male child would take us beyond the subject of my argument here. It is relevant to any development of the issues I am introducing, however. In schematic terms, the mother is presumed to desire the phallus. One of the dangers to the child is that he will identify with her desire, thereby disturbing his successful resolution of the Oedipus complex. Such dangers are especially present if the mother in any way encourages the child in this respect. See Rifflet-Lemaire (87). The parallel to the situation between March and the boy seems clear.

11. An interesting introduction to the significance and potential of Kristeva's theories for recent psychoanalytic and feminist criticism is to be found in Eagleton (ch. 5).

12. Christopher Brown's study of gaze behavior in *The Fox* recognizes other significances than the sexual by equating *seeing* with *dominance*.

as our reading of the text develops those details that lead us to see the tale as an account of an adult "love" triangle, such a response to the language of eyes is appropriate. Unfortunately, by serving the interests of those "realistic" conventions inscribed in the text and supported by our habits of interpretation, such a reading must inevitably repress or suppress other details that direct us to construct the functional familial relationships among the figures.

If, on the other hand, we read the tale in the context of current research on the nature of preverbal maternal and infant relationships, then the languages of eyes and postures and the representation of sounds produce quite different interpretations. Within these other contexts we may more successfully account for and understand some of the foregrounded representations that are anomalous with respect to adult conventions.

For a good part of the gaze behavior between March and the boy is substantially different from dominant adult behavior in Western culture, in spite of the boy's apparent "maturity" as indicated by other textual details. It is, on the contrary, strikingly analogous to the gaze behavior studied in early child-mother interaction.[13] Among humans, for example, the new mother's eyes characteristically open wider, and she responds to her infant's gaze with a directness, intensity, and exaggeration of display that violate adult codes. One is tempted to place side by side the words of one investigator ("As she watched his face . . . her eyes opened a little wider and her eyebrows raised a bit . . ." [Stern 3]) and the words of the text ("But the shrewish look [of her mouth] was contradicted by the curious lifted arch of her dark brows, and the wideness of her eyes" [137]).

The frequent, prolonged, and intense seeking of March's eyes by the boy parallels and returns to that of the infant for whom it is characteristic, even crucial. In fact, it has been argued that such gaze behavior may play a role in evolution, since the infant's success in capturing and holding his mother's gaze helps assure his biological survival. Researchers have known for some time that such eye contact releases "strong positive feelings" in the mother toward her child (Robson 16; Stern 37–38). March's response to the boy's gaze, uncharacteristic of adult behavior to the extent that it has been called "mystical" (Ruderman, "*Fox*" 257), finds its proper analogue in this repertoire of maternal "language."

The emphasis in the text on entering through the eyes is a well-known part of human preverbal behavior. At a certain point in the infant's development,

13. Experimental studies of the early relationships between mother and infant appear to uncover a repertoire of complex interactions involving sounds, gaze behavior, and body positions. Gaze behavior especially appears to be different in kind from that of adults (Stern 18–19). It should, however, be seen in relationship to these other modes of communication and is, in fact, so represented in *The Fox*.

for example, the mother experiences the impression that the child is looking literally into her eyes—with dramatic effects on her response.[14]

We should consider as part of this semiotic such related signals as the childlike roundness of the boy's eyes in *The Fox,* the "invisible smile gleaming on his face" (129), the steadiness of his gaze, and the "alert, forward-reaching look on his roundish face" (127). All belong to the body language in the text and parallel remarkably what has been learned about infant-mother communication. The infant's smile, for example, is a signal to maintain interaction. Moreover the singular representation of sounds and of human responses to sounds in the tale combines with gaze behavior and should be read in the context of infant-mother communication. In the interaction between mother and infant, both participants are, in the words of one investigator, "predisposed to attend to the sound of the other." Nor is the child simply imitating the mother in this repertoire: it initiates and "leads the dance." In film studies of this relationship, the infant is actually seen as "fractionally ahead" (Halliday 171). A close study of the representation of postures in the text would reveal other foregrounded details understandable in the context I am developing. Among those to be noted are ones that represent both the fox and the boy as *looking up* at March. The boy also attempts to engage March's eyes by leaning forward just as the child leans forward in order to capture its mother's gaze.

Significantly the Banford, who reads fitfully with her weak eyesight, wears glasses. The languages of eyes and of sounds represented in the text are inaccessible to her. Moreover this semiotic excludes verbal language and undermines the authority and power of patriarchal culture. In one passage, the contrast in seeing is subtly clear in the shift in the occupations of the characters:

And she [Banford] returned to her book. In her thin, frail hair were already many threads of grey, though she was not yet thirty. The boy did not look down, but turned his eyes to March, who was sitting with pursed mouth laboriously crocheting, her eyes wide and absent. (137)

March is also represented in *The Fox* as being "drawn" to a very large extent by the sounds of the boy's voice as well as attending raptly to the "singing" of the fox with which he is identified. In experimental studies of infant vocalization, the infant is observed to make calling sounds in order to attract the visual attention of the mother. He alternates this calling with periods of intense looking, and the mother's eyes open in response. "Listen" to but one of the representations of such behavior in *The Fox:*

14. The mother's positive response to the gaze of the newborn and his "approach behavior" is essential, it has been argued, for successful human development (Riess 388).

All the time, while she was active, she was attending to the youth in the sitting-room, not so much listening to what he said as feeling the soft run of his voice. She primmed up her mouth tighter and tighter, puckering it as if it were sewed, in her effort to keep her will uppermost. Yet her large eyes dilated and glowed in spite of her; she lost herself. (121–22)

Such representations of a nonverbal semiotic between March and the boy can be traced in many details of the text from which the reader constructs its central events and characters and identifies the maternal-child relationship of the familial isotopy. But this semiotic is everywhere significant. It appears in the very sounds we would hear if *The Fox* were read aloud. We can in fact identify the play of this semiotic in the first important opposition of sounds that appears in the text: the *ma* hidden in the name March, and—assimilating the voiced /b/ to the voiceless /p/—the *pa* hidden in Banford.[15] Perhaps we hear the echo (the ghost) of that primary set of binary oppositions considered by some to be essential to the very development of a system of significant sounds in language. These oppositions emerge eventually in the variations of *papa* and *mama* that occur in natural languages[16]—and which in this tale first identify the familial isotopy.

The relationship between the boy-mother figures that continues to the very end of this tale may well account for the mixed responses commentators have offered in their analyses of the conclusion of *The Fox*. The Oedipal murder that manifests itself in our perhaps unconscious constructions of the familial isotopy of the text can be disturbing, for in classical psychoanalytic terms the triumph of the boy over the Banford must be seen as unacceptable in Western culture, for he gains sexual access to the forbidden Mother. In addition this murder is related (in Lacan's terms) to a disturbing refusal of the powers of patriarchal language—of the powers of symbolization, of the insertion of the subject into the Symbolic—a refusal of the appropriate roles and relationships of Culture. At the same time, the gesture appears liberating, a rejection of ancient, no longer adequate patriarchal Law, an ambivalent return to the powers of the matriarchal. But something seems lost as Lawrence confronts these antinomies and develops his text: after the murder, the "Henry Grenfel" of the tale remains "the boy," while March is reduced to weeping like a child.

15. The distinction between voiced and voiceless sounds appears later in the infant's development. See R. M. Jones, *System in Child Language,* cited in Fineman (58, n. 19).

16. But the original /pa/, the infant's first production of that binary opposition necessary to the structure of language, remains buried under the structures of signification. The ghost of its presence may forever disturb meaning. On this point I am indebted to Fineman's analysis of the opening of *The Canterbury Tales.* Fineman observes that the infant's /pa/ signifies only the ability to produce the "maximum binary opposition of which the mouth is capable" (57). When /pa/ is "promoted to the level of significant signifier" by the introduction of another set of oppositions in /ma/, it is "utterly unrelated to the first simply diacritical /pa/ that it replaces" (59).

I would argue that the critic's construction of the familial isotopy from significantly foregrounded details of *The Fox* is central to an understanding of various strong readings of the tale and to the development of others. In some Lacanian contexts, the recognition of the displaced family structure and the identification of a primal scene, as well as scenes of seduction and castration, would bring an analysis close to an understanding of the nature of narrative as it is practiced by Lawrence. But the tracing I have offered of a representation of the preverbal semiotic in the mother-child relationship introduces into an evaluation of the end of the tale further explanations of the fierce ambivalences Lawrence expresses there. To reject the Law of the Father is to turn one's back on the power and the authority but also on the crippling restrictions of language (Culture). To return to the Mother raises questions about the unknown functions of desire in a structure that—tentatively—accommodates them. It is altogether appropriate that March and Henry have not yet sailed.

WORKS CITED

Brown, Christopher. "The Eyes Have It: Vision in 'The Fox.'" *Wascana Review* 15 (1980): 61–68.

Davis, Robert Con. "Critical Introduction: The Discourse of the Father." *The Fictional Father: Lacanian Readings of the Text.* Ed. Robert Con Davis. Amherst: U of Massachusetts P, 1981. 1–26.

Eagleton, Terry. *Literary Theory: An Introduction.* Minneapolis: U of Minnesota P, 1983.

Eco, Umberto. *Semiotics and the Philosophy of Language.* Bloomington: Indiana UP, 1984.

Fineman, Joel. "The Structure of Allegorical Desire." *October* 12 (Spring 1980): 47–66.

Gallop, Jane. *The Daughter's Seduction: Feminism and Psychoanalysis.* Ithaca: Cornell UP, 1982.

Halliday, M. A. K. "One Child's Protolanguage." *Before Speech.* Ed. Margaret Bullowa. Cambridge: Cambridge UP, 1979. 171–88.

Jameson, Fredric. "Imaginary and Symbolic in Lacan: Marxism, Psychoanalytic Criticism, and the Problem of the Subject." *Literature and Psychoanalysis: The Question of Reading: Otherwise.* Ed. Shoshana Felman. Baltimore: Johns Hopkins UP, 1982. 338–95.

Kristeva, Julia. *Desire in Language: A Semiotic Approach to Literature and Art.* Ed. Leon S. Roudiez. Trans. Thomas Gora et al. New York: Columbia UP, 1980.

Lacan, Jacques. *Écrits: A Selection.* Trans. Alan Sheridan. New York: Norton, 1977.

Lawrence, D. H. *The Fox. Four Short Novels of D. H. Lawrence.* New York: Viking, 1965. 111–79.

Ragland-Sullivan, Ellie. *Jacques Lacan and the Philosophy of Psychoanalysis*. Urbana: U of Illinois P, 1987.

Riess, Anneliese. "The Mother's Eye: For Better and for Worse." *The Psychoanalytic Study of the Child*. Vol. 33. Ed. Albert J. Solnit et al. New Haven: Yale UP, 1978. 381–409.

Rifflet-Lemaire, Anika. *Jacques Lacan*. Brussels: Dessart, 1970.

Robson, Kenneth S. "The Role of Eye-to-Eye Contact in Maternal-Infant Attachment." *Journal of Child Psychology and Psychiatry* 8 (1967): 13–25.

Ruderman, Judith. "Prototypes for Lawrence's *The Fox*." *Journal of Modern Literature* 8 (1980): 77–98.

Ruderman, Judith. "*The Fox* and the 'Devouring Mother.'" *D. H. Lawrence Review* 10 (1977): 251–69.

Ruderman, Judith. *D. H. Lawrence and the Devouring Mother: The Search for a Patriarchal Ideal of Leadership*. Durham, N.C.: Duke UP, 1984.

Stern, Daniel. *The First Relationship: Infant and Mother*. Cambridge: Harvard UP, 1977.

CHAPTER 10

"The Individual in His Pure Singleness": Theme and Symbol in The Captain's Doll

FREDERICK P. W. McDOWELL

As Jane Nelson suggests in the preceding essay, Lawrence developed challenging ideas about sexual relationships after the Great War. These ideas, with their social and political ramifications, can be disturbing and strident: they represent sincere but potentially violent assertions of Lawrence's self. Lawrence expounds these values in discursive works, *Psychoanalysis and the Unconscious* (1921), *Fantasia of the Unconscious* (1922), and *Studies in Classic American Literature* (1923), to mention the most important. These books extend the concepts formulated in his earlier nonfiction, *Study of Thomas Hardy*, "The Crown," "The Reality of Peace," and in the great novels before 1920. A fear of woman as predator and an insistence on man as the spiritual leader in intimate relationships are, however, new—or newly emphasized—concepts developed in the nonfiction and dramatized in the fiction of the early 1920s, especially in the novellas *The Ladybird, The Captain's Doll, The Fox, St. Mawr,* and the long short story "The Princess."

The psychic and intellectual dislocations engendered by the Great War animated both the nonfiction and the fiction of Lawrence's leadership phase from about 1919 to 1925, and he felt compelled to counteract his own disillusionment and the sterile life of the age—in short, to become a prophet to a generation torn from its moorings in tradition. In *D. H. Lawrence: The Artist as Psychologist* (1984), Daniel J. Schneider formulates the crisis that underlies the anxieties and frustrations so vividly projected in Lawrence's work during these years: "how can man achieve health and wholeness in a world that denies the unconscious sources of his behavior?" (8). The hero and heroine of *The Captain's Doll* do achieve health and wholeness, but the odds have been against them, and they have had to make difficult choices. They both become responsive to the unconscious elements in their psyches and thus recognize the primacy of instinct.

Although acknowledging *The Captain's Doll* as a notable accomplishment, critics have discussed it less than the other novellas. F. R. Leavis has written more extensively on *The Captain's Doll* than any other critic (*D. H. Lawrence* 242–78; *Thought* 92–121), and his magisterial treatment of it may have deflected further discussion. In his view Captain Alexander Hepburn is the self-sufficient protagonist whose very presence spiritually reorients his mistress, Hannele (the Countess Johanna zu Rassentlow). The Captain is, granted, her guide and mentor, and she is his intelligent and malleable disciple; but this interpretation diminishes her stature. Graham Hough (177–79) and J. I. M. Stewart (571–77) regard the tale similarly. More recent critics interpret the novella variously. Gerald Doherty stresses Hannele's limitations, unduly in my view, but defines with much penetration the role of comic conventions in undercutting the characters. W. R. Martin emphasizes, as I do, Hannele's intellectual stature, whereas Sandra Gilbert, skeptical of the Captain's authority, sees him as fearful of women and as a man who must in compensation dominate his mistress.[1]

In my view the strength of *The Captain's Doll* resides in Lawrence's exploration of the relationship between a man and a woman who have intrinsic strengths and who express potent insights, but who also reveal weaknesses that they must acknowledge and overcome. Kingsley Widmer (157–65) and Janice Harris (157–62) express this view in their books on Lawrence's short fiction, as do Elgin Mellown and, in briefer compass, H. M. Daleski and R. P. Draper. However, important aspects of this tale call for more extended analysis: the significance of the major symbolic entities (the moon, the doll, and the glacier), the impact of nature on the characters, Lawrence's development in them of a psychology based on both power and love, the precise definition of the relationship existing between them, and the tale's larger implications.

The pervasive doll symbolism is effective principally because it applies to all four main characters, just as the doll image in Ibsen's *A Doll's House* has implications for all his principal personages. Hannele is a life-serving woman living by her instincts, but she reaches fulfillment from the pulsating depths that she finds in her lover's psyche. Carried away in spite of some misgivings about him, she responds to his charismatic force, his mystery, his aloofness, his air of self-sufficiency—in short, his magic.

There is something extraordinary about the Captain, a preternatural or supernatural aspect, a suggestion that outside powers centered in the heavenly

---

1. Judith Ruderman interprets Lawrence similarly, though she does not discuss *The Captain's Doll*.

bodies operate through him, a hint of the demonic (as Widmer maintains) that gives him reserves of authority and makes him indifferent at many times to the women in his life. At the beginning he overwhelms Hannele as he gazes on her "with his black eyes and that curious, bright, unseeing look that was more like second sight than direct human vision," as if he can divine truths denied to the faculties of ordinary mortals (*CD* 189). He manifests a ruggedness of spirit, an objectivity, and a contempt for mundane trivialities when he turns "as if he heard something in the stars," and when he speaks in a "slow, musical voice, with its sing-song note of hopeless indifference" (216, 200). It is as if he heard the music of the spheres and as if for him "all the morning stars sang together." His air of mystery piques Hannele, and he seems to her "as if one of the men from Mars were loving her." She loses all volition as she falls under his hypnotic spell: "And she was heavy and spell-bound, and she loved the spell that bound her. But also she didn't love it" (193). He has her fundamental being in his grasp, making her, as it were, a psychic prisoner of a phantom or demon lover: he is to her "as unreal as a person in a dream, whom one has never heard of in actual life" (198). When he comes back to her in the Austrian Alps, she again reacts to his mystery and to a remoteness in him, at once formidable and fascinating, as she sees him "standing a long way off from her, beyond some border-line" (250), seemingly an otherworldly visitant or a cherished phantom in human form. Sometimes his influence is Satanic as she identifies him and her passion for him with the serpent, in Lawrence's view "the symbol of the fluid, rapid, startling movement of life within us" that can be "half-divine, half-demonish" (*Apocalypse* 123). "She could feel the snake biting her heart" (*CD* 216) when her desire mounts and she succumbs in thought to his charm.

Yet at times she detects in her lover less than a full commitment to her, and she dramatizes her inchoate reservations about him by making the doll. This doll is a work of art, Hannele having obtained a local reputation for her craft and having earned her living by it. The Captain initially congratulates her, saying that she has really "got" him, thinking to himself that it "was an extraordinary likeness of himself, true even to the smooth parting of his hair and his peculiar way of fixing his dark eyes" (188). He ultimately feels dissatisfied with this image precisely because Hannele has not really "got" him in his depths. She senses, with justification, however, that her lover is in part a doll, "a barren . . . dead puppet" (199), since he is unwilling at this point to express in the domain of personal relationships his capacious inner powers. Her resentment translates outward into her actions as she fashions the doll, working with pins, treating it roughly, and sexually demeaning her lover by fashioning tartan trews to cover in the effigy the legs about which she had developed a fetishlike fixation.

Despite the richness of his elemental being, the Captain has become, with respect to his wife, the slave of convention; his wife has made an automaton of him. Hannele senses the falsity of her lover's existence with his wife after the latter comes to "rescue" him from an entanglement with a German woman. In a well-known comic sequence Mrs. Hepburn mistakes the identity of the mistress after her polite boast to Hannele that "we Irish all have a touch of second sight, I believe" (211). Mrs. Hepburn is sure that her rival is Mitchka, Hannele's friend and roommate; Mrs. Hepburn's complacency, vulgarity, manipulativeness, and hypocrisy appall Hannele. She is even more aghast when Mrs. Hepburn reveals that her husband had sworn to her on bended knee that he would devote his life to making her happy.

Later in the tale the Captain admits that his wife had in fact made a doll of him and so confirms Hannele's intuitions that had led her also to make a doll of him. His acquiescence in a joyless lovemaking with his wife alienates Hannele. He has been false, she feels, to his better nature; in her view he should either have renewed the marital relationship with enthusiasm or ended it. In acting out an empty ritual, he becomes a hypocrite and, as Widmer observes, "Eros as a natural desire for pleasuring someone else stands antithetical to all authentic passion and being" (159). If Hannele had not caught in the doll all her lover's depths, she had nevertheless captured some of them as well as something of the mechanical quality of his present emotional life. After Mrs. Hepburn's revelations of the "adoration-lust"[2] that Alexander had displayed toward her, Hannele is radically disillusioned with him. Despite her overpowering disenchantment, she has enough perspective to realize that the illusion of passional fulfillment which she has experienced with him relates to the true depths of his being. If this satisfaction has been an illusion, yet it is, she thinks, more genuine than her revulsion at this moment. The spell with which he charmed her still holds her though she has become restive after she sees him with his wife: "And the strange gargoyle smile, fixed, when he caressed her with his hand under the chin! Life is all a choice. And if she chose the glamour, the magic, the charm, the illusion, the spell!" (218). She faces a dilemma, for her instincts draw her to the Captain even when her intelligence sees him disparagingly as the husband "of that little lady." When his wife fortuitously falls out a hotel window and dies, the Captain finds himself emotionally drained, and he can no longer respond to the sensual depths in his mistress that had previously entranced him.

Before he goes, the Captain talks to Hannele about his wife, despite Hannele's reluctance to hear about her. If Hannele had envisioned the Captain as being in part a doll, she also recognizes that Mrs. Hepburn had been much more of one. In appearance, she had seemed altogether artificial with her excess of tinkling jewelry and her shallow but assertive opinions. Her per-

---

2. This phrase is from *The Ladybird* (82).

missive attitude toward sex represents, in reality, a titillation, "sex-in-the-head" as Lawrence would regard it. She can jauntily accept the notion of her husband's infidelity, because she herself knows what it is, she tells Hannele, to sail in casual encounters *"very* near the flame" (207). Her ostensible sophistication is really hypocrisy because propriety determines all that she does. She thus reacts like a puppet to her experiences. Apropos of her request to purchase the doll that Hannele has made of Hepburn, Hannele cannot help thinking, "What a doll she would make herself! Heavens, what a wizened jewel!" (218). Yet Mrs. Hepburn has some depth and is not altogether a travesty of a woman. Hepburn had discovered in her an unwillingness to play the role demanded of her by society, even though she had never had the force to rebel against it and so remained a prisoner in the cage of society's conventions. Though a free spirit, she could not express the dynamic impulses that might have liberated her. The Captain thus regards her accidental death as a release from a burden that she had found increasingly heavy.

Despite the independence and genuineness of her responses, Hannele is also something of a doll. Whereas she scorns her lover's subjection to his wife, she regards his initial prostration before his mate as "almost a necessary part of the show of love" (214). When Hannele resists the regenerated Captain at the end of the tale, she cannot at first put aside the expectations engendered in her by traditional romantic love as the basis for a permanent relationship. She could love Alexander, she thinks, but she refuses to be bullied: "he must go down on his knees to her if he wanted her love" (251). She gradually becomes less absolute in her expectations and leaves behind the puppetlike aspects of her psyche, agreeing to accept Hepburn more or less on his own terms.

The Austrian official, the Herr Regierungsrat von Poldi, to whom Hannele is engaged when Hepburn returns to reclaim her, is entirely an automaton, defining his life in terms of traditional culture rather than instinct. He represents the overripe, complacent, stagnant, debilitated, and quasi-decadent culture of the early twentieth century, especially in Germany and Austria, which did not have the vigor to survive the devastation of the Great War. His is a dead-end cynicism, for he sees nothing to replace the genteel civilization that produced him, though he recognizes its ineffectuality. Like a noble Roman of the late empire, he has moral probity, but no possibilities for a meaningful existence open out for him, so that in all he says and does "there seemed a bigness, a carelessness based on indifference and hopelessness that laughed at its very self" (230).

The Herr Regierungsrat appeals to the doll-like side of Hannele, and she responds to his adulation. He makes her feel like "a queen in exile." If he wants her to be a doll, she would not object to becoming one in exchange for dominion over him. He would thereby become her doll, undoubtedly kneeling to her early in their projected marriage, and she would enjoy, somewhat sadistically, such abasement: "How he would abandon himself to her!—terribly—wonderfully—perhaps a little horribly" (232). His artificial values are no longer relevant to the extremities of the postwar situation, but he attracts her by his "subtle stoicism," his "unsentimental epicureanism," and his "reckless hopelessness"—in short, by assimilating so completely the corroding postwar disillusionment. But he has no elemental force or reserves of inner power; in choosing him, Hannele would have become a puppet in a charade. To attain fulfillment, she must reject him and elect the risk-fraught course of resuming a relationship with Hepburn. Harris describes Hannele's choice as one "between difficult salvation and easy perdition" (160); she must commit herself to a man who can "save" her rather than drift with one who will flatter her and gratify her somewhat ignoble cravings to dominate the male.

At his core Captain Alexander Hepburn is life-enkindling despite his entrapment in a meaningless marriage. The darkness that Hannele finds enveloping him cloaks a fierce light within, a darkness that gives him the power to venture into the unknown. The genuine instincts of his psyche lead him to a life-enhancing woman, Hannele, though at first he had refused to regard her with full seriousness. Mrs. Hepburn is not the only psychic prisoner in the marriage; her husband is also one until her sudden death frees him. The "adoration-lust" with which he had enshrined her continues to exert its influence over him; her death but accentuates the apathy he had felt in her presence. He rejects, however, the titillations offered by the nubile women who would adore him as a mate, just as he had adored his wife; and he reasserts his basic self, acting in the same spirit as Lawrence did in *Studies in Classic American Literature,* when he distinguished his own vital identity from the conformism implicit in Benjamin Franklin's attitude:

"That I am I."

"That my soul is a dark forest."

"That my known self will never be more than a little clearing in the forest."

"That gods, strange gods, come forth from the forest into the clearing of my known self, and then go back."

"That I must have the courage to let them come and go."

"That I will never let mankind put anything over me, but that I will try always to recognize and submit to the gods in me and the gods in other men and women." (22)

The Captain, like Lawrence himself, assumes a vatic stance when he bursts beyond the artifices of his society and in his own way illustrates the motivations that Lawrence ascribed to the Europeans in coming to America: "To slough the old European consciousness completely" and then "To grow a new skin underneath, a new form" ("Fenimore Cooper's Leatherstocking

Novels," *SCAL* 58). Hepburn, like Hannele, attains a reordered psyche; they both also participate in a mythic journey as Lawrence formulates it: "True myth concerns itself centrally with the onward adventure of the integral soul" (*SCAL* 69). The modern individual, discouraged by lifeless tradition and materialism, often lacks the courage "to withdraw at last into his own soul's stillness and aloneness, and *then,* passionately and faithfully, to strive for the living future" (*Fantasia* 160). Once he attains such mastery and such vision, Hepburn senses still an incompleteness, and so he attempts to encompass the secondary law of all organic life as Lawrence articulates it in *Studies in Classic American Literature*: "each organism only lives through contact with other matter, assimilation, and contact with other life" (71).

Realizing that "man doth not live by bread alone" and that "he lives even more essentially from the nourishing creative flow between himself and another or others" (*Psychoanalysis* 46), Hepburn finds, after his wife dies and he leaves the army, that memories of Hannele flood his being. He cannot now deny his demonic creativity, and with a flash of intuition he perceives that his future must lie with the most vital woman he has known. A proud isolation and a demonic intensity are not incompatible, the Captain discovers, with dynamic commitment to another human being. He now admits that "conscience is the being's consciousness, when the individual is conscious *in toto,* when he knows in full. . . . Every man must live as far as he can by his own soul's conscience" (*Fantasia* 165).

He is actively seeking to realize the Holy Ghost in his own being as Lawrence described it in *Fantasia of the Unconscious:* "the individual in his pure singleness, in his totality of consciousness, in his oneness of being: the Holy Ghost which is with us after our Pentecost, and which we may not deny" (165). He must extricate himself from the grooves of convention and venture forth into the unknown, as he had begun to do earlier with his astronomy. He recognizes that such advance into the uncharted realms of his spirit must now be his binding motivation. At the end of the tale he will leave behind a decadent Austria and an exhausted England and travel to Africa, and while there, he will pursue even more ardently his studies of the heavens.

On his return to Munich, Hepburn sees the doll in a shop window, and he is at once repelled and fascinated by it, fascinated because it captures uncannily his exterior mien, repelled because it seems now, in light of his altered consciousness, to be a kind of sacrilege, an invasion of his sacrosanct identity. The doll mesmerizes him, so that he does not act quickly enough to purchase it and thus loses it forever.

The German painter Wropswede bought the doll and used it as a model for a painting, featuring the doll as part of a fashionable modernist still life: "two sunflowers in a glass jar, and a poached egg on toast" (228). In using the doll in such a painting, Wropswede has, Hepburn senses, altered still further his essential identity; but for all his repulsion, he carries it with him as a kind of penance. He concludes that the doll and his own mistaken attitudes that it had epitomized must be eradicated. After he surmounts the glacier and survives his ordeal, Hannele proposes to burn the painting as a ritualistic celebration of the Captain's completion of his rite of passage. The destruction of the painting exorcises all elements of artifice that had obscured the Captain's fundamental being.

The doll provides a measure of the Captain's development. In his revised views on sex and marriage, he repudiates the idea of becoming a doll in a romantic relationship: given her conventional expectations, he thinks, a woman proceeds to nullify her husband's inner existence, absorbing him into her own self. Hepburn emerges at the end of the tale with a surer insight into human relationships than does Hannele—so Lawrence would have us believe. When Hepburn looks at the painting, he knows that no love is possible between him and Hannele—at least on the old basis of the artifices that they had cherished when she had fashioned the doll. He now argues for an association wherein intimacy will alternate with fierce independence, each partner respecting the separateness of the other. Though Hepburn asserts that Hannele must promise to honor and obey him rather than merely love him, he also says that he will cherish such a gifted woman so long as she does not attempt to obliterate his identity. The subordination of the woman signifies patriarchal domination, but Hepburn also tries to encourage in marriage an integral selfhood for each person and to abjure the possessive element that had in the past eroded his sexual relationships.

The other range of symbols in the novella derives from nature: it comments chiefly on Hepburn's resort to nature as a source of renewal, discovering there the sources of his own positive energies and the forces capable of destroying an outworn culture. But nature can also be inimical, destructive not only of the impediments to vitality but of valuable expressions of it. Nature must therefore be seen in full perspective. It can provide not only unlimited spiritual reserves, as the moon does for the Captain, but it can also be annihilating, as the Captain discovers the mountains to be. Nature can even mock human pretensions, thwart the individual as he aspires to mystical authority, and emphasize his insignificance when set against the cosmos. Mystic aloofness in nature, furthermore, can result not only in transcendence but in spiritual passivity and atrophy of will. To some extent, then, one must circumvent its power as well as court it.

The nature images intensify the meaning of the tale. There are, for example, the images drawn from astronomy as they suggest the Captain's personality and aspirations. His interest in astronomy allows him to escape from the tepid monotony of his marriage, much as in Strindberg's *The Father* the Captain's scientific pursuits provide a refuge from the frictions of domesticity. They allow Hepburn, even at the beginning, to express his deepest, instinctual self. The telescope is life-enhancing, a phallic emblem: Hannele fingers its barrel in the Captain's absence and thinks of his charismatic personality. His kinship with the moon countermands the barrenness of his intimacy with his wife, who cannot bear to look at it: its great distance from earth awakens in her the vertigo to which she becomes a victim. In contrast to the prison of his marriage, the moon signifies for the Captain the sacredness of his individuality. Its aloofness also encourages in him a stoic endurance that allows him to persevere in a relationship from which the vitality has vanished. His remoteness and self-sufficiency, which Hannele finds irresistible, have their correlative in the moon. Quite appropriately, he plans to write a book on the moon in Africa, where he intends to go with Hannele. There is, moreover, a "curious white light [that] seemed to shine on his eyes" (189), which suggests that the moon constantly informs his demeanor, to establish something ineffable and mysterious about him.

Lawrence often associates the moon with female energies as, for example, he does with Ursula in *The Rainbow* and *Women in Love*. So the Captain must come to terms with femininity and conquer it. He must try to secure for himself the largeness of the vital woman's soul, associated with the moon, but he must also dominate her before he can achieve wholeness of being as a man. Hannele is a source of vitality for the Captain, as the golden light falling on her hair as she sews the doll would suggest; her face at this time "seemed luminous, a certain quick gleam of life about it" (185). Although she is timorous about getting out on the roof to look at the moon, she responds, like other charismatic women in Lawrence's fiction, to its enchantment and beauty, "bewitched . . . by the great October moon and the sky full of resplendent white-green light" (201). Hepburn must appropriate her vitality without letting her drain his own, as might happen if she were to exert upon him the parasitic domination of his former wife. Hannele becomes at once a source of the Captain's greatest possible fulfillment and a threat to his integrity; she is for him not a "rosy love" but rather "a hard destiny" (226).

She is superior to the sensual youths with whom she is swimming in the Tyrol when Hepburn returns to her; she offers not only sensuality but a strength that is sui generis. The strength, nevertheless, would not exist without the sensual richness, emphasized when Hepburn comes upon her like a latter-day Venus arising resplendently from the waters: "Her legs were large and flashing white and looked rich, the rich, white thighs with the blue veins behind, and the full, rich softness of her sloping loins" (236). Amid "the sense of flesh everywhere, and the endless ache of flesh" (233), she embodies a vibrancy of which she is only partly conscious, in her half-hearted plans to ally herself with the placid Herr Regierungsrat.

During his marriage the Captain cultivated his integral self in isolation from his wife, but he had yet to learn how union with a woman strong enough to stand alone could reinforce his essential instincts and purposes. Even as he repudiates romantic love, he has intimations that sex will allow his inner powers to exfoliate. Although Lawrence was to urge that woman submit to man's tutelage in achieving the deepest intimacies, he also recognized in the contemporary *Fantasia of the Unconscious* that sexual gratification for both man and woman is indispensable to attaining fulfillment outside of and beyond the physical:

> It cuts both ways. Assert sex as the predominant fulfilment, and you get the collapse of living purpose in man. You get anarchy. Assert *purposiveness* as the one supreme and pure activity of life, and you drift into barren sterility, like our business life of today, and our political life. You become sterile, you make anarchy inevitable. And so there you are. You have got to base your great purposive activity upon the intense sexual fulfilment of all your individuals. . . . But you have got to keep your sexual fulfilment even then subordinate, just subordinate to the great passion of purpose. . . .
> (145)

The imagery in the early part of the tale underscores the Captain's glamor, vitality, animal energies, and intrinsic force. His hands covered with dark hair, his hairy breast, his dark eyes, his black and glossy hair, "the soft, melodious, straying sound of his voice" (*CD* 191), all attract Hannele as signs of physical grace and masculinity. The brilliant scarlet cactus flowers in his room convey his warmth and sensual power—and a sense of his isolate individuality. Hannele appreciates, moreover, the shapeliness of his legs, having carefully molded them when she made the doll and its tartan trews.

Lawrence establishes the Captain's spontaneous force by aligning him with the cat image, much as he does with other commanding men in his fiction at the time, Ciccio in *The Lost Girl* or Count Dionys in *The Ladybird*.[3] The gaze behavior that Jane Nelson analyzes in the preceding essay (pp. 137–39) appears with different emphasis in *The Captain's Doll*—as impersonal feline allure—for when the Captain stares at the moon through the telescope, he is "like a great cat." His eyes dilate like a cat's at night, he straddles the stool before the telescope like a tomcat, and his touch on Hannele's face seems to her that of a kitten's paw. Earlier, she hears from the stairwell "the slow, straying purr of his voice" (201, 199). In the mountains he impresses her as she registers "the queer, blank, sphinx-look with which he gazed out beyond himself"; and he displays also a "feline" aspect as he looks at the glacier before he climbs it (244, 242).

At other times the Captain suggests a conquering, imperial presence. His

---

3. See, for example, Lady Daphne's view of Count Dionys as "a little wild cat" and her perception of his eyes with "the invisible, cat-like fire stirring deep inside them" (*Ladybird* 68).

first name, Alexander, is of course that of a world conquerer (Mellown 273), and early in the relationship he had appeared to Hannele as a Caesar or a Germanicus. Shortly thereafter, his masterful presence is undercut for her by his subservience to his wife, so that Hannele wonders which is the true man, "the husband of the little lady" or that "queer, delicate-breasted Caesar of her own knowledge" (*CD* 218). In his apathy toward sex with his wife, Hannele regards him as hardly human, rather as a sort of "psychic phenomenon like a grasshopper or a tadpole or an ammonite" (203). But such derogatory comparisons reflect the Captain's deviation from a norm that he ought by rights to exemplify more consistently. These contradictory images betoken his vacillating conduct and values in his early phase and also Hannele's ambiguous reactions to him.

Some of the majestic strength of the mountains characterizes Hepburn at the novella's end, though he consciously rejects their harshness and impersonality. On the heights he not only draws sustenance from the cosmos and attains a significant rapport with it, but he also challenges its indifference and latent hostility. The landscape, everywhere alive but full of torpor, effuses menace rather than benevolence. Its evident but mostly dormant powers make it a formidable antagonist that seemingly negates the exertions of animate beings: the glacier is "coldly grinning in the sky" (237); an alpine river "shouted at the bottom of a gulf" as "bristling pine trees stood around" (240); the water "rushed like a beast of prey" (241); the high air "bit him in his chest, like a viper" (242); "the great fangs and slashes of ice and snow thrust down into the rock, as if the ice had bitten into the flesh of the earth"; and from its source in "the fang-tips" of the beast, the "hoarse" water cries "its birth-cry, rushing down" (244).

Despite the prodigal energies suffusing these images, the milieu is fundamentally sinister and suggests annihilation and death, when for example Hepburn and Hannele traverse the upper "valley of the shadow of death" (240). For Hepburn the alpine scene is threatening, "as if a dark wing were stretched in the sky, over these mountains, like a doom" (237). The great spaces hint at the possibility of a new life with limitless horizons, but from the streams and glaciers a raw force emanates that is inimical to the serene spirit and the subtle moral intelligence. The mountains fascinate and repel Hepburn; so does the glacier that he and Hannele have, in particular, come to see.

The Tyrol is beautiful but the life-spirit there, as the narrator observes, seems to be "squirming, bleeding all the time" (230). The mindless vigor of the youthful bathers recalls the dead-end sensuality symbolized by the African statuette in *Women in Love*. Hepburn and Hannele are here in the presence of two opposing modes of spiritual death (as Birkin defines them in "Moony" in *Women in Love*), though only Hepburn divines the extremity of these forces. Death by fierce sensuality, characterizing the tropical mode of life, is counterpointed against death by ice-abstraction, characterizing the arctic mode of life.

Hannele in her affinity with the unrestrained bathers and her ecstatic reactions to the beauty of the mountains disregards these disruptive influences, whereas Hepburn resists both the physicality of the tourists and the frozen grandeur of the mountains. He recoils from the aggressive heartiness of one hiker who suggests a Tannhäuser, a Siegfried, or a Balder; Hepburn judges as mechanical the *"Bergheil* business" that his hiker and the other holiday-makers—as makeshift heroes—represent. Hannele's voice also refracts the "high strident sound of the mountain" (242) as she becomes enraptured with the peaks in their beauty and regards the glowering glacier as "great silent, living" and as "hold[ing] the key to all glamour and ecstasy" (253). When she and Hepburn quarrel in the mountains, she reflects the arctic aspect of the scene with "her face naked as the rain itself with an ice-bitter fury" (248). At this point the fire in his face seems to her irrelevant, but this element is needed to thaw her temporarily frozen spirit. His face seems "like a dark flame burning in the daylight and in the ice-rains: very ineffectual and unnecessary" (249), but it is in fact necessary to dissipate the fixedness of some of her principles.[4] In this connection Lady Daphne Apsley in *The Ladybird* is more fully aware of Count Dionys's therapeutic value to her spirit than Hannele is of the Captain's: "The Count had something that was hot and invisible, a dark flame of life that might warm the cold white fire of her own blood" (99).

Hepburn now becomes the hunter suggested by his previous identification with the cat. An aggressive, partly sexual force is present for him in the mountains, a force that is rugged, partly destructive, and untamed. Thus the waters, as a masculine shattering force, enter the solid rock and cut out the valley clefts, penetrating ever deeper into the rock in apparent sexual friction as these waters cause the rock to disintegrate:

This valley was just a mountain cleft, cleft sheer in the hard, living rock, with black trees like hair flourishing in this secret, naked place of the earth. At the bottom of the open wedge for ever roared the rampant, insatiable water. The sky from above was like a sharp wedge forcing its way into the earth's cleavage, and that eternal ferocious water was like the steel edge of the wedge, the terrible tip biting in into the rock's intensity. Who could have thought that the soft sky of light, and the soft foam of water could thrust and penetrate into the dark, strong earth? (241)

The waters united with the sky in their motions suggest the movement of the phallus, but the corrosive effect of the water in this passage also denotes the force of the female principle as the waters wear away the rock masses with

4. In "The Two Principles" Lawrence asserts that "if we must imagine the most perfect clue to the eternal waters, we think of woman, and of man as the most perfect premiss of fire" (*Phoenix II* 234).

their suggestion of masculine strength. The glacier, as frozen water, is also female. Mounting the glacier becomes a sexual act, a test of survival for Hepburn, and an essay at mastery for him in the duel of sex. His eyes dilate with excitement (recalling the cat image) as he mounts the glacier, as if for "ordeal or mystic battle" (253).

The glacier symbolizes the powers of inanimate nature that assume an animate guise, as if to underscore its strength and vindictiveness. The glacier is as if alive, a beast that Hepburn must track down and overthrow, "like some great, deep-furred ice-bear lying spread upon the top heights, and reaching down terrible paws of ice into the valley" (252). In the hot summer atmosphere "the great monster [is] sweating all over, trickles and rivulets of sweat running down his sides of pure, slush-translucent ice" (253); the surface, as Hepburn climbs its "curved back," is "like a soft, deep epidermis" (254). It is also a great fish or porpoise with holes in the snow acting as gills. But if it is alive it is frozen and immobile, fostering no life except the glacier fleas. The glacier is either subhuman or superhuman, and it causes the animal potencies to atrophy or else suppresses them (despite the emphasis on its sexual attributes). The alpine milieu arrests rather than elicits the intense currents of the free psychic life, the spontaneous expressions of the unconscious.

The surmounting of the glacier tests the Captain's fortitide, bravery, and masculinity. It also signifies that he has overcome a major challenge in forming a new identity: the threatening female as her force is congealed in the glacier. As Lawrence expressed it in *Fantasia,* the central problem in the relationship between the sexes is this: "is he [man] lord of life" or "is she [woman] the supreme Goddess" (133). Too many men, Lawrence insisted, regard woman as the only source of life, the prime being, and are too active in her service. Hannele's decision to burn the modernist painting featuring the doll signifies the elimination of a major obstacle in Hepburn's attaining harmony with her and also signifies that she is at least partly willing to submit to his mastery. A man who is somewhat frail in physique conquers the glacier: the female attributes in their strongest guise have yielded to his persistence, and he is thus no longer in any sense a doll.

Hepburn has had his surfeit of the ecstasy-inducing but dehumanized mountains, preferring to their sublime and static beauty the more common-place world "where cabbages will grow on the soil" (256). Whereas "the savage cat-howling sound of the water" and "those awful flanks of livid rock" produce a sympathetic response in Hannele, Hepburn recoils from the sound of the water, the relentless air, and the "dark-blue, black-blue, terrible colour of the strange rich monkshood," the color of which poisonous flower is reflected in the blue depths of the glacier pools (242, 244).

As he undergoes his trial on the glacier, the Captain is not prepossessing but is ridiculous in some part, a mock hero. The comic elements undercut but also reinforce the tale's significance as a parable. The Captain's boast that he is larger than the mountains is amusing, but it is also true that the human spirit, enriched by the working of the Holy Ghost within, can move mountains. His own destiny concerns him more than objects of beauty or of potential veneration outside him. Paradoxically, he does acquire some of the grandeur of the mountains as he meets their challenge, and Hannele, for whom they induce rapture and a bodiless ecstasy, becomes more human as Hepburn overcomes their threat to him.

Both characters exist at first in a state of arrested development, and the effectiveness of the tale lies partly in its depiction of a protagonist and a heroine who attain awareness and reject the spurious (or puppetlike) parts of their psyches. At first they are, in R. P. Draper's words, "both of them a little unreally self-contained" (128); both must become less passive and more aggressive in defining their essential selves. They attain, finally, a sensuality and a freedom that are genuine, thorough, and absolute.

Sensing the inadequacies of romantic love as a basis for human relationships, Lawrence stressed the need to attain a balance between love—in his view, primarily sexual attraction—and power, the conscious cultivation of the sources within that would lead to the most responsible expression of individuality. Rawdon Lilly's definition of power in *Aaron's Rod* applies here: "Not intellectual power. Not mental power. Not conscious will-power. Not even wisdom. But dark, living, fructifying power" (297). Throughout his career Lawrence insisted that we use our talents creatively in order to achieve such inner command. He emphasized the obligation of the creative soul to find a rapprochement with another individual in sex, in order to experience not only sexual fruition but the fullest possible realization of human powers. The need to attain to a star-equilibrium, as Birkin propounds it in *Women in Love,* is never quite obliterated in Lawrence's furtherance of patriarchal values, though Ursula even in that novel complains that Birkin seems to want a woman to be a satellite rather than an equal.

For Captain Hepburn and Hannele, the active realization of their individualities—their souls in separateness yet combining with one another in significant union—provides the assurance that their new understanding will be blessed. Each has allowed the Holy Ghost, whose vestiges appear in every person, to guide the self. The implication is that life on the African farm for Alexander and Hannele will be dynamic and forever changing, that they will respond not only to all manifestations of the profane but to the sacred as well. The two will experience, at least intermittently, intimations of transcendence to complement a full expression of their sensual selves.

Each person contributes to the dynamic quality of such a union by acting in accord with his or her inviolable self, with the Holy Ghost within: "Each must be true to himself, herself, his own manhood, her own womanhood, and let the relationship work out of itself. This means courage above all things: and then discipline" ("Morality and the Novel," *STH* 174–75). The Captain and Hannele possess such courage and discipline, or they come to possess these attributes as their association with each other deepens. They thereby earn their salvation, though the road to ultimate understanding has not been easy for either of them.

They dramatize in their experiences and conflicts not only Lawrence's own difficult pilgrimage after the Great War, but they are also on the way to an encompassing peace that Lawrence himself was only fitfully to attain. Hepburn and Hannele both establish the "living organic connections" celebrated in the last paragraph of the posthumously published *Apocalypse:* "What we want is to destroy our false, inorganic connections, especially those related to money, and re-establish the living organic connections, with the cosmos, the sun and earth, with mankind and nation and family. Start with the sun, and the rest will slowly, slowly happen" (149). Hepburn and Hannele begin with the moon and the night heavens, and their struggles to reach an authentic mode of life are convincing. They look back to the past to recover the unlimited possibilities present to the unfallen—and even to the fallen—Adam and Eve; and they herald a future in which the opportunities for a regenerate mankind will be immense. They are sensitive, imaginative, and conscientious, and they enact a progress that leads them always forward into the unknown. As such questing individuals, they become archetypal figures, serving as models for the present-day man or woman who might wish to regain—or reaffirm—his or her elemental identity.

WORKS CITED

Daleski, H. M. "Aphrodite of the Foam and *The Ladybird." D. H. Lawrence: A Critical Study of the Major Novels and Other Writings.* Ed. A. H. Gomme. New York: Barnes & Noble, 1978. 142–58.

Doherty, Gerald. "A 'Very Funny' Story: Figural Play in D. H. Lawrence's *The Captain's Doll." D. H. Lawrence Review* 18 (1985–86): 4–18.

Draper, R. P. *D. H. Lawrence.* New York: Twayne, 1964.

Gilbert, Sandra M. "Potent Griselda: 'The Ladybird' and the Great Mother." *D. H. Lawrence: A Centenary Consideration.* Ed. Peter Balbert and Phillip L. Marcus. Ithaca: Cornell UP, 1985. 130–62.

Harris, Janice Hubbard. *The Short Fiction of D. H. Lawrence.* New Brunswick, N.J.: Rutgers UP, 1984.

Hough, Graham. *The Dark Sun: A Study of D. H. Lawrence.* London: Duckworth, 1956.

Lawrence, D. H. *Aaron's Rod.* Ed. Mara Kalnins. Cambridge: Cambridge UP, 1988.

Lawrence, D. H. *Apocalypse and the Writings on Revelation*. Ed. Mara Kalnins. Cambridge: Cambridge UP, 1980.

Lawrence, D. H. *The Captain's Doll*. *Four Short Novels*. New York: Viking, 1965. 181–266.

Lawrence, D. H. *Fantasia of the Unconscious*. *Psychoanalysis and the Unconscious and Fantasia of the Unconscious*. New York: Viking, 1960. 51–225.

Lawrence, D. H. *The Ladybird*. *Four Short Novels*. New York: Viking, 1965. 41–109.

Lawrence, D. H. *Phoenix II: Uncollected, Unpublished and Other Prose Works by D. H. Lawrence*. Ed. Warren Roberts and Harry T. Moore. New York: Viking, 1968.

Lawrence, D. H. *Psychoanalysis and the Unconscious*. *Psychoanalysis and the Unconscious and Fantasia of the Unconscious*. New York: Viking, 1960. 1–49.

Lawrence, D. H. *Studies in Classic American Literature*. Harmondsworth, Eng.: Penguin, 1983.

Lawrence, D. H. *Study of Thomas Hardy and Other Essays*. Ed. Bruce Steele. Cambridge: Cambridge UP, 1985.

Leavis, F. R. *D. H. Lawrence: Novelist*. New York: Knopf, 1956.

Leavis, F. R. *Thought, Words and Creativity: Art and Thought in Lawrence*. New York: Oxford UP, 1976.

Martin, W. R. "Hannele's 'Surrender': A Misreading of *The Captain's Doll*." *D. H. Lawrence Review* 18 (1985–86): 19–24.

Mellown, Elgin. "'The Captain's Doll': Its Origins and Literary Allusions." *D. H. Lawrence Review* 9 (1976): 226–35.

Ruderman, Judith, *D. H. Lawrence and the Devouring Mother: The Search for a Patriarchal Ideal of Leadership*. Durham, N.C.: Duke UP, 1984.

Schneider, Daniel J. *D. H. Lawrence: The Artist as Psychologist*. Lawrence: UP of Kansas, 1984.

Stewart, J. I. M. *Eight Modern Writers*. Oxford: Clarendon, 1963.

Widmer, Kingsley. *The Art of Perversity: D. H. Lawrence's Shorter Fiction*. Seattle: U of Washington P, 1962.

CHAPTER 11

Lawrence as Reader of Classic American Literature

LYDIA BLANCHARD

Even admirers of D. H. Lawrence as a literary critic see little if any method informing *Studies in Classic American Literature* (1923), instead judging the work as brilliant but intuitive and impressionistic. Nevertheless, the important and growing influence of *Studies* on our understanding of American literature rests as much on a strong methodological base as it does on the power of Lawrence's insights. Perhaps surprisingly, Lawrence shares a number of critical assumptions with E. D. Hirsch, whose understanding of interpretation offers one of our most influential approaches to literary texts. Like Hirsch, Lawrence grounds his response to literature in genre; he believes that genre classifications are based on the writer's purpose and a reconstruction of the writer's horizon. Moreover, Lawrence shares with Hirsch two other assumptions: that the goal of valid interpretation is consensus, and that the goal of criticism is to illuminate meaning and to apply that meaning to life. Although Lawrence places his emphasis on criticism rather than on interpretation, this criticism is grounded in an understanding of the writer's intentions, as an analysis of Lawrence's reading of American literature indicates. The personal and idiosyncratic style of *Studies* should not mislead us. Whereas Lawrence believed the touchstone of criticism was emotion, the account of the feeling produced in the critic was to be reasoned. Lawrence fulfills his own criterion.

I

In the hands of a brilliant reader, impressionistic criticism may be effective; and a man of genius, such as D. H. Lawrence in *Studies in Classic American Literature*, may intuitively arrive at valid conclusions which a less gifted critic could reach only through extended and careful analysis. (172)

The judgment is Maurice Beebe's, but it could have been written by almost any one of the many American commentators on D. H. Lawrence's criticism of classic American literature, who agree that Lawrence reads American literature brilliantly but with little discernible method.[1] In Beebe's defense, any inadequacies in judgment would have been academic in 1960, when he wrote the above, for although Lawrence's reading of American literature has always had American admirers, initial reaction to *Studies* was definitely mixed. Before 1960, few saw Lawrence's readings of American literature as serious or significant.

But in 1960, Leslie Fiedler, in *Love and Death in the American Novel*, called Lawrence "of course" the critic of American literature "closest to the truth"; only Melville "more precisely identified the nature of the American novel" (14, 15). Fiedler's enthusiasm called attention to a phenomenon that had been building with little notice: citations of Lawrence's work in important studies of American literature were growing (in 1955, for example, R. W. B. Lewis had quoted *Studies* in a controlling epigraph for *The American Adam*), and Lawrence's ideas about our major nineteenth-century writers had begun to shape—often without acknowledgment—the direction of criticism in American studies. By 1975, although Michael Colacurcio thought it might be "too academic to say that there is a 'School of Lawrence'" in American studies, his review essay in the *American Quarterly* of that year provided a strong case for identifying it. Lawrence's influence, he said, was "showing up all around" (488): Richard Poirier, for example, called *Studies* the "crucial study of American literature" (37), and for Quentin Anderson, it began "the serious discussion" (134).[2]

---

1. Most studies of Lawrence's literary criticism follow Beebe's judgment that if Lawrence has a method, it is impressionistic or instinctive. Richard Foster writes that Lawrence "did have a method, though it was really half unconscious, or more accurately, instinctive" (321). Although recognizing that Lawrence wrote *Studies* "to make [his intuitive knowledge] stand up by some system or language that will not betray the quality of its truth" (284), Richard Swigg still believes that Lawrence's system is impressionistic. Peter Bien argues that Lawrence's literary criticism is more systematic than has been acknowledged, but limits his analysis to aesthetics; his emphasis differs significantly from Lawrence's.

2. Few American critics before 1960 shared F. R. Leavis's enthusiastic judgment that Lawrence was "the finest literary critic of our time" (233), but important exceptions were Edmund Wilson and Richard Chase. In 1943 Wilson called *Studies* "one of the few first-rate books that have ever been written on the subject" (906); and in 1959 Chase called Lawrence "one of the best [readers] ever to turn his attention to the American novel" (9). In *D. H. Lawrence and America* (91–99) Armin Arnold details the more typical mixed reaction that *Studies* initially received. By 1969, however, David Cavitch could call *Studies* "the most influential piece of criticism written on the subject" (105). Following the lead of Lewis, critics such as Leo Marx had begun to use *Studies* not for occasional citations, as they did before 1960, but as the source of central ideas. Colacurcio's review essay traces Lawrence's influence on Poirier, Anderson, Crews, Fiedler, Joel Porte, and Richard Slotkin. Even critics who find Lawrence's

Still, even when critics agree with and admire Lawrence's insights into American literature, they often continue to view *Studies* as fundamentally a gloss on Lawrence, worth reading not for its insights into classic American texts, but rather, in Nathan Scott's words, "for what it tells us of Lawrence and the world within which his own spirit was contained" (168).[3] This reading is understandable. *Studies*, with its fragments and exclamation points, its Carlylean capitalizations and short paragraphs, certainly looks like impressionistic criticism. With its frequent apparent digressions from the texts, it also seems like Lawrence's indulgence of his love affair with (in the 1918–19 *English Review* version) and subsequent disenchantment with (in the 1923 version) America, not America's literature.[4] As Cowan (24–32) shows, *Studies* even provides a forum for Lawrence to develop ideas about blood-knowledge rather than texts. Nevertheless, to call Lawrence's methodology "impressionistic" limits our understanding of the real methodology that underlies *Studies*.

Colacurcio provides an important framework for understanding why *Studies* is now a seminal book. Using the critical vocabulary of Hirsch, Colacurcio identifies Lawrence's method as a probing for "symptomatic meanings," involuntary accompaniments to meaning, and argues that Lawrence's symptomatic criticism ("reading the classics . . . for what they reveal . . . of some deep cultural malaise") is the source of Lawrence's usefulness and "one vital source of Lawrence's excitement" (491). But Colacurcio also sees Lawrence's insistence on cultural significance as "the source of serious methodological difficulties" (491) and argues for the "absolutely crucial hermeneutic distinction between 'intentional' and 'symptomatic' meanings":

I personally see no way to avoid the conclusion [of E. D. Hirsch] that before we can know what a work "reveals," even in relation to the psyche of an individual writer, we have got to develop some adequately historical sense of what it could possibly have been intended to "mean," as a complex of intention designed rationally to communicate between an individual writer in history and an audience, also in history. (494)

---

criticism seriously flawed now begin by acknowledging the centrality of his work (see, for example, Axelrad and Wellek).

3. For example, Robert Pierle writes: "Nathan Scott probably had the right idea" (340). Michael Small writes: "In the process of attempting to rescue Hawthorne's tale from Hawthorne, Lawrence has at least partially rewritten the romance. Recognizing that he will not find confirmation of his views in those of Hawthorne, the teller, he too readily seeks confirmation of his views in the tale" (56). Richard White writes that Lawrence "tended to judge another's work *not* according to the intentions of the author but according to his own demands of what a novel should be" (174).

4. For an analysis of the differences between these two versions of *Studies*, see Arnold; in his edition called *The Symbolic Meaning*, Arnold collects the 1918–19 *English Review* essays. Swigg (283) presents a brief publishing history. See also Clark 180–206.

I quote at length from Colacurcio because he is, to my knowledge, the first critic to gauge the extent to which Hirsch helps in understanding *Studies*.[5] Certainly there seems much immediate evidence for seeing Hirsch and Lawrence, as Colacurcio sees them, at opposite poles, illuminating each other through contrast. Consider Lawrence's most quoted dictum from *Studies:* "Never trust the artist. Trust the tale. The proper function of a critic is to save the tale from the artist who created it" (8). The argument seems to place Lawrence with those critics who see a text as autotelic, to be understood only within itself and not by any outside standard, including the author's. Nothing apparently could be further from Hirsch's stress on the author as the deter- miner of a work's meaning: "Permanent meaning is, and can be, nothing other than the author's meaning" (*Validity* 216).

Similarly, Lawrence insists on reading for symbolic meaning: "You *must* look through the surface of American art, and see the inner diabolism of the symbolic meaning" (89). His apparent stress on rescuing the tale from the teller also seems to argue that the author is not a privileged reader of his own work. Lawrence seems to favor W. K. Wimsatt and M. C. Beardsley's famous argument for the intentional fallacy: "The design or intention of the author is neither available nor desirable as a standard for judging the success of a work of literary art" (468). Consequently, most critics looking at Lawrence have understood his approach to American literature as subjective, impressionistic, reader-centered. Again it is understandable that Lawrence has been viewed as an early advocate of ignoring intention. The epigrammatic nature of *Studies* makes it one of the most quotable of critical works. How- ever, in their habitual choice of epigram ("Trust the tale"), critics of *Studies* have distorted Lawrence's methodology and thus Lawrence's insights into American literature. Quite simply, *Studies* needs to be read in the order in which it is presented.

II

If we start at the beginning of *Studies in Classic American Literature* and follow Lawrence's own priorities, his connection with Hirsch becomes quite different from what Colacurcio maintains, his methodology much more sys- tematic. For Hirsch, validity of interpretation is constituted by determining genre: "Valid interpretation is always governed by a valid inference about genre" (*Validity* 113). Similarly, Lawrence would agree with Hirsch that "every disagreement about an interpretation is usually a disagreement about

5. In *D. H. Lawrence as a Literary Critic*, David J. Gordon anticipates the connection in his discussion of Lawrence's understanding of the intentional fallacy: in his criticism, Lawrence "is hostile to the apparent intention. But he understands it perfectly well" (37).

genre'' (98). Therefore, at the outset of *Studies*, in ''The Spirit of Place,'' Lawrence identifies the mistake in genre that has kept many readers of American literature from valid interpretation: ''We like to think of the old-fashioned American classics as children's books'' (7). He then sets out to identify, instead, the meaning of a writer by correctly identifying the genre to which the work belongs.

Lawrence understands genre in complex ways. Consider the diversity of writers he includes in *Studies* (Franklin and Melville, Crèvecoeur and Whitman, for example). Lawrence connects these writers because, like Hirsch, he understands genre in terms of common elements in a limited group of historically related texts. Moreover, whereas Lawrence's selection of writers covers a broader period of time than Hirsch might allow, he locates his ''most important unifying and discriminating principle in genres'' (*Validity* 100) in a determination of purpose. Here Lawrence's interest in the Americans is dramatically clarified, for he believes that the classic writers have a common bond in their engagement with moral issues: American art is ''all essentially moral'' (*SCAL* 180).

Lawrence rarely uses standard generic labels (Hirsch himself finds them useful only as heuristics), but when he does, he stresses the moral issue. As an example of Lawrence's argument, he tells us that *The Scarlet Letter* is not romance but variously a parable, a satire, an allegory. Lawrence's use of all three terms may suggest that he is trying to broaden generic classification, but it is the shared interest that parable, allegory, and satire have with the moral basis of human behavior that concerns him. The three genres are, in fact, not fully separated, parable being a subcategory of allegory and allegory moving into satire. For Northrop Frye, ''allegory in reverse gear gives us [satire]'' (''Nature'' 20), and Lawrence perceives Hawthorne in *The Scarlet Letter* as moving into that reverse gear.

Even so, how can Lawrence justify ignoring Hawthorne's own use of the term *romance* for *The Scarlet Letter*? I will return to this question, but let me begin the answer by referring again to the opening lines of ''The Spirit of Place.'' Here Lawrence shares a second fundamental assumption with Hirsch, that the reader comes to validity in interpretation, including determination of genre, by reconstructing a writer's ''horizon.'' Recognizing the impossibility of discovering a writer's thought at the moment of creation, Hirsch uses Husserl's concept of the horizon, ''a system of typical expectations and probabilities . . . derived from the explicit meanings present to consciousness'' (*Validity* 221), as a way to reconstruct the circumstances of creating a text and thus its meaning. Similarly Lawrence stresses ''spirit of place,'' recognizing the difficulty for readers removed by time and location to hear what any writer says: ''The old American art-speech contains an alien quality, which belongs to the American continent and to nowhere else.'' The reader will not hear this quality if he approaches the text with the wrong generic expectations: "So long as we insist on reading the books as children's tales, we miss all that" (*SCAL* 7). This point is so essential that, in the second paragraph of "The Spirit of Place," Lawrence compares the difficulties of a twentieth-century Englishman in understanding classic American literature with the difficulties of late Romans in understanding Lucretius, Apuleius, and other writers interested in religious and ethical questions, who were separated from their audience in time and place and who—like American writers— frequently used satire or irony.

Given these two important assumptions shared by Hirsch and Lawrence in his first paragraph—that our reading must be based on a proper generic classification and that validity in interpretation depends on that classification and on a determination of the writer's horizon—Lawrence seems to recognize limits to the interpretation of a text. His understanding is similar to that of Frank Lentricchia, who has criticized Hirsch's "rationalist faith in types" because it implies that the only thing valid to say about a text is the genre itself, after which "we have run up against the limits of cognition" (268). As if anticipating the criticism, Lawrence moves quickly from interpretation (discussion of meaning, "the whole verbal meaning of a text") to criticism (discussion of significance, "textual meaning in relation to a larger context" [Hirsch, *Aims* 2–3]). This mixture of interpretation and criticism is one that Hirsch allows. Whether Lentricchia and Lawrence are right that statements about genre constitute the extent of validity in interpretation and that emphasis will thus always be on significance, Lawrence does lay the groundwork for discriminating between interpretation (meaning) and criticism (significance). Lawrence's dictum "Never trust the artist" must be understood in this context.

In his dictum, Lawrence considers classic American literature for its *significance*, for what it has to tell his contemporary reader. It is in distinguishing the text's meaning from its significance that Lawrence argues both that "art-speech is the only truth" and that art-speech "prevaricates so terribly" (*SCAL* 8): the contradiction is only a surface one. Art-speech tells the truth about the author's day (the author's horizon, which provides insight into his meaning), but it lies to the reader who tells himself lies about the text's significance. Because art-speech (and artists) prevaricate, readers need to be trained to see through the subterfuge.

Looking through the subterfuge, concentrating on significance—where differences in judgment occur—Lawrence argues that art has two great functions, to provide an emotional experience and to become a mine of practical truth. Because so much previous attention has been given to feelings, he chooses to emphasize practical truth, truth that can guide action. For Lawrence *practical* retains close connections with the Greek *praktikos*, "fit for doing, active." Despite the danger in quoting from what Lawrence wrote about literature on other occasions (he may have changed his mind), he does not seem to have modified his insistence that literature provides impetus to social change. In 1913 he told Arthur McLeod that he wrote because he wanted English folk "to alter, and have more sense" (*Letters* I: 544). His position is consistent with his statement twelve years later, in "Morality and the Novel," that "the novel can help us to live, as nothing else can" (*STH* 175). Again the emphasis is consistent with Hirsch's argument that "the value of interpretation lies in its *application*. . . . The job of criticism is both to illuminate meaning (when necessary) and to indicate some valuable application of meaning" (*Aims* 156).

Although Lawrence is interested primarily in the cultural significance of a text, which is determined by the time and place of the reader, he continues to discuss significance in generic classifications. His readings show the possibility of reconciling different interpretations by tracing how different critics, on different paths, can lead toward the same genre. The goal of valid interpretation, for Hirsch, is consensus, a goal Lawrence implicitly accepts and works toward. This is another important connection between Hirsch and Lawrence.

The Scarlet Letter again offers a good example because it is a perplexing classic, a text that has led critics to disagree in apparently irreconcilable ways. Frederic Carpenter's classification of these interpretations (traditional moralist, romantic enthusiast, transcendental idealist) offers at least a start for showing how Lawrence's reading of the novel is a reconciliation, an achievement of consensus. Carpenter himself faults Hawthorne for not making the novel clearer, but Lawrence—with his generic expectations—shows how to reconcile the contradictions Carpenter classifies. For traditional moralists, *The Scarlet Letter* is a study of the effects of sin, in this case adultery; for romantic enthusiasts, the sin is society's for calling Hester's moral code an evil one; for transcendental idealists, Hester has committed a sin of dishonesty rather than passion, keeping Chillingworth's identity a secret from Dimmesdale and thus effecting their destruction. Lawrence shows Hawthorne "meaning" all three, reconciling the interpretations by showing how they all lead to satire as the text's purpose. *The Scarlet Letter* holds up all three possibilities to exaggeration and thus ridicule. First, the novel *is* about the effects of sin, but the effects exaggerated: Dimmesdale's anguish about his guilt is masturbation. Second, *The Scarlet Letter* argues that consciousness of adultery, not the act itself, is the novel's sin: mind-knowledge is satirized. Third, Hester's sin is her destruction of Dimmesdale by taking upon herself the decision to conceal Chillingworth's identity: the novel satirizes strong women. All three readings, if taken toward satire, can be reconciled; the novel satirizes the mind-consciousness of allegory.

III

But that leads back to the question: Is Lawrence justified in reading *The Scarlet Letter* as satire (or parable or allegory), however brilliant the reading, when Hawthorne himself called the book a romance? We can defend Lawrence on a number of grounds, the simplest being that, as F. O. Matthiessen argues, Hawthorne's definition of romance "bears only tangential relation" to the other definitions current during his lifetime (266). Certainly Hawthorne's romance has little in common with Northrop Frye's formulation, in *Anatomy of Criticism*, of the mythos of summer. Lawrence himself does not deny that the novel is a romance, arguing only that it is not a "pleasant, pretty romance," but rather "a sort of parable, an earthly story with a hellish meaning" (*SCAL* 89). There is support for such a reading of the genre. Eleanor Terry Lincoln argues that any understanding of romance must include a sense of both vision and nightmare (5), and Daniel Hoffman has suggested that the romance can "absorb or become" other genres (including satire) without losing its distinctive character (354). But Lawrence's definition also needs defense from his own explanation of what makes *The Scarlet Letter* a satire.

Lawrence could have made his case most easily by focusing on "The Custom-House," which is clearly satire, but he prefers to ground his understanding of genre in those characteristics the novel shares with other classic American texts. He credits Hawthorne with knowing that he was writing on two levels in *The Scarlet Letter*—"Nathaniel knew disagreeable things in his inner soul. He was careful to send them out in disguise" (89)—and Lawrence finds this split between the deliberate consciousness and the under-consciousness in all the texts he considers. A common characteristic of writers discussed in *Studies* is their ability to resolve the split: "They give tight mental allegiance to a morality which all their passion goes to destroy. Hence the duplicity which is the fatal flaw in them" (180). Thus, Lawrence argues, we must read through the surface of *The Scarlet Letter* for "the inner diabolism of the symbolic meaning," and in finding that diabolism, we will see that the text is a satire: "Otherwise it is all mere childishness" (89). But precisely what is this symbolic meaning and, more important for the connection with Hirsch, has it been determined by the author's intention?

In *Studies* Lawrence implicitly rejects two popular understandings of "symbolic meaning," those of Charles Feidelson and Frederick Crews, who in different ways deny the author's intention as privileged in determining the meaning of his text. In *Symbolism and American Literature* Feidelson argues that to regard a literary work as a symbol is to consider it autonomous as well as, within itself, creative: "It is quite distinct both from the personality of its author and from any world of pure objects. . . . It brings into existence its own meaning'' (49). However, such a stress on the literary work as a ''piece of language'' is contrary to Lawrence's attempt in *Studies* to extract a purpose for each one of his writers from Franklin to Whitman. Nor do symbolic or unconscious meanings reflect an author's repression, as Crews has argued about Hawthorne in *The Sins of the Fathers*. Although Lawrence does write about the ''disagreeable things'' Hawthorne knew ''in his inner soul,'' he— unlike Crews—had little interest in Hawthorne's unresolved Oedipal conflicts. Lawrence specifically rejected Freudian readings of his own work and had little desire to consider other writers in similar terms.[6]

Nevertheless, those ''disagreeable things'' are part of the text's symbolic meaning, and for Lawrence that symbolic meaning is its cultural meaning. One of the best sources for understanding this connection is Lawrence's introduction to Frederick Carter's *The Dragon of the Apocalypse*. Although the introduction was not finished until January 1930 and published posthumously, Lawrence received Carter's manuscript the summer he published *Studies* and, in correspondence with Carter in 1923, formed many of the introduction's ideas. Of the Apocalypse, Lawrence writes that its intentional, Christian meaning, a superficial allegorical meaning, is defied by the work's symbols; his argument about the relationship between intentional and symbolic meaning is similar to his argument about classic American literature.

In the introduction Lawrence usefully distinguishes between allegory and symbolism: allegory uses images as terms in an argument, ''nearly always for a moral or didactic purpose''; but it ''takes centuries'' for these images to become significant symbols. The writer, then, does not invent symbols (''He can invent an emblem . . . but not symbols''); generations of readers create symbols. To read for ''symbolic meaning'' is to read for both the author's intention and the historical accumulation of significance that has turned a text's images into symbols: ''Some images, in the course of many generations of men, become symbols . . . carried on in the human consciousness for centuries'' (*Phoenix* 295–96). In *Studies* Lawrence aims to awaken the reader— ''when men become unresponsive and half dead, symbols die'' (*Apocalypse* 49)—and so keep the symbols of classic American literature alive, dynamic, ''belonging to the sense consciousness of the body and soul'' (48).

Lawrence's understanding of symbol, then, is based on a separation of meaning and significance consistent with Hirsch's system. Lawrence anticipates Hirsch's vocabulary when he argues that orthodox interpretations of the Apocalypse are ''the final intentional meaning of the work'' (47). Hirsch would not, of course, share Lawrence's judgment that meanings are superficial and a bore, and Lawrence is far more interested than Hirsch in the

---

6. See Lawrence's letter of 16 September 1916 to Barbara Low about the *Psychoanalytic Review* essay on *Sons and Lovers* (*Letters* II: 655).

growing, dynamic, unbounded symbol and its significance. But they would agree, I think, that Hawthorne created an emblem in the scarlet letter that is fixed, understood as part of the text's meaning, and separable from what it becomes as a symbol or part of the text's significance.

Hawthorne himself seems to intend a similar insight into meaning and significance from the moment he discovers the rag of scarlet cloth in the custom-house:

My eyes fastened themselves upon the old scarlet letter, and would not be turned aside. Certainly, there was some deep meaning in it, most worthy of interpretation, and which, as it were, streamed forth from the mystic symbol, subtly communicating itself to my sensibilities, but evading the analysis of my mind. (62)

Within a few moments, the rag turns from the capital letter A, an image that can be measured and described, into a symbol with the force of a red-hot iron, its diabolical under-consciousness already manifested. Lawrence called *The Scarlet Letter* "the most perfect American work of art" (180), perhaps because the novel demonstrates Lawrence's own understanding of how image becomes symbol.

Lawrence categorized *The Scarlet Letter* as satire on this presentation of the varied perceptions of meaning and significance in the scarlet A. In Lawrence's reading, Hawthorne holds up to ridicule those excesses of Hester, Dimmesdale, and Chillingworth that result from their inability to move the scarlet A out of the realm of image (or emblem or metaphor) into the realm of symbol. They never allow the letter to free them, to release their imaginations, to arouse their deep emotional selves, because all are involved in the mind-consciousness in which allegory operates. To respond to a blood-consciousness of the scarlet A would move the emblem into the liberating world of the symbol, but this never happens in the novel. The duplicity of Hawthorne is that he denies that liberation to his characters while he celebrates it for himself. His own perception of the scarlet A as symbol frees him for the imaginative act of writing *The Scarlet Letter*.

Thus Lawrence sees that meaning and significance are fused in determining genre (at least in those American texts that must be read for symbolic meaning), and in doing so he suggests a sterility in the Cartesian divisions of Hirsch's system. Lawrence sees that the strength of the generic concept, at least in the case of satire, rests not only on our ability to fix the text's meaning in its genre, but also on our recognition of indeterminacy in a text's ability to grow and respond and disrupt generic expectations. Moreover, such a dark under-consciousness of the text may well be—and with Hawthorne certainly is—part of the author's "intention."

However, this difference between Hirsch and Lawrence should not obscure the extent to which Lawrence's priorities anticipate *Validity in Interpretation*.

Like Hirsch, Lawrence understands the importance of determining genre and horizon and distinguishing meaning from significance. Moreover, in concentrating on significance and in questioning whether future generations will see in classic American texts the significance he sees, Lawrence seems to accept Hirsch's argument that ''verbal meaning is determinate, whereas significance and the possibilities of legitimate criticism are boundless'' (*Validity* 57).

IV

''Boundless'' does not mean that all criticism, all discussions of significance, are of equal interest, however, and surely one reason for the influence of *Studies* is that Lawrence does not abuse his interest in the significance of literature as a ''compelling penetration of history'' (Stern 195). That is, unlike many commentators, Lawrence does not turn that interest into license to air personal prejudices. Rather, anticipating Hirsch, he bases his discussion of significance on a clear understanding of the text's meaning. That is why we continue to find his concerns about significance our concerns as well.

In some areas, in fact, we have had to catch up with Lawrence. Although Lawrence's central position in Cooper and Whitman studies is well established, his influence on our interpretation of Hawthorne is more recent. Traditionally Hawthorne scholars have not paid much attention to Lawrence because they have read the novel with different generic expectations, seeing the text as romance or novel rather than satire.[7]

As romance or novel, *The Scarlet Letter* is a sympathetic treatment of religious torment. Its undertones reinforce, rather than work against, Hawthorne's preoccupations with sin, light and dark, good and evil. In this reading the drama focuses on Dimmesdale and his tragic journey to an acknowledgment of sin and subsequent redemption. Like Stuart Sherman, whose *Americans* (1922) Lawrence reviewed as he worked on the final version of *Studies*, most Hawthorne critics see Dimmesdale's unresolved guilt as the ''main tragic problem'' of *The Scarlet Letter*. Dimmesdale is, as Sherman argues, unquestionably ''the figure of primary importance'' (146), the character who ''affects us as most unquestionably human'' (147). Similarly, for Harry Levin, ''the recognition-scene where Dimmesdale lays his soul bare to the multitude'' is the culmination of the novel (xix). James Mellow stresses Dimmesdale's autobiographical connections with Hawthorne (306). Richard Harter Fogle sees the conclusion as an ''unresolved contradiction.'' The sin of *The Scarlet Letter* is ''the original sin, by which no man is untouched . . .

---

7. Critics like Geoffrey Moore, who accept Lawrence's generic determination, immediately grasp the relevance of his remarks about Hawthorne. Writing about religious satire in *Elmer Gantry*, for example, Moore finds himself going back to Lawrence's comments in *Studies* (66).

human beings by their nature must fall into error—and yet it would be better if they did not'' (132–33). Dimmesdale's death scene is thus "climactic" (146). Even for critics like Hyatt Waggoner, *The Scarlet Letter* remains a "tale of human frailty and sorrow," a negative judgment of the Puritans by their own Christian standards (155). Reading the novel as a romance, Richard Chase rejects a feminist interpretation of the novel, arguing that it is a mistake to treat Hawthorne ''as if he were a political or social writer'' (73).

Lawrence's reading is, of course, different. Approaching the novel with the generic expectations of satire, he sees the exaggerated suffering of Dimmesdale not as torment with which the reader should feel sympathy, but as masturbation, excessive agonizing that should be ridiculed. Chillingworth shows the failure of the intellectual tradition; he has "only intellectual belief in himself and his male authority" (105). Most important, Lawrence argues that *The Scarlet Letter* is a satire of strong women, of the way in which men allow women to make fools of them.

This reading is Lawrence's most controversial discussion of the novel's significance. Armin Arnold, who generally prefers the earlier *English Review* version of *Studies* to the familiar 1923 version, calls the revised *Scarlet Letter* section "Lawrence at his poorest" (*SM* 122). In the 1923 version, he argues, Lawrence becomes hysterical: "Hester Prynne is the great nemesis of woman" (95). For Lawrence, she is variously the "KNOWING Ligeia risen diabolic from the grave" (95), a demon, a devil, Hecate, the hell-cat, a witch—bolstering man "from the outside," destroying him "from the inside" (99). Her surface appearance of nurse, of divine maternity, is Hawthorne's "goody-goody," "lovey-dovey," deceptive surface through which we must look to find the witch (89). Similarly, Pearl is the "continuing of [Hester's] female revenge on life. . . . America is a whole rope of these absolutely immaculate Pearls, who can't sin" (104, 109). The practical truth that Lawrence mines from *The Scarlet Letter* indicts strong women and the men who do not control them. Such women send out "waves of destructive malevolence which eat out the inner life of a man, like a cancer. It is so, it will be so, till men realize it and react to save themselves" (99).

Lawrence did not restrict his interest in gender relationships to the Hawthorne section of *Studies*. Some of his most perceptive criticism of Cooper and Crèvecoeur, for example, discusses their treatment of women as a comment on the culture's treatment of women. Such critical questions, based as they are on gender or power relationships, had little effect, however, until feminist literary critics sensitized readers to their importance. Although Lawrence's reading of *The Scarlet Letter* is hardly a typical feminist reading, Lawrence defined the issues of the novel as feminists would.

For example, Nina Baym's seminal book *The Shape of Hawthorne's Career* (1976), though not specifically feminist, reads *The Scarlet Letter* with an attention to gender problems consistent with Lawrence's identification of the central issues in the novel. Baym argues that Hawthorne's interests are not religious but secular (9); they reflect his desire "to represent a basic difference in the status of men and women within a patriarchal structure" (128).[8] For Baym, as for Lawrence, Dimmesdale's offense is to have repudiated patriarchal rule by acknowledging Hester's matriarchal dominion: Hawthorne's world is one of strong women and weak men. Pearl's significance is that she has located herself in a world inhabited entirely by women. When Pearl tells the Boston patriarchs that she was plucked from the wild rosebush, she defines her birth as an event that can occur apart from men. Again, for Baym as for Lawrence, Pearl is isolated in her purity, born, as it were, from an immaculate conception, a virgin unto herself.

Like Lawrence, Baym views Dimmesdale as hypocritical. His hypocrisy is thinking that his sin is religious when he is really acting, Baym argues, to maintain himself as a favorite in the power structure. Although Baym does take Lawrence to task for misreading Hester—"as a dark lady with an appetite for corrupting pure men" (136)—her argument is not against calling Hester dark but against calling Dimmesdale pure. For her, Dimmesdale's fall began before he met Hester. Whereas Lawrence thinks Dimmesdale lost his manhood, Baym thinks he never had it. Baym celebrates Hester and Lawrence fears her; Baym believes matriarchy will strengthen and Lawrence thinks it will destroy America. These differences are clearly important, but less important than the belief Baym and Lawrence share that Hawthorne writes as a feminist with secular, gender-related, and political concerns. For Baym, as for Lawrence, the novel ends not with Dimmesdale's confession and death but, on the last page of the novel, with Hester's speculation that at some brighter period

a new truth would be revealed, in order to establish the whole relation between man and woman on a surer ground of mutual happiness. . . . The angel and apostle of the coming revelation must be a woman . . . [and will come] not through dusky grief, but [through] the ethereal medium of joy; and showing how sacred love should make us happy.

I cannot predict the extent to which this feminist reading will be preferred to earlier readings of *The Scarlet Letter* as a study of the anguish of unconfessed sin. However, Lawrence's record in identifying areas of significance is impressive.[9] Certainly his influence on American studies stems from his

8. In her preface, Baym credits Crews for his "declaration of independence from then-standard readings of Hawthorne" (10). As I have argued, however, Crews's psychoanalytic criticism is inconsistent with Lawrence's emphases.

9. A review essay entitled "Hawthorne and Melville: Some Recent Studies in Classic American Literature" asserts that Baym's arguments—secular, pro-feminist, concerned with the in-

ability to identify ways in which our classic American writers have penetrated history and isolated cultural characteristics that direct our actions. Whether it is the American obsession with youth or the destructive impulse underlying our national character, whether it is our ambivalent feeling about the irreconcilability of democracy and elitism or the sterility of our preference for things scientific, whether it is the basis on which relationships between men and women should be constituted or our inability to achieve a balance in those relationships, Lawrence seems to have found, in our classic American writers, the grounds for a continued mining of practical truth.

Lawrence's achievement in *Studies in Classic American Literature* is based, then, not on an instinctive genius, but on a clear set of priorities that make him more systematic in his criticism than has been acknowledged. Like Hirsch, Lawrence accepts the primacy of interpretation of genre and horizon, of determining genre through identification of a group of common traits in historically related texts, of working toward consensus in interpretation, of distinguishing between meaning and significance. Most important, he shares with Hirsch an interest in the application of texts, an acknowledgment of the value of literature in shaping our lives. Unquestionably Lawrence believed, as he wrote in his essay on John Galsworthy, that criticism cannot be a science, that the touchstone is emotion rather than reason, but he never eliminated reason from his criticism: "Literary Criticism can be no more than a *reasoned* account of the feeling produced upon the critic by the book he is criticising" (*STH 209*, emphasis added). No more, but also no less.

Studies offers Lawrence's most comprehensive statement of his critical position. Although my analysis has centered on Lawrence's interpretation of Hawthorne, the same points could be made for any of the other writers discussed in Lawrence's work. Moreover, *Studies* is Lawrence's most persuasive statement that criticism, even when it is systematic, need not be dull. Lawrence succeeds in getting away, as he wants to get away, from what he calls "critical twiddle-twaddle," from "all this pseudo-scientific classifying and analysing of books" (*STH* 209).

But again, his lively, impressionistic, nonscientific language should not mislead us as readers. Hirsch himself is the best authority on this point, for he has presented the strongest case for synonymity, for the fact that "identical meaning [can be expressed] through different linguistic forms" (*Aims* 50). Although Lawrence's conception of the act of interpreting and criticizing a text is by no means identical with that of Hirsch, he shares with him a number of "reexpressible propositions" (*Aims* 73). The rigor of those reexpressible

---

dividual struggle against authoritarian society—are "strong and often suggestive" (Asals 69). In the introduction to the Viking Penguin reprint of *The Scarlet Letter* (1983), Baym strengthens her case for a secular reading of *The Scarlet Letter*.

propositions and the interest of Lawrence's own style have created the achievement that is *Studies in Classic American Literature*. Our understanding of Lawrence as a literary critic, and of his influence on America's reading, will be stronger if we recognize the importance of both.

WORKS CITED

Anderson, Quentin. *The Imperial Self: An Essay in American Literary and Cultural History*. New York: Knopf, 1971.

Arnold, Armin. *D. H. Lawrence and America*. New York: Linden, 1958.

Asals, F. J. "Hawthorne and Melville: Some Recent Studies in Classic American Literature." *University of Toronto Quarterly* 49 (1979): 65–78.

Axelrad, Allen M. "The Order of the Leatherstocking Tales: D. H. Lawrence, David Noble, and the Iron Trap of History." *American Literature* 54 (1982): 189–211.

Baym, Nina. *The Shape of Hawthorne's Career*. Ithaca: Cornell UP, 1976.

Beebe, Maurice, ed. *Literary Symbolism: An Introduction to the Interpretation of Literature*. San Francisco: Wadsworth, 1960.

Bien, Peter. "The Critical Philosophy of D. H. Lawrence." *D. H. Lawrence Review* 17 (1984): 127–34.

Carpenter, Frederic I. "Scarlet A Minus." *College English* 5 (1944): 173–80.

Cavitch, David. *D. H. Lawrence and the New World*. New York: Oxford UP, 1969.

Chase, Richard. *The American Novel and Its Tradition*. 1957. New York: Gordian Press, 1978.

Clark, L. D. *The Minoan Distance: The Symbolism of Travel in D. H. Lawrence*. Tucson: U of Arizona P, 1980.

Colacurcio, Michael J. "The Symbolic and the Symptomatic: D. H. Lawrence in Recent American Criticism." *American Quarterly* 27 (1975): 486–501.

Cowan, James C. *D. H. Lawrence's American Journey: A Study in Literature and Myth*. Cleveland: Case Western Reserve UP, 1970.

Crews, Frederick C. *The Sins of the Fathers: Hawthorne's Psychological Themes*. New York: Oxford UP, 1966.

Feidelson, Charles, Jr. *Symbolism and American Literature*. Chicago: U of Chicago P, 1953.

Fiedler, Leslie A. *Love and Death in the American Novel*. 1960. New York: Stein and Day, 1975.

Fogle, Richard Harter. *Hawthorne's Fiction: The Light and the Dark*. Norman: U of Oklahoma P, 1964.

Foster, Richard. "Criticism as Rage: D. H. Lawrence." *A D. H. Lawrence Miscellany*. Ed. Harry T. Moore. Carbondale: Southern Illinois UP, 1959. 312–25.

Frye, Northrop. *Anatomy of Criticism: Four Essays*. 1957. New York: Atheneum, 1969.

Frye, Northrop. "The Nature of Satire." *Satire: Theory and Practice*. Ed. Charles A. Allen and George D. Stephens. Belmont, Calif.: Wadsworth, 1962. 15–30.

Gordon, David J. *D. H. Lawrence as a Literary Critic*. New Haven: Yale UP, 1966.

Hawthorne, Nathaniel. *The Scarlet Letter*. New York: Viking Penguin, 1983.

Hirsch, E. D., Jr. *The Aims of Interpretation*. Chicago: U of Chicago P, 1976.

Hirsch, E. D., Jr. *Validity in Interpretation*. New Haven: Yale UP, 1967.

Hoffman, Daniel. *Form and Fable in American Fiction*. New York: Oxford UP, 1961.

Lawrence, D. H. *Apocalypse and the Writings on Revelation*. Ed. Mara Kalnins. Cambridge: Cambridge UP, 1980.

Lawrence, D. H. *The Letters of D. H. Lawrence*. Vol. 1: *September 1901–May 1913*. Ed. James T. Boulton. Cambridge: Cambridge UP, 1979.

Lawrence, D. H. *The Letters of D. H. Lawrence*. Vol. 2: *June 1913–October 1916*. Ed. George J. Zytaruk and James T. Boulton. Cambridge: Cambridge UP, 1981.

Lawrence, D. H. *Phoenix: The Posthumous Papers of D. H. Lawrence*. Ed. Edward D. McDonald. 1936. New York: Viking, 1968.

Lawrence, D. H. *Studies in Classic American Literature*. Harmondsworth, Eng.: Penguin, 1983.

Lawrence, D. H. *Study of Thomas Hardy and Other Essays*. Ed. Bruce Steele. Cambridge: Cambridge UP, 1985.

Lawrence, D. H. *The Symbolic Meaning: The Uncollected Versions of "Studies in Classic American Literature."* Ed. Armin Arnold. New York: Viking, 1964.

Leavis, F. R. "The Wild, Untutored Phoenix." *Scrutiny* 1937. Rpt. in *The Common Pursuit*. 1952. Harmondsworth, Eng.: Penguin, 1963. 233–39.

Lentricchia, Frank. *After the New Criticism*. Chicago: U of Chicago P, 1980.

Levin, Harry M., ed. *The Scarlet Letter*, by Nathaniel Hawthorne. Boston: Houghton Mifflin, 1960.

Lewis, R. W. B. *The American Adam: Innocence, Tragedy, and Tradition in the Nineteenth Century*. Chicago: U of Chicago P, 1955.

Lincoln, Eleanor Terry, ed. *Pastoral and Romance: Modern Essays in Criticism*. Englewood Cliffs, N.J.: Prentice-Hall, 1969.

Marx, Leo. *The Machine in the Garden: Technology and the Pastoral Ideal in America*. New York: Oxford UP, 1964.

Matthiessen, F. O. *American Renaissance: Art and Expression in the Age of Emerson and Whitman*. New York: Oxford UP, 1941.

Mellow, James R. *Nathaniel Hawthorne in His Times*. Boston: Houghton Mifflin, 1980.

Moore, Geoffrey. "Sinclair Lewis: A Lost Romantic." *The Young Rebel in American Literature*. Ed. Carl Bode. London: Heinemann, 1959. 51–76.

Pierle, Robert C. "D. H. Lawrence's *Studies in Classic American Literature*: An Evaluation." *Southern Quarterly* 6 (1968): 333–40.

Poirier, Richard. *A World Elsewhere: The Place of Style in American Literature*. New York: Oxford UP, 1966.

Scott, Nathan A., Jr. *Rehearsals of Discomposure: Alienation and Reconciliation in Modern Literature*. New York: King's Crown, 1952.

Sherman, Stuart. *Americans*. New York: Scribner's, 1923.

Small, Michael. "The Tale the Critic Tells: D. H. Lawrence on Nathaniel Hawthorne." *Paunch* 40–41 (1975): 40–58.

Stern, Milton R. "Nathaniel Hawthorne: 'Conservative after Heaven's own fashion.'" *Essays in Honor of Russel B. Nye.* Ed. Joseph Waldmeir. East Lansing: Michigan State UP, 1978. 195–225.

Swigg, Richard. *Lawrence, Hardy, and American Literature.* London: Oxford UP, 1972.

Waggoner, Hyatt H. *Hawthorne: A Critical Study.* 1955. Cambridge: Harvard UP, 1963.

Wellek, Rene. "The Literary Criticism of D. H. Lawrence." *Sewanee Review* 91 (1983): 598–613.

White, Richard. "D. H. Lawrence the Critic: Theories of English and American Fiction." *D. H. Lawrence Review* 11 (1978): 156–74.

Wilson, Edmund, ed. *The Shock of Recognition: The Development of Literature in the United States Recorded by the Men Who Made It.* Garden City, N.Y.: Doubleday, Doran, 1943.

Wimsatt, W. K., Jr., and M. C. Beardsley. "The Intentional Fallacy." *Sewanee Review* 54 (1946): 468–88.

CHAPTER 12

Lawrence and the Clitoris

MARK SPILKA

My pre-text for this literary sermon is the concluding chapter, "Uncoding Mama: The Female Body as Text," in *Semiotics and Interpretation*, a recent intertextual gambit by my friend and colleague, and in many respects my double, Robert Scholes.[1] I should say at once, in the Leavis manner, that I admire the chapter and the author, and that I agree with and applaud much of what he says. In these latter days of the feminist movement most of us are in favor of uncoding Mama, along with Papa, to whom Scholes attends in the previous chapter ("Decoding Papa," 110–26). But as an aging Lawrentian and eclectic humanist of a fast-fading school, I am troubled by the ethnocentric biases of the newer critical modes that my double advances so ably and so reasonably. Though his chapter is nothing if not historical as it explores language codes for the clitoris from the Greeks, Hindus, and Muslims on down to modern times, it offends my own sense of the vagaries of recent sexual history and my own regard as well for what Lawrence actually contributed to the raised consciousness from which the chapter emanates. And of course, like any proper double, I want to fill in my disregarded underside of the uncompleted argument.

But first I must explain, as best I can, my double's side. Professor Scholes subtitles his chapter "The Adventures of an Organ in Language and Literature." The adventures are semiotic in that Scholes disqualifies himself as an expert in human sexuality and discounts also his role as a feminist critic. He is rather a semiotician interested in "certain signs of sexuality as they function in language, in psychoanalytic discourse, and in literature"—cultural signs of codes that operate as ingrained conventions "in our perception of our own

---

1. I might mention here, with regard to doubling, that until recently Professor Scholes and I were both balding graybeards who taught different aspects of modern fiction and literary theory at Brown University, where at different times we both chaired the English Department and made fortunate second marriages (he to a biologist who taught sex education in a local high school, I to a psychiatric social worker) at about the same time in life that the less fortunate Lawrence died of tuberculosis. Since then we have diverged considerably.

176

bodies.'' Though his concern is ''only indirectly with the realities'' of human sexuality, he obviously hopes to change our approach to those realities by uncoding cultural myths about the clitoris, and to supplement and advance thereby the terms of recent feminist discourse (126).

He begins accordingly with a familiar feminist target, the Freudian myth of human socialization. At a crucial moment in Freudian childhood, he explains, the infant notices the genitals of a member of the opposite sex and becomes aware of either an absence or a presence. The result is penis envy in the female seeing a presence she lacks, and castration anxiety in the male seeing an absence he fears. This binary opposition enables children ''to join the social community,'' says Scholes, ''with their libidinal energies tamed by fear and envy.'' But as Freud understood through his professional knowledge of anatomy, there is a part left over, the clitoris, which fails to fit into his binary scheme; it mars the symmetry, and must therefore be trivialized, criticized, and removed ''from the discourse of sex.'' Thus Freud calls it ''the real little penis of the woman,'' which—though normal—is ''felt to be inferior,'' and proceeds to erase it by ingenious means (128–29).

Scholes postpones these ingenuities so as to consider the fortunes of the term *clitoris* in pre-Freudian history. He finds that the word has not been ''naturalized in English''; that it has no slang equivalents beyond the abbreviation ''clit'' in recent times and the word ''cockey'' in Joyce's masturbatory letters to his common-law wife Nora. Even its lexicological origins are confusing since the primary meaning of the Greek *kleitoris* is said to derive from the verb ''to shut or bar,'' whereas the secondary meaning of ''jewel'' or ''gem'' accords more favorably with the nouns ''bar'' or ''key'' and with such related adjectives as ''splendid'' or ''famous,'' which in turn accord with male metaphors for the penis. ''We are dealing,'' says Scholes, ''with a widespread process of censorship—not a political conspiracy but a semiotic coding that operates to purge both texts and language of things that are unwelcome to the men who have had both texts and language in their keeping for so many centuries.'' This powerful and unconscious coding derives its energy, he concludes, ''from a deeply felt fear of feminine sexuality'' (129–31).

Of the many forms such fear may take Scholes chooses as ''the simplest and perhaps most benign . . . the feeling that women experience a deeper, more thorough gratification from sex than men do.'' He cites in this regard the small-boned Japanese lover in a recent story by Angela Carter who felt ''like a small boat upon a wide, stormy sea'' when in bed with a large-boned Anglo-Saxon woman; and, as an example of how the awe men feel at ''full female sexual response'' may turn nasty, he cites the British lover who said ''I would have enjoyed it more had you enjoyed it less'' when terminating an affair. Then he turns to the different forms this estimate of female sexual pleasure may take in different cultures, beginning with the famous quarrel between Jove and Juno in Ovid's *Metamorphoses*, where Tiresias is brought in to settle the question of which sex has the greater pleasure, and continuing with the similar Hindu myth of Bhangāsvana, the Talmudic prohibition against widows owning male slaves or dogs, and the Islamic practice of clitoridectomy, or female castration, once widespread and still found in North Africa. And in all these estimates he finds that men tend to oppose female pleasure with male power (131–33).

Next he turns to the real matter of his essay: how in Western Europe from the Enlightenment on, this castration process, this "ritual acting out of male fears," "has been primarily a semiotic one, not enacted on the suffering bodies of actual women but inscribed in texts" which have created their related share of suffering; and to illustrate his thesis he chooses for semiotic analysis three exemplary texts, John Cleland's *The Memoirs of Fanny Hill* (1749), Freud's *Three Essays on Sexuality* (1905), and Lawrence's *Lady Chatterley's Lover* (1928).

In Cleland's pornographic novel, Scholes tells us, erasure occurs primarily through the male fantasy that females are dependent for their deepest sexual satisfaction on the male organ. Thus "a woman cannot achieve full satisfaction alone; nor can two women together achieve it," whether by digitation or other means; only the "male machine" "can appease the desire of an aroused woman," and that on a quid pro quo basis, with no allowance for the woman's greater capacity for multiple orgasms. At one point, interestingly, Cleland does allow that a "soft fleshy excrescence" exists in Fanny's "soft-pleasure conduit pipe," but he misplaces it deep inside that channel, "where it ought to be" in the male fantasy world he has constructed (134–36).

Sigmund Freud knew better but arrived at a comparable male arrangement. The spasms of the clitoris by which small girls discharge their sexual excitement are repressed at puberty, he claimed, and then more or less anesthetized as women put aside "their childish masculinity" and transfer their excitability from the clitoris to the vaginal orifice. This myth of anesthesia suggests to Scholes that Freud had become the prisoner of his own binary code of female absence and male presence (136–38). It is this code or scenario that Lawrence fleshes out with "dramatic interaction" in *Lady Chatterley's Lover* (140).

Scholes cites three passages from the unabridged "popular" edition of the novel (1929) to make his case. The first is from the introduction, where Lawrence tells us that the real point of his book is to make us "*think* sex fully, completely, honestly and cleanly" as a kind of complement to our personal struggles for complete sexual satisfaction, holding that years of such effort will at last bring our sexual thoughts and acts into harmony, so that one doesn't interfere with the other. Scholes calls this an ambitious program for liberating us "from our sexual inhibitions," and claims that two passages from the novel will ''provide most of the answer'' as to how close Lawrence comes to achieving it (138). For expediency's sake let me observe that Scholes not only commits the intentional fallacy here, he also reduces the scope of Lawrence's stated intention to his own narrow focus on the reduction of inhibitions. But surely to *think* sex honestly and fully, as Lawrence intends it, is to deal with a wide range of attitudes and feelings, with exploitations as well as inhibitions—willed passivities and aggressions, egoisms and hostilities—which Lawrence later codifies as ''self-importance'' and ''self-will''; and beyond that, it involves an *''adjustment in consciousness''* toward that ''proper reverence for sex'' and that ''proper awe of the body's experience'' which Lawrence then calls for as an antidote to the mind's contempt for the body's sexual powers. The male awe Scholes invokes for a woman's full sexual response is a reflection of the former idea, or of its literary variant in Leopold Bloom's molliolatry in *Ulysses*, which may accord better with Scholes's background as a Joycean scholar. Perhaps such unacknowledged ''codifications'' in his own text explain why Scholes credits Joyce's letters for the word ''cockey,'' but says nothing at all about Joyce's failure to celebrate the clitoris in his own fictive attempts to free us from sexual inhibitions. But then Lawrence, who never poses as a value-free novelist like Joyce, may be fairer game. If he too exposes false cultural expectations, like a good semiotician, he also posits a peculiar ideal—''our real and accomplished chastity''—for the kind of complete satisfaction he has in mind—a more pronounced and kinetic form of ''absence,'' certainly, than Bloom's worshipful abstinence, which again better suits and perhaps even graces Scholes's merely biological idea of independent female pleasure.

For his second limited and selective reading Scholes chooses the famous passage wherein Mellors compliments Connie on her proud, womanly ''arse,'' strokes ''the two secret openings of her body,'' and tells her that he is glad she shits and pisses. Here Scholes oddly finds only two points to be noted: first, that ''Connie's femininity is defined against an opposed masculinity'' since her tail is not ''like a lad's''; and second, that ''something is missing'' from the ''anatomy lecture'' that Dr. Mellors delivers ''in his charming northern dialect'': namely, an organ that ''has too much of the 'lad' in it to belong on a 'proper woman's arse' '' (138–39).

We may forgive Scholes his modest levity here but not, I think, his cultural shortsightedness. He shows no awareness, here or elsewhere, that the critique of cloacal associations with human sexuality that Lawrence made in the 1920s has any bearing on the cultural ambience of the 1980s. Yet surely all that shit and piss from the past had to be cleared away by brave writers like Joyce and Lawrence before we could even discuss the neglected clitoris. To speak now of the ''pornotopic brush'' removing blemishes from the scene is thus, in terms of cultural history, more than a little ingenuous (139). A prideful arse, unashamed of its several natural functions, seems to me an obvious precondition for a prideful clitoris; and we might even note in passing that Mellors's regard for it does not suggest a man who fears that women experience greater gratification from sex than men do. Those "button-arsed lasses as should be lads" whom he callously dismisses would presumably be less threatening than this amply proportioned woman, this wider, stormier sea for small male craft; and that Japanese locution, previously cited, recalls in turn still another oceanic passage worth mentioning, wherein Connie is likened to the sea, "nothing but dark waves rising and heaving, heaving with a great swell, so that slowly her whole darkness was in motion, and she was ocean rolling its dark, dumb mass," while far down inside her the deeps part and roll asunder in heavy billows until "the quick of all her plasm" is touched by the frail Mellors's plunging penis (*LCL* 229)—a passage, needless to say, that Scholes erases from his textual memory, perhaps because it tends to contradict his chosen version of male fears.

Nevertheless male fears abound in this novel, and with his third quotation—his pièce de résistance—Scholes raises questions of real substance about them. As with Cleland and Freud, the missing clitoral organ surfaces in Lawrence's novel as Mellors tells Connie about his marriage to the "terrible" Bertha Coutts, who liked to "grind her own coffee" in the act of love. Here is the "dramatic interaction" by which Lawrence "simply" fleshes out "the bare bones of a Freudian scenario" (140):

But she treated me with insolence. And she got so's she'd never see me when I wanted her; never. Always put me off, brutal as you like. And then when she'd put me right off, and I didn't want her, she'd come all lovey-dovey, and get me. And I always went. But when I had her, she'd never come off when I did. Never! She'd just wait. If I kept back for half an hour, she'd keep back longer. And when I'd come and really finished then she'd start on her own account, and I had to stop inside her till she brought herself off, wriggling and shouting, she'd clutch clutch with herself down there, an' then she'd come off, fair in ecstasy. And then she'd say: That was lovely! Gradually, I got sick of it: and she got worse. She sort of got harder and harder to bring off, and she'd sort of tear at me down there, as if it was a beak tearing me. By God, you think a woman's soft down there, like a fig. But I tell you the old rampers have beaks between their legs, and they tear at you with it till you're sick. Self! Self! Self! all self! tearing and shouting! They talk about men's selfishness, but I doubt if it can ever touch a woman's blind beakishness, once she's gone that way. Like an old trull! And she couldn't help it. I told her about it, I told her how I hated it. And she'd even try. She'd try to lie still and let *me* work the business. She'd try. But it was no good. She got no feeling off it, from my working. She had to work the thing herself, grind her own coffee. And it came back on her like a raving necessity; she had to let herself go, and tear, tear, tear, as if she had no sensation in her except in the top of her beak, the very outside top tip, that rubbed and tore. That's how old whores used to be, so men used to say. It was a low kind of self-will in her, a raving sort of self-will: like

in a woman who drinks. Well, in the end I couldn't stand it. We slept apart. (*LCL*
260–61)

And here is Scholes's response to it:

The supposed masculinity of Mrs. Mellors is what makes her so terrible—a masculinity expressed in her desire to take charge, to be in control of the sexual scene, but
concentrated physically in her clitoral orientation, presented metaphorically as a predatory beak. It is just such an orientation that Connie herself has given up, in moving
from her earlier, unsatisfactory lover to Mellors. Exactly as Freud does, so Lawrence,
too, orders the clitoris to cease and desist, orders women to be more ''feminine,'' to
become the perfect binary opposites that men require, and to become less sexual in the
process. (140)

"Exactly" may seem inexact, given Lawrence's well-known quarrel with
Freud, but Scholes confidently insists that their "texts are governed by the
same masculine code," shaped by the same fear of feminine sexuality, and by
the same "need to define woman as lacking what the male possesses and as
perpetually deficient without the presence of the male" (140). This easy
conflation is the "major point" of the chapter, which now concludes on a
welcome cautionary note: if—thanks to Masters and Johnson, Shere Hite, and
others—the female body may seem to have been at last uncoded in our time,
"we would perhaps do better to wonder what we have lost or hidden by this
very finding" (141). I shall speak presently to the lost or hidden assumptions
behind Scholes's semiotic argument; but for the moment I want to add to its
apparent weight.

Lawrence's desire to polarize sexual identities, even allowing for his overt
concern with bisexuality, suggests a binary message that might indeed have
affected "many other minds and texts" (140–41). In *The Plumed Serpent*
especially he rails against the kind of "white, phosphorescent ecstasy" (422)
in modern women, frictional and beakish, that seems to correspond with
Bertha's predatory ecstasy; and in the second version of *Lady Chatterley*,
called *John Thomas and Lady Jane*, he even reveals a peculiarly Freudian
trauma, as when Mellors—frightened at an early age by a glimpse of the
provocative Bertha's pubic bush—is unable to make love to her, after their
marriage, until she shaves it off—as if to prove the absence of a rival presence
there (*JTLJ* 225–26).[2] In the third *Lady Chatterley* the same sense of rivalry

2. Here too the gamekeeper explicitly complains of Bertha, "an' when she did sleep with me,
she wanted it all her own way, I was nowhere: as if she was the man, an' me the woman"
(226)—a passage that supports the fear of Bertha's masculinity in Scholes's argument, but also
indicates that greater fear of losing male identity I discuss in later pages, which seems to me to
go beyond castration anxiety. I think also that Lawrence consciously subordinates the masculinity
issue, so prominent in *John Thomas and Lady Jane*, so as to focus the *Chatterley* version of the
Bertha story on the instrumentalization problem discussed later.

seems evident in Mellors's hatred of lesbians and in his desire to kill those proto-lesbians who "put you out before you really 'come,' and go on writhing their loins till they bring themselves off against your thighs" (262). The animus is unmistakable, but the form it takes is not so much a fear of castration, or of deficiency, as of displacement, dysfunction, or exclusion from what ought to be a mutual process. And indeed the principle of mutuality is oddly absent from Scholes's discussion of the female pleasure problem, where a kind of separate but greater policy seems very much in evidence—separate, that is, from the expendable male penis and the expendable male presence. Where Lawrence claims in a lovely essay, "We Need One Another," Scholes and others now say, "No, We Don't." Their finely calibrated pleasure-meters are designed to record oral, digital, or frictional satisfactions for which either sex is serviceable, or no partner at all—as if sex were quite simply a terminal pleasure and had no bearing on the expression, deepening, and enrichment of our closest personal relations. Perhaps this is a fit response to the very real damages that women have sustained from overweening patriarchal pride and power, whether in bed or out—a kind of declaration of biological independence, our bodies being our selves, as Lawrence surely taught us; but it is a sad or at best a provisional response if the terms of mutuality are to be enriched and furthered. It is moreover an ironic response if it simply moves us from the "tyranny of the orgasm," which critics old and new have accused Lawrence of promoting, to the further "tyranny of the multiple orgasm," the Big MO, which he is now in effect accused of not promoting by my double-daring double!

The damages of the separate but greater policy are what concerned Lawrence most, I think, in his development of the Bertha story. And damages too are oddly missing from Scholes's view of the pleasure process. They are inflicted by Lawrence and Freud, of course, in their several inscriptions, but there is no evidence that other kinds of problems might affect our sexual pleasures. As most thoughtful readers of Lawrence know, there are a number of constants in his fiction that inform the wider drama of human intercourse in which sexual relations occur. He believes in and makes felt our extreme vulnerability, for instance, to emotional damages through sexual relations. On the other hand, he believes that we all bring emotional problems into such relations, and that our need to work through those problems makes conflict essential as well as hazardous to their progress. In other words, he believes that sexual conflict is not only necessary and inevitable, but that it can be creative as well as destructive, can nourish as well as diminish our emotional well-being. The Bertha story is in fact part of a longer history of destructive conflicts that Mellors recites to Connie; it matches our knowledge of her own sexual history, whereby both lovers can be likened to "a couple of battered warriors" in the modern sexual fray (264); and it is instructive to note that

Scholes nowhere places it in this context, that he ignores that "uniqueness of the literary text" he hoped in his preface to "guard against" losing (xi). But then he also loses any sense of the conflictual nature of even the most creative sexual relations, and with it the process of change, growth, and development which is Lawrence's chief concern in dealing with Connie and Mellors. It is possible to parody that concern, and to reduce it in turn to a hazardous semiotic coding, as Stephen Heath does in *The Sexual Fix* (esp. 125–28); but for the moment I want to take it seriously as it applies to the Bertha story.

Scholes touches on this process when he remarks on how Connie moves "from her earlier, unsatisfactory lover to Mellors." Connie's earlier experience with one of Clifford's parlor cronies, the stray-dog playwright Michaelis, is a complement to Mellors's experience with Bertha. But actually Michaelis is not an unsatisfactory lover, in Scholes's terms; he gives Connie her sexual satisfaction, but like the British lover in Scholes's anecdote he turns nasty when terminating their affair. Thus Michaelis uses his premature ejaculations and his fear of emotional commitment as secret excuses for accusing Connie of running the whole sexual show. But Connie is not a beakish, predatory, or controlling lover, as Michaelis charges and as Scholes implies; she is instead the injured and innocent party who had no other choice, and whose "whole sexual feeling" for her lover, "or for any man," is temporarily crushed by her lover's nastiness (*LCL* 94). It is Michaelis, then, and not Mellors, who fits Scholes's coding of the man who fears greater female sexuality. Mellors is by deliberate contrast a man with greater delaying powers who seeks sexual commitment with his wife, and his similar complaint against her as a woman who uses her clitoris as a weapon in the sexual fray, even as men use their penises, seems to be well taken.

As Mellors tells Connie, his earliest experiences before marriage were with two educated women who "loved everything about love, except the sex" (259). These experiences reflect the novel's concern with Victorian inhibitions, the overall attempt to break with taboos on sexuality from the past, especially as they apply to the sexual needs and feelings of "decent" women—a pervasive aspect of the novel that Scholes reduces to the shits and pisses passage. Then came Mellors's marriage to the commoner Bertha Coutts, a woman who wanted sex as much as he did, but whom he later likened to the "old whores" in a kind of throwback to Victorian sex and class divisions. Mellors tells Connie that he entered that marriage "in a state of murder" (260), and later admits to her that he is inwardly mistrustful, a "broken-backed snake" himself with women who wanted to love him "properly" but couldn't (265). More interesting still, when Connie says he may have had "too much of a good thing" with Bertha, which corresponds with Scholes's charge of male fear of female sexual response, Mellors says that he would rather have Bertha than "the never-never ones" (262).

The long sequence on Bertha (259–62) bears these many-sided matters out. It is Bertha who is so displeased with Mellors's inordinate sexual pleasure, for instance, especially when he brings her breakfast in bed, that she begins to despise him for it, treats him with insolence, puts him off until he doesn't want sex, then becomes "lovey-dovey" (260), but with the new twist of deliberately holding back until he finishes, even when he keeps back himself for half an hour. Meanwhile their sexual antagonism alternates with murderous kitchen battles. What Mellors objects to then is the breakdown of mutuality between them, whether in bed or out. He attributes this breakdown to her selfishness and self-will, as expressed through the blind beakishness of her separate comings. That his own willfulness has contributed equally to the vicious conflict is underscored, a bit later, when he accuses Connie of self-importance, and she finds him guilty of the same fault, then acts to resolve *their* quarrel by asking what has come between them. The answer of course is the Bertha story itself, which has revived all those murderous feelings in Mellors (266–67).

It is not so much Bertha's masculinity that makes her "terrible," then; nor does her clitoris per se trouble Mellors: it is the willful, hardened, and perhaps "common" way she uses her pelvis to reduce him to a mere instrument for her own sexual pleasure, a power game that men also play, as Lawrence had previously shown with the machismo industrialist Gerald Crich in *Women in Love*. In asking Bertha to let him control their love-making, moreover, Mellors is opting for that mutual satisfaction through vaginal orgasm that Lawrence considered "proper" in the 1920s, with the male in the old missionary position and the female mutually active. He could not have known at that time—it was not confirmed till the Masters and Johnson reports of 1966 and 1970—that the clitoris triggers even vaginal orgasms, a much debated issue in the 1960s and 1970s but not before.[3]

It seems clear, nonetheless, that Mellors mistrusts female predominance of any kind, including the female superior position and those oral-genital shenanigans, so popular in our time, which he doesn't even try to imagine. It is here that Scholes's charges, as I am now going to qualify them, hold most weight. What Lawrence could not seem to allow, along with female predominance, was the extension of mutuality to the kind of sequential satisfactions that occur, among today's unselfish lovers, either as variations or when simultaneous orgasms fail to happen. He was by our current promiscuous standards a relatively inexperienced lover, with only two known partners and

3. See William H. Masters and Virginia E. Johnson, *Human Sexual Response* (1966) and *Human Sexual Inadequacy* (1970), both published in Boston by Little, Brown. See also my essay, "Lessing and Lawrence: The Battle of the Sexes," *Contemporary Literature* 16 (1975): 218–40.

two never-nevers before the long marriage with Frieda and the late impotent pass at Dorothy Brett. Even that "battered warrior" Mellors, though he alludes to wider experience, cites only three women he has known carnally before Connie. And like Lawrence himself he also suffers from oral as well as anal hangups, only the latter of which have received much attention.[4] These curiously limiting conditions for sexual prophecy may help to explain the novel's present quaintness as a guide to sexual pleasures, whether for male *or* female readers.

They are the conditions, nonetheless, through which Lawrence spoke with prophetic acuteness to contemporary problems. Mellors's fear of female predominance is our own case in point. As his anal hangups help to show, he is trying to work through insecurities as to male identity—problems of shame, self-doubt, and hostility that require purging if he is to affirm selfhood and eschew dominance himself, and that also require a woman willing to make the same hazardous struggle.[5] This attempt to separate identity from dominance in both sexes is, I think, what makes *Lady Chatterley* still interesting in our time, especially when we consider its connection with the smashing of traditional values in the First World War, when the expendability of men and marriage was made so evident through mass slaughter in the trenches and mass promiscuity at home and abroad. It was in that disruptive context that Lawrence tried to redefine marriage as essentially a sexual bond, and to ensure its mutuality by securing both male and female identities from their power-seeking propensities and, conversely, their threatened loss.

However one feels about that impressive effort, it does help to explain, if not exonerate, Mellors's tenacious hold on male presence and on the male superior position, and his insistence too on being the more active partner. But more important is his invocation, in the Bertha chapter, of warmheartedness in lovemaking, another easy target for semiotic coding until we remember its connection with vulnerability, on the one hand, and with necessary conflict on the other. The one thing Mellors believes, that through warmhearted fucking "everything would come all right," is not then an oversimple prescription but an invocation of what makes the novel revolutionary even today: its attempt to achieve heartfelt intimacy through sexual relations, without benefit of

4. See, however, Judith Ruderman's comments on Lawrence's oral problems in *D. H. Lawrence and the Devouring Mother: The Search for a Patriarchal Ideal of Leadership* (Durham, N.C.: Duke UP, 1984), especially pages 8–16 on his life and, for example, 94–96 on his work.

5. See in this regard my essay, "On Lawrence's Hostility to Willful Women: The Chatterley Solution," in *Lawrence and Women*, ed. Anne Smith (New York: Barnes & Noble, 1978), 189–211; and chapter 3 of Michael Squires's *The Creation of "Lady Chatterley's Lover"* (Baltimore: Johns Hopkins UP, 1983), which traces the gamekeeper's insecurity through the three versions of the novel.

previous courtship and in defiance of the kind of asexual intimacy that
Clifford Chatterley posits as the real basis of marriage. This dramatized but
unstated premise is the *Chatterley* experience par excellence, and is today for
better and perhaps worse a contemporary *modus amandi*. Our secret desire,
indeed our secret need, is to release and express our repressed affections
through sexual relations, and it has been so ever since the Victorians made
the affections hazardous to mental and emotional health, as Lawrence early
understood.

"Shall I tell you what you have . . . that will make the future?" says
Connie to Mellors in the penultimate chapter. "It's the courage of your own
tenderness . . . like when you put your hand on my tail and say I've got a
pretty tail" (346). We may wish now that he had said "pretty clitoris" instead
of "pretty tail," but the fact that it takes courage to praise either the region
or the organ, and that tenderness is thereby expressed, indicates how afraid
we have become of all such tender feelings. And here Mellors's persistent fear
of female affections, along with his own, seems to me more significant for the
novel, and for our time, than any proposed fear of female sexuality.[6] My
double to the contrary notwithstanding, sexuality is what Mellors is sure of;
it's real, it's solid, it's deep, it's where love itself is to be found in our crazy
age, if we can agree on the right way to do it, without discovering beforehand
who we are and why we want as well as need each other. All we know now,
thanks to Lawrence, is to find a pridefully tender sparring partner who won't
do us in, and to be one ourselves: a formula that has worked for gays and
lesbians as well as heteros in recent times, again largely thanks to Lawrence,
and may serve us all till the affections too are liberated and can emerge—as
they now seem to be doing—from their long cultural hibernation.

WORKS CITED

Heath, Stephen. *The Sexual Fix*. New York: Schocken, 1984.
Lawrence, D. H. *John Thomas and Lady Jane*. New York: Viking, 1972.
Lawrence, D. H. *Lady Chatterley's Lover*. New York: Grove, 1959.
Lawrence, D. H. *The Plumed Serpent*. Ed. L. D. Clark. Cambridge: Cambridge UP,
    1987.
Scholes, Robert. *Semiotics and Interpretation*. New Haven: Yale UP, 1982.

6. See in this regard my essay, "Lawrence's Quarrel with Tenderness," *Critical Quarterly* 9
(1967): 363–77.

CHAPTER 13

Lawrence and Recent American Poetry

ALAN GOLDING

Few Lawrentians have ever defended R. P. Blackmur's notorious and influential essay "D. H. Lawrence and Expressive Form" (1935). I wish to do that. I believe Blackmur understood Lawrence's poetics better than is usually acknowledged, and better than even he himself admitted. After all, he describes accurately what most later critics have thought a central virtue of Lawrence's poetry, finding in the work "a kind of furious underlying honesty of observation" (297) and praising the way Lawrence "intensified his private apprehension," even though, in Blackmur's view, he failed to develop "an external form" to match it (290). And beneath this railing against Lawrence's inadequacies as a poetic craftsman, Blackmur seems to know that Lawrence's alleged technical slackness was a conscious rhetorical strategy. He found in Lawrence an "increasing disregard of the control of rationally conceived form" (296); but the "absence of the advantages of craft," he saw, "is not particularly due to [Lawrence's] inability to use them, but to a lack of interest" (288). Terms like "increasing disregard" and "lack of interest" presume just the kind of artistic self-consciousness in Lawrence that Blackmur spends most of the essay denying. Indeed, in "Lord Tennyson's Scissors" (1951) Blackmur allows that Lawrence left "lasting poems naked as the sensibility itself," "self-willed marvels of craft" with an "absolute flair for meaning by rhythm" (433). Even in denouncing Lawrence, Blackmur calls him "one of the most powerfully articulate minds of the last generation," a poet of real "potential magnitude" ("D. H. Lawrence" 293, 290). All of these remarks suggest that Blackmur may have taken Lawrence's poetry more seriously than he claims, and that he understood certain features of Lawrence's poetics perfectly well.[1]

---

1. After I completed this essay, another appeared that touches on similar topics: Roberts W.

I have mentioned the ways in which Blackmur understood Lawrence's poetry accurately to contrast with what I find most striking about his essay: his failure to pursue this germinal understanding. In his wariness of the biographical fallacy and his New Critical commitment to tight structure, tonal complexity, and density of implication, he cannot finally account for poems that are not intended as well-wrought urns. The limitations of his method lead him to make his misguided remarks on, for instance, Lawrence's "uneven, lopsided metrical architecture" ("D. H. Lawrence" 291). Donald Davie's apt response to this comment is representative of later critics who are more sympathetic to Lawrence:

> This is true, and it is well said. It is also quite irrelevant. The whole notion of "metrical architecture," all the cluster of metaphors and analogies which lies behind such an expression, was entirely foreign to Lawrence's way of thinking about what it was he did when he wrote poems. (*Thomas Hardy* 146)

Fine critic though he was, Blackmur lacked the flexibility to bring other tools to bear on reading Lawrence's poetry when his own didn't work.

Further evidence that modernist critical assumptions could not accommodate Lawrence's poetry appears in I. A. Richards's *Practical Criticism*. Richards used Lawrence's "Piano" in his famous experiment with Cambridge undergraduates, and only one poem out of the thirteen he used received a higher number of unfavorable responses. Like Blackmur a few years later, Richards's young readers, who clearly prided themselves on their close reading ability, objected to Lawrence's supposed technical incompetence. Some sample comments: "A good example of feeling without artistry. The man evidently means everything he says, but he doesn't know how to say it"; "I find some charm in the thoughts but *none in the verse or very little*" (104); "the subject matter is appealing; the picture given in the first verse is vivid and original. *The metre, however, detracts considerably from the* poem" (107).

Blackmur's essay and Richards's experiment are only two well-known examples that illustrate a general trend in the reception of Lawrence's poetry. Sandra Gilbert summarizes one reason for that reception:

> Perhaps a major reason for the prolonged neglect of Lawrence's verse is that . . . his view of poetry was the exception rather than the rule in the earlier part of this

---

French, "Lawrence and American Poetry," *The Legacy of D. H. Lawrence: New Essays*, ed. Jeffrey Meyers (New York: St. Martin's, 1987) 109–34. French and I overlap in some of our concerns—Lawrence's relationship to Karl Shapiro, Theodore Roethke, Charles Olson, and confessional poetry, and his violation of New Critical reading canons. But I have chosen to devote more space than does French to the latter three topics. Furthermore, unlike French, I have tried to focus as much on matters of style and structure as on matters of theme and philosophical stance. This seems to me the most reliable way to establish one poet's influence on another.

century. He himself was well aware that as a poetic theorist he consistently opposed contemporary critical opinion and, to a lesser extent, prevailing poetic practice. For one thing, his view of a poem as a pure act of attention, an act of absolute surrender to the visionary image, was very much at odds with the emerging belief of critics—and of many influential poets—that the essential qualities of poetry are irony, ambiguity, and paradox. (9)[2]

Many critics have countered Blackmur's view especially, usually occupying one of the two positions laid out by Ross Murfin (xi) in his book on Lawrence's poetry. Position One is that, far from "being frenzied, hysterical, and without craftsmanship," the poems are "carefully and even rather traditionally crafted." Position Two is "that technique is not the *sine qua non* of all great poetry" (a view proposed, interestingly, by that consummate technician W. H. Auden).

Both these positions, especially the second, are valid defenses of Lawrence. But still a third is possible: namely, to assess the value of Lawrence's poetry and poetic theory by way of its importance to the poets who have come after him. Although Lawrence's differences from most other Anglo-American modernists have led to critics underestimating or misreading his poetry, those differences have also made him a powerful influence on recent American poets looking for alternative or additional poetic models outside the intimidating examples of Yeats, Eliot, Pound, and Stevens. There is one significant exception to the claims I will make about Lawrence's differences from his peers: William Carlos Williams. Among the major modernists, it is Williams who most resembles Lawrence in his poetics, and in many ways his importance to later poets has paralleled or complemented Lawrence's. Lawrence favorably reviewed *In the American Grain* (*Phoenix* 334–36) and recommended it to friends (Nehls 290); Williams thought equally well of Lawrence, and wrote a moving elegy on his death.[3] Yet even Williams, or at least the

2. For reinforcement of Gilbert's view, see A. Walton Litz, "Lawrence, Pound, and Early Modernism," *D. H. Lawrence: A Centenary Consideration*, ed. Peter Balbert and Phillip C. Marcus (Ithaca: Cornell UP, 1985): "When ['Poetry of the Present'] and the poems of *Look! We Have Come Through!* are read against the poetry and criticism Pound and Eliot were writing at the time, a series of either/or choices emerges that has determined the shape of later criticism, not only of Lawrence but of modernist literature in general: either openness or closure, either the temporal sequence or the spatial image, either expressive form or the rational inspiration, either the confessional mode or a poetry of 'impersonality'" (27–28).

3. Williams's "An Elegy for D. H. Lawrence" is given its own section in *The Collected Earlier Poems of William Carlos Williams* (New York: New Directions, 1966) 359. Mike Weaver discusses Williams's interest in Lawrence in *William Carlos Williams: The American Background* (Cambridge: Cambridge UP, 1971) 149–51. Donald Davie argues for the influence of *Studies in Classic American Literature* on *In the American Grain* in "The Legacy of Fenimore Cooper," *Essays in Criticism* 9 (1959): 222–38; so too does Thomas R. Whitaker in *William*

pre-*Paterson* Williams, was a poet of his age in stressing craft, the poem as a made object. Lawrence might have described a poem as "a small (or large) organism made of words." Unlike Williams, he would never have described it as "a small (or large) machine made of words," and unlike Williams he never preached the high modernist value of "perfect economy" (Williams 256). From the other poets mentioned Lawrence was even further removed, and at this distance his work anticipates many of the characteristics that separate much postmodern American poetry from the modernism of the twenties and thirties. The features of Lawrence's poetry that did separate him from his modernist contemporaries and that have attracted recent poets are my subject in this essay.

First, I should justify my focus on recent *American* poets. Highly regarded as a novelist, Lawrence as a poet has remained a prophet without honor in his own land. His influence on Ted Hughes is generally acknowledged, and, surprisingly, one can sometimes detect his presence in Philip Larkin's work. But although D. J. Enright, Elizabeth Jennings, and Edward Lucie-Smith have all written sympathetically on Lawrence, their own poetry shows little evidence of his influence, and generally one can trace few convincing lines of connection between Lawrence and most established post–World War II British poets.[4] Between Lawrence and American poets, however, those lines are many.

Commentary abounds on Lawrence's poetic roots in Whitman, Hardy, Swinburne, Shelley, and Blake—all poets, incidentally, whose stock plummeted during the modernist era. Less has been written on his importance to poets who followed him, and much of that criticism assumes that Lawrence affected later poetic theory more than poetic practice, that his influence has

---

Carlos Williams (Boston: Twayne, 1968) 78. The relationship between Williams's and Lawrence's poetry is discussed in two reviews of Williams's *Collected Poems* (1938) by Horace Gregory, *New York Herald Tribune,* 5 Feb. 1939, Books Section, p. 10, and Ruth Lechlitner, *Poetry* 54 (1939): 326–35.

4. The absence of any strong Lawrentian influence in recent British poetry is argued at greater length by William Chace, "Lawrence and English Poetry," *The Legacy of D. H. Lawrence: New Essays,* ed. Jeffrey Meyers (New York: St. Martin's, 1987) 54–80. For thorough commentary on Lawrence and Hughes, see Randy Brandes, "The Myth of the Fall in the Poetry of D. H. Lawrence and Ted Hughes," Diss. Emory U, 1985; for a shorter but more easily available discussion see Keith Sagar, *The Art of Ted Hughes* (Cambridge: Cambridge UP, 1975) 38–45. On Lawrence and Larkin, see Terry Whalen, "Lawrence and Larkin: The Suggestion of an Affinity," *Modernist Studies* 4 (1982): 105–22. Larkin mentions his enthusiasm for Lawrence's poetry at a number of points in his *Required Writing: Miscellaneous Pieces 1955–1982* (New York: Farrar, Straus & Giroux, 1984). Enright, Jennings, and Lucie-Smith discuss Lawrence in, respectively, *Conspirators and Poets* (London: Chatto & Windus, 1966) 95–101; *Seven Men of Vision: An Appreciation* (London: Vision, 1976) 45–80; and "The Poetry of D. H. Lawrence— With a Glance at Shelley," in *D. H. Lawrence: Novelist, Poet, Prophet,* ed. Stephen Spender (London: Weidenfeld & Nicholson, 1973) 224–33. For a dissenting opinion on Lawrence's influence on Enright, see M. L. Rosenthal, *The New Poets: British and American Poetry Since World War II* (New York: Oxford UP, 1967), who argues that Enright "sometimes sounds a more rational Lawrence" (222).

been attitudinal or philosophical rather than technical. M. L. Rosenthal, for instance, thinks Lawrence has had an "extraordinary influence" on recent poets, but not because of his style, since "of all modern poets of real standing, he is perhaps the shakiest as a master of his craft" (160, 168). Similarly, R. P. Draper argues that in England the influence of Lawrence's poetry has been "greater on the thought and feeling of writers than on their methods of composition" (169). Donald Davie observes that "Lawrence's use of free verse or of 'open form' is in no way a paradigm of what has been and is still normal practice in these modes" (*Thomas Hardy* 146). And W. H. Auden writes that when he first read Lawrence in the late 1920s, he was more impressed by Lawrence's "message" than his technique (278).

Balancing this view is the testimony of a poet like Theodore Roethke, who learned some of his major stylistic lessons from Lawrence. Roethke, who first read Lawrence in 1930, learned especially from his predecessor's handling of rhythm and the poetic line. In the essay "Some Remarks on Rhythm" (1960) he describes how the free-verse poet "can vary his line length, modulate, he can stretch out the line, he can shorten." Roethke thought Lawrence "a master of this sort of poem," relating his own penchant for successively shortening or lengthening lines to the extreme variety of line length in Lawrence's mature work (*On the Poet* 82–83). As an example of his debt to Lawrence, Roethke uses one of his best-known poems, "Elegy for Jane." Here is its first stanza:

> I remember the neckcurls limp and damp as tendrils;
> And her quick look, a sidelong pickerel smile;
> And how, once startled into talk, the light syllables leaped for her,
> And she balanced in the delight of her thought,
> A wren, happy, tail into the wind,
> Her song trembling the twigs and small branches.
> The shade sang with her;
> the leaves, their whispers turned to kissing;
> And the mold sang in the bleached valleys under the rose.
>   (*Collected Poems* 98)

Roethke details his use of Lawrentian techniques thus:

"I remember," then the listing, the appositions, and the absolute construction. "Her song trembling," etc. Then the last three lines in the stanza lengthen out. . . . A kind of continuing triad. In the last two stanzas exactly the opposite occurs. . . . There is a successive shortening of the line length, an effect I have become inordinately fond of, I'm afraid. (*On the Poet* 82)

Roethke clearly alludes in this account to a stanza of "Tortoise Shout," which begins seven of its first nine lines with the phrase "I remember" and then continues via "listing" and "appositions":

I remember the scream of a terrified, injured horse, the sheet-lightning,
And running away from the sound of a woman in labour, something like an owl
    whooing,
And listening inwardly to the first bleat of a lamb,
The first wail of an infant,
And my mother singing to herself. . . .

(*CP* 366)

The stanza ends with that "shortening of the line length" that Roethke says
he habitually uses:

And the first tenor singing of the passionate throat of a young collier, who has
    long since drunk himself to death,
The first elements of foreign speech
On wild dark lips.

In "Some Remarks on Rhythm" Roethke explains his position further by
quoting Lawrence's well-known letter of 1913 to Edward Marsh: "It all
depends on the *pause*—the natural pause, the natural *lingering* of the voice
according to the feeling—it is the hidden *emotional* pattern that makes poetry,
not the obvious form" (*Letters* II: 104). Also relevant here is another letter of
1913 to Marsh, again reprinted widely enough for Roethke to have known it:
"I think, don't you know, that my rhythms fit my mood pretty well, in the
verse. And if the mood is out of joint, the rhythm often is. I have always tried
to get an emotion out in its own course, without altering it" (*Letters* II: 61).
Roethke translates these principles into the assertion that the poet must work
with "the breath unit, the language that is natural to the immediate thing, the
particular emotion" (*On the Poet* 83). Thinking of Lawrence's stress on the
immediate, the particular, and at the same time commenting on his own poetic
goals and what he calls in one poem his "terrible hunger for objects" (*Collected Poems* 212),[5] Roethke adds, "We need the eye close on the object, and
the poem about the single incident—the animal, the child. We must permit
poetry to extend consciousness as far, as deeply, as particularly as it can" (*On
the Poet* 83). As Jenijoy La Belle has shown (145–48), the effect of Lawrence's intense particularity and concentration shows especially in Roethke's
poems about animals. La Belle convincingly links Lawrence's "Snake" (*CP*
349) with Roethke's "The Meadow Mouse" (*Collected Poems* 219),
"Lizard" and "St. Mark" (*CP* 524, 323) with "The Lizard" (*Collected
Poems* 218), "Fish" (*CP* 334) with "The Pike" (*Collected Poems* 225), and

5. Compare with this phrase from Roethke's "The Abyss" Lawrence's "this ache for being
is the ultimate hunger" (*CP* 265).

"Red Geranium and Godly Mignonette" (*CP* 690) with "The Geranium" (*Collected Poems* 220).[6]

In my view Lawrence—primarily the Lawrence of *Look! We Have Come Through!* and later volumes—has influenced the theory *and* practice of many recent poets. Although his overall impact may not have been as great as that of Pound, Williams, or Stevens, there remain certain features of postmodern poetry that Lawrence anticipated more fully than any other modernist. I have already hinted at the first such feature: the reduced stress on the poem as artifact. When Lawrence describes a peach, he takes pleasure in the fact that it is not "round and finished like a billiard ball"—or, we might say, like a certain kind of poem. But, he adds, "it would have been if man had made it" (*CP* 279). In his most important poetic manifesto, "Poetry of the Present," he programmatically rejects a poetry of "exquisite form" and "perfect symmetry," the "crystalline, pearl-hard jewels" and "unfading timeless gems" that a New Critic like Blackmur looked for in poetry (*CP* 182–83). Throughout his comments on poetry, as indeed throughout his career in all genres, Lawrence equates perfect, finished form with death. Years before the "Poetry of the Present" essay, in 1913, he had written to Edward Marsh, "Remember skilled verse is dead in fifty years" (*Letters* II: 61). And in a letter of 1909 to Blanche Jennings, he set "beautiful dying decadent things with sad odors" against his own ambition to write "live things, if crude and half formed" (*Letters* I: 108).

This desire to shatter the well-wrought urn resurfaced in many later American poets, from an established figure like Robert Lowell, who shifted his style in the 1950s due to his impatience with a density of craft that stifled poetic emotion, to a more marginal but still influential figure like Charles Olson. Lowell suggests strongly that Lawrence influenced his move toward greater prosodic freedom in *Life Studies*. He writes of "Lawrence's bird and animal poems" as being among those poems, along with the work of Whitman, Pound, and Williams, that proved to him "the glory of free verse," "poems that would be thoroughly marred and would indeed be inconceivable in meter" (124). Olson's important manifesto "Projective Verse" echoes the attacks in "Poetry of the Present" (also published under the title "Verse Free and Unfree") on what Lawrence called "restricted, limited unfree verse" (*CP* 184). Olson translates Lawrence's distinction between "free" and "unfree" verse into one between "projective" (or "open") and "closed" verse. Lawrence's example encouraged Olson and others to court formal untidiness, to write purposely unpolished poetry. As he

---

6. Cf. also Jerome Mazzaro, *Postmodern American Poetry* (Urbana: U of Illinois P, 1980): "Roethke's handling of nature is closer to the Lawrence of *Birds, Beasts and Flowers* . . . than to any other modern poet" (71).

writes in the poem "These Days," Olson felt committed to leaving the rough edges on his work:

> Whatever you have to say, leave
> the roots on, let them
> dangle
> And the dirt
>   just to make clear
>   where they came from.

(Archaeologist 13)

Lawrence provides a precedent for such a poetics. He said of his own free verse, "There is some confusion, some discord. But the confusion and the discord only belong to the reality as noise belongs to the plunge of water" (*CP* 184). Typically Lawrence compiles an accurate description through lists of images and similes, none of which he accords the privilege of being "right." He exploits a combination of accumulation, substitution, and repetition. Often he will use an anaphoric list: "this small bird, this rudiment, / This little dome, this pediment / Of all creation, / This slow one" (*CP* 356). Just as often, he will repeat a phrase and either add or substitute modifiers—"Made of thick smooth silver, / Made of sweet, untarnished silver" (*CP* 298). Elsewhere he will repeat but invert: "Rock, waves of dark heat; / Waves of dark heat, rock" (*CP* 302). Lawrence also relishes multiple oxymorons that verge on flat contradiction, as in the image of fig-tree branches "dull / With the life-lustre" of a "dim light" "that is always half-dark" (*CP* 298). Often he will foreground the difficulty he has finding *le mot juste* by using adjectives like *weird, queer,* or *strange.* He will undermine the authority of his own perspective ("I had made a mistake" [*CP* 338]), and will even correct himself in mid-poem but not edit out his "mistake": "I say untarnished, but I mean opaque—" (*CP* 298). As Wayne Booth remarks earlier in this volume (pages 11–12), this procedure risks that a reader may mistake a conscious poetic strategy for more of the slack copy editing that sometimes characterizes Lawrence's writing, and thus "take as careless much that is actually deliberate and fresh." But the apparent carelessness is very frequently rhetorical strategy. In Olson's words, these various tropes of "confusion and discord" show how Lawrence leaves the roots and the dirt on, how the poems preserve or discuss the process of their own creation.[7]

In rejecting the poem as artifact, many recent poets have come to see poetic form as a process rather than a product. Again Lawrence provides them with a model. In "Poetry of the Present" Lawrence describes formally traditional poetry as "the poetry of the beginning and the poetry of the end" (*CP* 181).

---

7. For an extended discussion of this feature of Lawrence's style, see Gilbert (131–46).

These terms mean little as description, but they do suggest a poetry distanced from the "present" of the individual writing. Lawrence's alternative is "the poetry of that which is at hand: the immediate present," a poetry of "the immediate, instant self" (*CP* 182, 185). One central characteristic of the poetry of the present is that it cannot be planned, shaped in the imagination before the actual writing. As Lawrence writes in "The Work of Creation," "Even an artist knows that his work was never in his mind, / he could never have *thought* it before it happened" (*CP* 690). This view of form as something evolving, unpredictable, in flux is central to much postmodern American poetry. One can again turn to Olson for its most influential recent articulation. Olson's dogma about what a poetry of "the immediate present" requires is by now familiar:

ONE PERCEPTION MUST IMMEDIATELY AND DIRECTLY LEAD TO A FURTHER PERCEPTION. It means exactly what it says, is a matter of, at *all* points (even, I should say, of our management of daily reality as of the daily work) get on with it, keep moving, keep, speed, the nerves, their speed, the perceptions, theirs, the acts, the split second acts, the whole business, keep it moving as fast as you can, citizen. And if you also set up as a poet, USE USE USE the process at all points, in any given poem always, always one perception must must must MOVE, INSTANTER, ON ANOTHER! (*Selected Writings* 17)

The rhythm of this passage from "Projective Verse," as much as its content, shows what Lawrence's stress on the "instant" and the "immediate" meant to Olson. Only a few months after writing "Projective Verse," Olson told Robert Creeley how compelling he found the implied assertion in both Creeley's and Lawrence's work that "I [the writer] don't know any more than you [the reader] do . . . where this is going to get us on the next page. . . ." Creeley agreed that Lawrence was at his best when he wrote "with no planned intent" but "deadly, when [writing] a calculated, planned for: gig" (Olson and Creeley III: 61; IV: 76).

The privilege that Lawrence accords the idea of form as process and the concomitantly reduced status of the poem as artifact result in a poetics that tends to deemphasize closure and to undermine the boundaries of the poem. The single poem becomes less important than the relationship between poems, and the poet works and thinks in sequences. Graham Hough suggested early that Lawrence's verse be read as an extended single poem or "long verse-journal," as "the development of an intelligible train of feeling through a number of fragmentary occasions" (195). It is "poetry rather than poems—a body of work poetically felt and conceived whose individual units rarely reach perfection or self-subsistence" (191). Certainly both Lawrence's poetry and his comments on it show that he wanted his work to be read as a sequence. Probably his best-known "sequence" is the six tortoise poems which Lawrence published as a separate book in America in 1921 before their appearance in *Birds, Beasts and Flowers*. The tendency to make a whole book out of sequences, however, appears as early as *Look! We Have Come Through!*[8] About this volume Lawrence said, "These poems should not be considered separately, as so many single pieces. They are intended as an essential story, or history, or confession" (*CP* 191). The satiric pieces of *Pansies*, Lawrence's "little bunch of fragments" (*CP* 417), and *Nettles* anticipate contemporary books of satiric epigrams like Edward Dorn's *Hello, La Jolla*, and *Yellow Lola*, which also depend on accumulation for their effect. And *Last Poems* consists of a sequence of sequences: the five poems on the relationship between body and spirit beginning with "Demiurge"; the four poems on the knowledge of self apart from God beginning with "The Hands of God"; the four meditations on salt beginning with "Salt." Not only are the poems in these last sequences related thematically, but it is not even clear that they need to be separate poems.

Lawrence's use of the sequence yields results different from poems like the *Cantos, Hugh Selwyn Mauberley*, or *The Bridge*, where each individual part is intended as a separate entity. Two of Lawrence's tortoise poems could be combined without detriment to either; two *Cantos* could not. The implied argument of Lawrence's sequences is that boundaries between poems are finally artificial, a position that many postmodern poets have found appealing. Here is Robert Creeley, who once remarked punningly that "Lawrence is worth 50,000 Pounds in any market" (Olson and Creeley II: 126), writing on a significant shift in his poetics: "Sometime in the mid-sixties I grew inexorably bored with the tidy containment of clusters of words on single pieces of paper called 'poems' " (*Was That a Real Poem* 103). The result of this shift for Creeley is that "the concept of poems as set instances of articulate statement yields to a sense of continuity" (Faas 186). Many of the poets most affected by Lawrence have worked in sequences as much as individual

8. Gail Porter Mandell has shown that Lawrence grouped poems in clusters or mini-sequences *within books* from the beginning; see Mandell, *The Phoenix Paradox: A Study of Renewal Through Change in the Collected Poems and Last Poems of D. H. Lawrence* (Carbondale: Southern Illinois UP, 1984) 10–12. Only with *Look!* did Lawrence start to think of a whole book as a sequence, and apparently came to view his whole canon as "a biography of an emotional and inner life" (*CP* 27) when he compiled the *Collected Poems* of 1928.

Two essays on Lawrence as self-consciously a writer of poetic sequences are Jeffrey Herrick, "The Vision of *Look! We Have Come Through!*" *D. H. Lawrence Reivew* 14 (1981): 217–37; and Jay Dougherty, " 'Vein of Fire': Relationships Among Lawrence's *Pansies*," *D. H. Lawrence Review* 16 (1982): 303–30. For a book-length argument that "the sequence is . . . a fundamental unit of poetic composition" and that Lawrence's sequences reflect an ongoing process of self-shaping, "a sequence of identities" or "a series of stories Lawrence told about himself," see Holly A. Laird, *Self and Sequence: The Poetry of D. H. Lawrence* (Charlottesville: UP of Virginia, 1988) x, viii. Laird's valuable study appeared too late for use in the current essay.

poems: some of Roethke's most highly regarded poetry occurs in "North American Sequence"; Olson's major work is a lifelong sequence, *The Maximus Poems;* Robert Duncan continued his "Passages" and "Structure of Rime" series until his death, scattering their individual parts apparently at random through the rest of his work; Creeley has organized much of his work since *Pieces* (1969) on the principle that a poet's work "all goes together as one continuing writing. To make divisions in it is a little specious . . ." (Creeley, *Contexts* 101).

Just as Lawrence often blurred the boundaries between poems, he also blurred the distinction between art and life in ways that are more typical of postmodernist than of modernist poetry. For Lawrence, this identification of poetry and life helps justify his writing in sequences. If a poet's words are to be identified with his life, then one cannot say where one moment or poem ends and the next begins. Creeley's *Pieces,* as I have suggested, is one recent book that embodies this belief. *Pieces* is a sequence of fragments, often only two or three words long. It is often impossible to separate individual poems; in fact, if we look for anything resembling the usual poem (with a title, and a visible beginning and end), we'll be lost. The book's form "comes and goes / in a moment," a process continually completing itself but, in the sense of achieving formal poetic closure, never actually completed (Creeley, *Collected Poems* 382).

One can put the identification of art and life another way: the voice of Lawrence the poet is the voice of Lawrence the man. Auden asserts that "it is doubtful if a writer ever existed who had less of an artistic *persona* than Lawrence" (288). Vivian de Sola Pinto implicitly agrees by titling his introduction to the *Complete Poems* "D. H. Lawrence: Poet Without a Mask." In this regard Lawrence was years ahead of his time. In 1913 he called for "passionate poets"; "the time to be impersonal has gone" (*Selected Literary Criticism* 74), when for his modernist contemporaries it had barely arrived. Of a Ralph Hodgson poem he complains, "Only here and there is the least touch of personality in the poem" (*Letters* II: 92). Not coincidentally, Eliot, that great champion of impersonality, criticized Lawrence's poetry more heavily than that of any other modernist poet. Yet Eliot, master of the ironic persona, has had less effect on contemporary American poetry than any of his peers, to the extent that Paul Bové can claim, too sweepingly but still with some accuracy, that "postmodern poetry . . . is modelled upon nonironic poets like Whitman, Lawrence, and W. C. Williams" (96).[9]

In describing the personal nature of his poetry, Lawrence remarks that many of his poems "are what one might call fictional" (*CP* 27) and play no

---

9. In further support of my discussion of Blackmur, Bové's third chapter contains an excellent analysis of why New Critical methods do not work on "open form" poetry like Lawrence's.

part in his biography. Elsewhere he writes of "the less immediate, the more fictional poems" (*CP* 850) that he wrote in more traditional forms. Lawrence could use a persona if he chose, just as he could write a well-crafted poem if he chose. He simply had little interest in doing so. He speaks *sincerely:* "Before everything I like sincerity, and a quickening spontaneous emotion" (*Letters* I: 63). Sincerity is a slippery notion, of course. Skeptical contemporary readers are likely to see it as a rhetorical strategy in itself. Most "sincere" poetry, from *Lyrical Ballads* to Robert Lowell's *Life Studies,* has also been highly self-conscious poetry. Nevertheless, many recent poets have valued personal presence, speaking *in propria persona* rather than in a borrowed persona such as Eliot's J. Alfred Prufrock or Stevens's Comedian as the Letter C. Lawrence, more than any other modernist, provided a model for such direct speaking. In particular, some of Lawrence's early love poems and *Look! We Have Come Through!* anticipate the so-called confessional poetry of Lowell, W. D. Snodgrass, Sylvia Plath, and Anne Sexton, even though these later poets laced their confessions with irony. Both Sandra Gilbert and Joyce Carol Oates have noted the continuity between Lawrence's work and this aspect of recent poetry; Oates argues that *Look!* is "perhaps the first of the frank, embarrassingly intimate confessional books of poetry commonplace today" (47).[10] As Lawrence writes in "Grapes," "Ours is the universe of the unfolded rose, / The explicit / The candid revelation" (*CP* 285). Typical of one dominant note in *Look!* are passages like this from "First Morning" that combine oppressive imagery and direct, first-person statement to detail the pain of personal relations:

> In the darkness
>> With the pale dawn seething at the window
>> through the black frame
>> I could not be free,
>> not free myself from the past, those others—
>> and our love was a confusion,
>> there was a horror,
>> you recoiled away from me.

> (*CP* 204)

Lawrence himself calls *Look!* "confession." And in his note written in 1928 to *Collected Poems,* he admits "many of the poems are so personal that . . . they make up a biography of an emotional and inner life" (*CP* 27)—not a claim that can be extended to other modernists, but one that can be extended to the more recent poets I have mentioned.

This passage from Lawrence's "Mutilation," in *Look!,* with its combina-

---

10. See Gilbert (60–69) for a longer discussion of Lawrence and confessional poetry, to which I am much indebted in this paragraph.

tion of violent imagery, short, end-stopped lines, and sense of horror barely controlled by the flatly declarative syntax, could easily come from any of the confessional poets that I have mentioned:

> A thick mist-sheet lies over the broken wheat.
> I walk up to my neck in mist, holding my mouth up.
> Across there, a discoloured moon burns itself out.
>
> I hold the night in horror;
> I dare not turn round.
>
> (*CP* 212)

In another poem from *Look!*, ''In the Dark,'' Lawrence shows his rare ability to give female anger toward the male a voice, doing so through images of darkness. Here the woman's tears are ''a sound subdued in the darkness,'' and she says to her lover, ''*Ah, you are horrible; / You stand before me like ghosts, like a darkness upright*'' (*CP* 210–11). Such a poem anticipates in tone and imagery Sylvia Plath's famous ''Daddy,'' in which Plath describes her father as ''the black man who / Bit my pretty red heart in two,'' a man symbolized by ''a swastika / So black no sky could squeak through'' (222). Plath was rereading Lawrence's poems in late 1962, while writing her own late poems. Judith Kroll (163, 231, 264) has shown, however, that Plath's interest was not limited to the explicitly confessional *Look! We Have Come Through!* She finds echoes of Lawrence's late ''Walk Warily'' (*CP* 707) in ''Getting There'' (Plath 247), and of ''Tortoise Shout'' (*CP* 363) in ''Burning the Letters'' and ''Stopped Dead'' (Plath 204, 230).[11] And Plath annotated or underscored remarks on love, marriage, and separation that she found throughout Lawrence's poetry.

   The personal openness that Lawrence anticipates in much recent poetry is one thing that the ''freedom'' of free verse implied to him: ''direct utterance from the instant, whole man'' (*CP* 184). Karl Shapiro, though not a confessional poet, has also found that openness instructive for his work. In his essay

---

   11. For further comments on the Lawrence-Plath connection, see Marjorie Perloff, ''*Angst* and Animism in the Poetry of Sylvia Plath,'' and Frederick Buell, ''Sylvia Plath's Traditionalism,'' *Critical Essays on Sylvia Plath*, ed. Linda W. Wagner (Boston: G. K. Hall, 1984) 109–24 and 140–54, respectively. Perloff argues that ''the process of self-communion found in the poetry of . . . Lawrence is precisely that which occurs in the later poetry of Sylvia Plath'' (111); and, more specifically, that ''it is Lawrence's flower poems—especially his 'Andraitx—Pomegranate Flowers'—that stand behind 'Poppies in October,' and his 'November by the Sea' contains in embryo the imagery of Sylvia Plath's 'Letter in November''' (122). Buell sees Plath, in ''Tulips'' and ''Poppies in July,'' describing nature ''in rhetoric that is a conscious echoing and inversion of D. H. Lawrence's'' (144). See also Tom Marshall, *The Psychic Mariner: A Reading of the Poems of D. H. Lawrence* (New York: Viking, 1970), who argues that Plath and the Lowell of *Life Studies* ''are, in a very real sense, Lawrence's heirs'' because of their concern with ''personal exploration'' in their poetry (249, 242).

"The Unemployed Magician" (1957) Shapiro undergoes an imaginary interview with the god of poetry, who at the essay's end turns out to be Lawrence himself. In response to the classic interview question, Shapiro says that Lawrence's poetry is the one book of poems that he would take to a desert island. Why? Because "Lawrence in his sincerity . . . broke through the facade of artistry and literary affectation and stood at the doorway of poetry itself" (244). In another essay, "The First White Aboriginal," Shapiro argues that "twentieth-century poetry is a poetry of perfections. It is the least spontaneous poetry since—whatever date for the birth of artificiality you call to mind" (193). Lawrence's unpolished personal speech, however, puts him outside this overcivilized tradition: "Lawrence made a magnificent leap across civilization into the aboriginal darkness. He is one of the supreme heretics of white, modern civilization" (187).[12]

In discussing the value both Lawrence and certain later poets have placed on sincerity, I used the term "personal presence." "Presence" is a matter not only of voice but also of attentiveness—in Lawrence's case, attentiveness to the world outside him as well as to the world within. His ability to attend to and identify with an animal or an object while respecting its otherness was initially important for a mid-century poet like Roethke in his volume *The Lost Son* (1948), and more recently for poets as diverse as James Schuyler and Gary Snyder. In a 1985 interview Schuyler said, "I've always liked looking at things and I'm very attracted to writers who share that infatuation with things, such as . . . D. H. Lawrence (in his poetry)" (qtd. in Hillringhouse 5). Lawrence "was certainly one of my greatest teachers," says Snyder. "He was my first modern poetry teacher." What struck Snyder first was the accuracy of Lawrence's writing about nature in *Birds, Beasts and Flowers:* "I grew up in a very poor, relatively uneducated rural background in Washington State, but I knew about the mountains and the trees. And so I read this book and I said: This man knows what he is talking about, and I was converted to the poetry right there, and to modern poetry" (Faas 119).

Certainly Lawrence's critics have remarked on this ability. Sandra Gilbert calls Lawrence's poems "acts of attention"; Alfred Alvarez cites his "rigorous but open alertness" (142); for Kenneth Rexroth, "the accuracy of Lawrence's observation haunts the mind permanently" (12); and Auden says that "Lawrence in his best poems is always concerned intensively with a single subject, a bat, a tortoise, a fig-tree, which he broods on until he has exhausted its possibilities" (288). Lawrence saw such attention as central to

12. Paradoxically, Shapiro seems to have based the last of these comments on Eliot's *After Strange Gods: A Primer of Modern Heresy* (New York: Harcourt, Brace, 1934), although he reverses Eliot's value judgment. Eliot describes Lawrence as lacking "orthodoxy of sensibility and . . . the sense of tradition" (40), and his characters "any moral or social sense" (39). Eliot's Lawrence, then, is "an almost perfect example of the heretic" (41).

poetry. In 1928 he wrote, "the essential quality of poetry is that it makes a new effort of attention" (*Phoenix* 255). Like the augury that he describes in *Etruscan Places*, poetry comes out of what he calls "an act of pure attention" (153), an attention that is one result of his "coming through" in "Song of a Man Who Has Come Through" (*CP* 250).

Charles Olson saw this sharpening of one's own attention and sympathetic penetration of the other as the main lesson that Lawrence could teach postwar American poets: "the clue: open, stay OPEN, hear it, anything, really HEAR it. And you are IN" (*Human Universe* 125). Writing to Creeley on 4 May 1951 and alluding to "Bavarian Gentians," Olson says, "i am always coming at [Lawrence] by way of his penetration of, flowers. That he did damn well give himself to what (whenever) it was before him" (Olson and Creeley VI: 38). In this and other comments, Olson praises what he elsewhere calls Lawrence's "stance toward reality." That stance involves reassessing our place in the physical universe and our relationship to nature, including our own nature— another important project for postmodern poets. For Olson, Lawrence is one of "the modern men who projected what we are and what we are in, who broke the spell. They put men forward into the post-modern, the post-hu-manist . . ." (*Additional Prose* 40). Lawrence had addressed the limitations of the humanist worldview as early as 1923: "We are prisoners inside our own conception of life and being. We have exhausted the possibilities of the universe, as we know it" (*Phoenix* 325). Or as he puts it in "Fish," "*I am not the measure of creation*" (*CP* 339). Lawrence's downplaying of the individual ego and his sense of the human as involved in rather than above nature proved appealing to many poets for whom humanist values had been shattered by World War II. In a 1967 discussion of myth in poetry, for example, Denise Levertov quotes Lawrence's "There Are No Gods." Lawrence begins this poem by parodying secular humanism in iambic pen-tameter, as if he can dissociate himself from that philosophy by using an uncharacteristic meter: "There are no gods, and you can please yourself" (*CP* 651). But then he counters this position:

> But leave me alone, leave me alone, to myself!
> and then in the room, whose is the presence
> that makes the air so still and lovely to me?
>
>   (*CP* 652)

Levertov uses Lawrence to sum up "what myth meant to me as a practicing poet" (62). She and a number of other recent writers have shared his attrac-tion to forces stronger and more mysterious than the human will or intellect. Furthermore, this reassessment of the relationship between the human and the nonhuman, and of what constitutes the human, involved Lawrence in a search that has also profoundly influenced recent American poets—the search for

alternative sources of cultural energy outside of either the Eastern or, especially, the Western traditions. Lawrence was the only modernist poet to
conduct such a quest. For their cultural ideals Yeats turned to Byzantium;
Pound to the Italian Renaissance, the America of John Adams, and Confucian
China; Eliot to the European literary tradition; Crane to American historical
figures treated stereotypically rather than archetypally. In contrast, for all his
reading in and creative use of Yoga, Hinduism, theosophy, and, secondarily,
Buddhism, and despite his re-creation of the Greek gods in the pieces beginning *Last Poems*, Lawrence largely saw "the East a dead letter, and Europe
moribund" (*CP* 371).[13]

At the risk of digressing, a distinction is in order with regard to *Last Poems*.
Admittedly Lawrence uses figures from Greek mythology throughout his
prose and poetry, including *Last Poems;* and to begin this sequence, he
envisions and imaginatively celebrates the return of Greek gods and heroes in
"The Greeks Are Coming!" "The Argonauts," "Middle of the World," and
"For the Heroes Are Dipped in Scarlet." He follows these poems, however,
with an explicitly anti-Platonic sequence in which he rejects the theory of
forms. Lawrence foreshadows this move in the opening lines of "For the
Heroes Are Dipped in Scarlet": "Before Plato told the great lie of ideals / men
slimly went like fishes, and didn't care" (*CP* 688). Then in "Demiurge" he
dismisses Platonic idealism at greater length and with the vehement judgment
"what nonsense it is!" (*CP* 689)—in which it is hard not to hear a pun on
"non-sense." Lawrence extends his critique to a pre-Socratic figure later in
Last Poems when he finds Anaxagoras full of "mental conceit and mystifi-

---

13. Gerald Doherty documents Lawrence's reading in and use of Eastern systems of thought
in a useful series of articles: "Connie and the Chakras: Yogic Patterns in D. H. Lawrence's *Lady
Chatterley's Lover,*" *D. H. Lawrence Review* 13 (1980): 79–93; "The Nirvana Dimension:
D. H. Lawrence's Quarrel with Buddhism," *D. H. Lawrence Review* 15 (1982): 51–76; and
"The Darkest Source: D. H. Lawrence, Tantric Yoga, and *Women in Love,*" *Essays in Literature*
11 (1984): 211–22. At the same time he carefully limits his claims for Lawrence's philosophical
adherence to these systems. Thus Lawrence " is wholly idiosyncratic in his exploitation of chakra
psychology as a diagnostic tool in his acerbic and often despairing onslaughts on modern civilization and its discontents" ("Connie and the Chakras" 81); "Buddhism was never central to
Lawrence's concerns" ("The Nirvana Dimension" 51); and although "yoga theory in relation
to the somatic basis of consciousness was to remain a staple of the Lawrentian metaphysical
construct," after *Women in Love* Lawrence never again made use specifically of Tantric yoga as
a model of sexual initiation ("The Darkest Source" 214ff.).

In arguing that "Lawrence's acquaintance with the real (Scriptural) Hindu thought was very
meager," acquired "through volumes on Hinduism, not directly through the Scriptures," Cha-
man Nahal makes an even more modest claim: "It is not suggested here that Lawrence was
influenced by Hinduism to any considerable extent. . . ." Nahal's aim is rather "to bring out the
deep affinities, irrespective of what Lawrence might or might not have known of Hinduism, that
exist between Lawrence's approach to life and the approach to life as signified in the Vedas." See
D. H. Lawrence: An Eastern View (New York: A. S. Barnes, 1970) 20–21.

cation / and nonsense'' (*CP* 708). ''Religion knows better than philosophy,''
he states in ''Demiurge'' (*CP* 689). He seems to have embraced Greek mythology and rejected Greek philosophy, using figures from both realms as
actors in a characteristic psychic melodrama pitting blood-consciousness
against mental consciousness.

Lawrence's attraction to so-called primitive cultures past and present—
Etrurian, Sardinian, Mexican, Indian, North American Indian—has been
thoroughly documented. He turned to these sources for a set of cultural
conditions that embodied the liveliness of perceptual and emotional attention
and the de-anthropocentrized view of humankind that I have already discussed. Later poets who wished to conduct a similar search could, among
Anglo-American modernists, turn only to Lawrence for a precedent. Lawrence's interest in earlier, non-Western cultures anticipates much of Robert
Bly's and Snyder's work; the ethnopoetics movement, represented in Jerome
Rothenberg's anthologies *Technicians of the Sacred* and *Symposium of the
Whole;* and again Olson, who turned to the Maya and to Sumer as Lawrence
turned to Etruria. Donald Davie has argued that ''Olson's most Lawrencian
book is his *Mayan Letters,* written from Central America to Robert Creeley,
when Olson was pursuing archaeological researches into the Maya civilization'' (*Poet* 180). Olson's attempt to ''read'' Mayan glyphs finds an earlier
parallel in Lawrence's essentially archaeological attempt to ''read'' and re-
animate the ancient culture ''embowered'' in cypresses:

> Tuscan cypresses,
> What is it?
>
> Folded in like a dark thought
> For which the language is lost,
> Tuscan cypresses,
> Is there a great secret?
> Are our words no good?
>
> The undeliverable secret,
> Dead with a dead race and a dead speech, and yet
> Darkly monumental in you,
> Etruscan cypresses.
>
> (*CP* 296)

In Olson's view, part of Lawrence's value for postmodern poets is that ''he
imagines states of being & geography divers from the modern'' (*Selected
Writings* 128). In fact, the foreword to *Fantasia of the Unconscious,* a seminal
text for Olson that underlies one of his own most important essays on poetics,
''Human Universe,'' inspired his study of ancient civilizations to the point
where Olson saw the two writers' interests as exactly parallel: ''his ETRURIA

(my, SUMERIA)'' (Olson and Creeley III: 64).[14] Again, Lawrence could speak
to later poets disillusioned with the cultural assumptions of classical humanism as most of his contemporaries could not.

I have often mentioned Charles Olson's name in this essay. Lawrence
affected him perhaps more powerfully than he did any other postwar American poet. That Lawrence should have influenced so strongly a man who is
perhaps the paradigmatic postmodern American poet, in addition to the other
writers I have mentioned, says much for his impact on contemporary verse.
That impact has generally been underrated. Describing his own poetry as a
chariot, Robert Duncan once said that it had four wheels: Pound, Williams,
Olson, and Lawrence (qtd. in Ginsberg 133). For a nonformalist poet writing
after 1950, the first three names are predictable. I have tried to show that the
fourth name has been more important to contemporary poetry than most
readers realize.

WORKS CITED

Alvarez, Alfred. *The Shaping Spirit: Studies in Modern English and American Poets.*
London: Arrow, 1963.

Auden, W. H. *The Dyer's Hand and Other Essays.* 1962. New York: Random House,
1968.

Blackmur, R. P. "D. H. Lawrence and Expressive Form." 1935. *Language as Gesture.* New York: Columbia UP, 1980. 286–300.

Blackmur, R. P. "Lord Tennyson's Scissors: 1912–1950." 1951. *Language as Gesture.* New York: Columbia UP, 1980. 422–40.

Bové, Paul A. *Destructive Poetics: Heidegger and Modern American Poetry.* New
York: Columbia UP, 1980.

Creeley, Robert. *The Collected Poems of Robert Creeley 1945–1975.* Berkeley: U of
California P, 1982.

Creeley, Robert. *Contexts of Poetry: Interviews 1961–1971.* Ed. Donald Allen. Bolinas, Calif.: Four Seasons Foundation, 1973.

Creeley, Robert. *Was That a Real Poem and Other Essays.* Ed. Donald Allen. Bolinas, Calif.: Four Seasons Foundation, 1979.

Davie, Donald. *The Poet in the Imaginary Museum: Essays of Two Decades.* Ed.
Barry Alpert. New York: Persea, 1977.

Davie, Donald. *Thomas Hardy and British Poetry.* New York: Oxford UP, 1972.

Draper, R. P. *D. H. Lawrence.* New York: Twayne, 1964.

14. Olson's letter to Robert Creeley (1 October 1950) forms the basis for his essay "The
Escaped Cock: Notes on Lawrence and the Real" (*Human Universe* 123–25). On the subject of
Lawrence and Olson, one coincidence that Olson would have appreciated is the fact that
Lawrence anticipated Olson's major sequence in the titles of two late poems, "Maximus" and
"The Man of Tyre" (*CP* 692–93).

Faas, Ekbert, ed. *Towards a New American Poetics: Essays and Interviews.* Santa Barbara: Black Sparrow, 1978.

Gilbert, Sandra M. *Acts of Attention: The Poems of D. H. Lawrence.* Ithaca: Cornell UP, 1972.

Ginsberg, Allen. *Allen Verbatim: Lectures on Poetry, Politics, Consciousness.* Ed. Gordon Ball. New York: McGraw-Hill, 1974.

Hillringhouse, Mark. "James Schuyler: An Interview." *American Poetry Review* 14 (1985): 5–12.

Hough, Graham. *The Dark Sun: A Study of D. H. Lawrence.* London: Duckworth, 1956.

Kroll, Judith. *Chapters in a Mythology: The Poetry of Sylvia Plath.* New York: Harper & Row, 1976.

La Belle, Jenijoy. *The Echoing Wood of Theodore Roethke.* Princeton: Princeton UP, 1976.

Lawrence, D. H. *The Complete Poems of D. H. Lawrence.* Ed. Vivian de Sola Pinto and F. Warren Roberts. New York: Viking, 1971.

Lawrence, D. H. *Etruscan Places. Mornings in Mexico* and *Etruscan Places.* Harmondsworth, Eng.: Penguin, 1971. 95–215.

Lawrence, D. H. *The Letters of D. H. Lawrence.* Vol. 1: *September 1901–May 1913.* Ed. James T. Boulton. Cambridge: Cambridge UP, 1979.

Lawrence, D. H. *The Letters of D. H. Lawrence.* Vol. 2: *June 1913–October 1916.* Ed. George J. Zytaruk and James T. Boulton. Cambridge: Cambridge UP, 1981.

Lawrence, D. H. *Phoenix: The Posthumous Papers of D. H. Lawrence.* Ed. Edward D. McDonald. 1936. New York: Viking, 1968.

Levertov, Denise. *The Poet in the World.* New York: New Directions, 1973.

Lowell, Robert. "On Freedom in Poetry." *Naked Poetry: Recent American Poetry in Open Forms.* Ed. Stephen Berg and Robert Mezey. Indianapolis: Bobbs-Merrill, 1969.

Murfin, Ross C. *The Poetry of D. H. Lawrence: Texts and Contexts.* Lincoln: U of Nebraska P, 1983.

Nehls, Edward, ed. *D. H. Lawrence: A Composite Biography.* Vol. 3. Madison: U of Wisconsin P, 1959.

Oates, Joyce Carol. *The Hostile Sun: The Poetry of D. H. Lawrence.* Los Angeles: Black Sparrow, 1973.

Olson, Charles. *Additional Prose.* Ed. George F. Butterick. Bolinas, Calif.: Four Seasons Foundation, 1974.

Olson, Charles. *Archaeologist of Morning.* New York: Grossman, 1973.

Olson, Charles. *Human Universe and Other Essays.* Ed. Donald Allen. San Francisco: Auerhahn Society, 1965.

Olson, Charles. *Selected Writings of Charles Olson.* Ed. Robert Creeley. New York: New Directions, 1966.

Olson, Charles, and Robert Creeley. *Charles Olson and Robert Creeley: The Complete Correspondence.* Vols. 2–4, 6. Ed. George F. Butterick. Santa Barbara: Black Sparrow, 1980–82, 1985.

Rexroth, Kenneth. Introduction to D. H. Lawrence, *Selected Poems*. New York: Viking, 1959. 1–23.

Richards, I. A. *Practical Criticism*. New York: Harcourt, Brace, 1929.

Roethke, Theodore. *The Collected Poems of Theodore Roethke*. 1966. Garden City, N.Y.: Anchor-Doubleday, 1975.

Roethke, Theodore. *On the Poet and His Craft: Selected Prose of Theodore Roethke*. Ed. Ralph J. Mills, Jr. Seattle: U of Washington P, 1965.

Rosenthal, M. L. *The Modern Poets: A Critical Introduction*. New York: Oxford UP, 1960.

Shapiro, Karl. "The First White Aboriginal." 1957–58. *In Defense of Ignorance*. New York: Random House, 1965. 187–204.

Shapiro, Karl. "The Unemployed Magician." 1957. *In Defense of Ignorance*. New York: Random House, 1965. 239–61.

Williams, William Carlos. *Selected Essays of William Carlos Williams*. New York: New Directions, 1969.

Notes on Contributors

Lydia Blanchard, Associate Professor of English at Southwest Texas State University, has contributed essays to the collections *D. H. Lawrence: The Man Who Lived, Lawrence and Women, D. H. Lawrence's "Lady,"* and *D. H. Lawrence's Literary Inheritors.* Her essays on Lawrence and on women and literature have appeared in *Mosaic, Modern Language Quarterly, Modern Fiction Studies, Studies in the Novel,* the *D. H. Lawrence Review,* and *Style.*

Wayne C. Booth is George M. Pullman Distinguished Service Professor in the Department of English, the Committee of Ideas and Methods, and the College at the University of Chicago; he is also past president of the Modern Language Association. His books include the classic study *The Rhetoric of Fiction, A Rhetoric of Irony, Modern Dogma and the Rhetoric of Assent, Critical Understanding, The Vocation of a Teacher,* and *The Company We Keep.*

Keith Cushman, Professor of English at the University of North Carolina at Greensboro, is the author of *D. H. Lawrence at Work,* the editor of Lawrence's *Memoir of Maurice Magnus,* and the coeditor of *The Letters of D. H. Lawrence and Amy Lowell.* He has published over two dozen essays on nineteenth- and twentieth-century literary figures and is at work on a biographical study of Lawrence's friendship with Earl and Achsah Brewster.

Paul Delany is Professor of English at Simon Fraser University. He is the author of *British Autobiography in the Seventeenth Century, D. H. Lawrence's Nightmare,* a biography of Lawrence during the war years, and *The Neo-Pagans,* a study of the Rupert Brooke circle. He is writing a book about money in the English novel.

Alan Golding is Assistant Professor of English at the University of Louisville. His essays on Edward Dorn, on Wallace Stevens and Louis Zukofsky, and on American poetry anthologies have appeared in books on Dorn and Stevens and in the collection *Canons.* He has also published on Oppen, the Language poets, Olson, Toomer, Poe, and canon formation. He is completing a history of the American poetry canon.

Janice H. Harris, Professor of English at the University of Wyoming, is the author of *The Short Fiction of D. H. Lawrence.* Her essays have appeared in the *Massachusetts Review, Modern Language Quarterly, Philological Quarterly, Modern Language Studies, Studies in Short Fiction, The Midwest Quarterly,* and the *D. H. Lawrence Review.* She is currently writing a book on feminism and Edwardian fiction.

Robert Kiely is Loker Professor of English and American Literature at Harvard University. His books include *Robert Louis Stevenson and the Fiction of Adventure,* *The Romantic Novel in England,* and *Beyond Egotism: The Fiction of James Joyce,* *Virginia Woolf, and D. H. Lawrence.* He is presently at work on a book entitled *The Reverse Tradition,* a postmodern reading of nineteenth-century fiction.

Frederick P. W. McDowell, Emeritus Professor of English at the University of Iowa, has edited *E. M. Forster: An Annotated Bibliography of Writings About Him* and has published books on Forster, Ellen Glasgow, Elizabeth Madox Roberts, and Caroline Gordon. He has also written on Shaw, Lawrence, Hardy, Auden, Conrad, and Angus Wilson.

Julian Moynahan, Professor of English at Rutgers University, is the author of *The Deed of Life: The Novels and Tales of D. H. Lawrence.* He has published four novels and a study of Nabokov, and has completed a book about nineteenth- and twentieth-century Anglo-Irish literature.

Jane A. Nelson is Professor of English at Northeastern University. Author of *Form and Image in the Fiction of Henry Miller,* she is currently writing a book on Emily Dickinson. Her articles on Whitman and Coleridge have appeared in the *Walt Whitman Quarterly Review* and *Studies in Romanticism.*

Mark Spilka is Professor of English at Brown University, where he edits *Novel: A Forum on Fiction.* He is the author of *The Love Ethic of D. H. Lawrence* and editor of *D. H. Lawrence: A Collection of Critical Essays.* Soon to appear are his collected essays on Lawrence under the title *D. H. Lawrence in Changing Times.* His other books are *Dickens and Kafka: A Mutual Interpretation, Virginia Woolf's Quarrel with Grieving,* and *Hemingway and Androgyny.*

Michael Squires is Professor of English at Virginia Polytechnic Institute and State University. He is the author of *The Pastoral Novel* and *The Creation of "Lady Chatterley's Lover,"* and coeditor of *D. H. Lawrence's "Lady."* Forthcoming are his edition of *Lady Chatterley's Lover* for Cambridge University Press and his edition of the correspondence of Frieda Lawrence and Jake Zeitlin for Macmillan.

John N. Swift is Associate Professor of English at Occidental College. His essays on Milton, Cather, and literary romanticism have appeared in *South Atlantic Quarterly, Western American Literature,* and the *Sewanee Review.*

M. Elizabeth Wallace is Assistant Professor of English at Western Oregon State College. The author of *Part-Time Academic Employment in the Humanities,* she has published essays in *College English, ADE Bulletin,* and the *D. H. Lawrence Review.* She is at work on a study of Lawrence and epistemology.

Index

ALCOHOL PROBLEMS